TESTAMENT OF MUSIC

ERNEST NEWMAN

TESTAMENT OF MUSIC

Essays and Papers

by

ERNEST NEWMAN

Edited by

Herbert Van Thal

NEW YORK: ALFRED A. KNOPF
1963

© 1963 by Mrs Ernest Newman
Printed in Great Britain by
Cox and Wyman Ltd · Reading

For
VERA

CONTENTS

ACKNOWLEDGEMENTS

Thanks are due to Cassell and Company Ltd., for permission to quote from *A Musical Critic's Holiday*.

INTRODUCTION

NEWMAN WAS a law unto himself. He was far more than a critic, his mastery lay in his complete understanding of music. No other critic of the subject has left as renowned a name as he: his life of Wagner is never likely to be surpassed and stands equal with the outstanding biographies of all times.

Newman was endowed with an almost unerring judgment, and even the opinions given in his earliest writings changed less than those of other critics. His writings of over sixty years cover a revolutionary period in the history of music, for he saw the perfection of the gramophone, the disappearance of the piano-player and the advent of wireless and television.

'Among the elements', wrote Desmond Shawe-Taylor, 'that went to the making of Newman's powerful intellect, two are of primary importance: a deep scepticism (he was a staunch agnostic of the old school) and a passion for accuracy. He was never prepared to accept something as true merely because it had not been questioned before, and he was never content with second-hand information when primary sources were available. His cast of mind was forensic and there is little doubt that he could have made a formidable barrister or judge.'*

Born on the 30th November, 1868, at Waterhouse Street, Everton, Lancaster, Newman was the son of a master tailor, Seth Roberts, and his wife Harriet. He was christened William, and

* The *Sunday Times*.

educated at St. Saviours School where he won the Bibby Scholarship to Liverpool University. Leaving the University in 1886, he intended sitting for the Indian Civil Service Examination but, owing to illness, was advised by his doctor that the climate of India would not suit him. He therefore became a bank clerk in 1889, a post he held over the next fourteen years, although he was writing continuously during the whole of this period. As 'Ernest Newman' he was a regular contributor to Bradlaugh's *National Reformer* (1889–93), and the *Free Review* (1893-97) as well as to his university magazine. He even wrote on banking subjects, but all this time music was becoming of increasing interest to him.

He was first married on 3rd February, 1894 to Kate Eleanor Woollett, the daughter of Henry Woollett, an artist. It was a happy marriage, but she died in 1918 and in the following year he married Vera Hands, the elder daughter of Arthur Hands of Birmingham, an equally successful match. There was no church ceremony to either marriage, for Newman, an ardent freethinker, never deviated from his dislike of the church. He was never gregarious, but a lone figure whose singleness of purpose was, as *The Times* said of him, that of 'an artist using criticism as his medium'.

When he became Musical Critic of the *Manchester Guardian* in 1905, he threw over all the traces of William Roberts – and became 'a new man in earnest'. A year later he joined the *Birmingham Daily Post*. He was for a while musical critic to the *Observer*, but in 1920 he joined the *Sunday Times*, to which paper he contributed until he retired in September 1958.

He was musically entirely self-taught, an astonishing achievement. He studied scores and every available book on the subject 'with an ardour with which schoolgirls used to read novels or schoolboys adventure stories'; and he further reveals that when he was about twenty 'I had in my simplicity the idea that it would be possible in another year or two to have learned outwardly all that really mattered.' 'I have never (read)', he wrote in his *Confessions of a Musical Critic*, 'and I do not suppose I knew that there was such a thing as musical criticism.' Yet he was soon able to read a musical score with the ease that most of us read an ordinary book.* He mastered the German language with equal facility, and also studied Russian, Latin, Greek, French, Italian, Spanish, Swedish and Hebrew!

Throughout his life he was never in any doubt about the importance of his work, and he was continually at pains to explain and drive home the essentials of musical criticism. As has already been said, he insisted that musical criticism must be literature above everything else, and not an attempt to repeat wrongly in one medium what has already been said rightly in another. The fundamentals of criticism were of the utmost interest to him. He complained that as 'a plyer of the nefarious trade of criticism' he was disliked by artists because he was a critic, while the contemporaries of his earlier years were equally uncivil because he was always trying to demolish current criticism. 'I am like Wotan, willing my own destruction; yet there is no Wagner to write a tetralogy upon the nobility and the cosmic significance of my self-immolation.'† Eight years later he was to crystallize his theories in his *A Musical Critic's Holiday*. 'Genuine criticism must always function in the past rather than the present. It is only from the past that aesthetic standards can come, and these are valid for any new form of the art. Let the critic leave the future alone. We do not know which of the speculative theories of our time will survive and be fruitful; but we can be pretty sure *which* of the music of our time will live.'‡

Despite his appreciation of the remarkable changes that were continually taking place in the musical world, his judgments were always very considered, and he never proclaimed that this or that unknown composer was the genius of the future. Not that

* Alfred Knopf in an essay on Newman in the *Saturday Review* wrote, 'he defended the proposition that for a musician loss of hearing is greatly preferable to loss of sight; he always concluded that he could more greatly enjoy a score by reading it quietly in that remarkable one-room building at Tadworth than by hearing a performance which except on the rarest occasions would fall short of the perfection always demanded.'

† *New Witness*, August 1917.
‡ *A Musical Critic's Holiday*, p. 11.

these changes were in any way solely true of his time, since we need only look at 1961 and compare the choice of programme of the Promenade Concerts with that of 1960, or the opening concert at the Edinburgh Festival with that of previous years. He must have influenced many minds, for there had not existed, as far as contemporary opinion was concerned, a responsible musical literature until he and Shaw led the way.

Newman sparred with his contemporary Edwin Evans, but he paid tribute to the *Manchester Guardian*'s music critic, Arthur Johnstone, who died on the 8th December 1904, at the early age of forty-four, but as this century progressed a very considerable literature on music both critical and otherwise has been contributed by a number of outstanding writers.

Cardus among others has had plenty to say of the function of the musical critic. 'The critic's responsibility', he has written, 'is not such a burden that he need wear a long face perpetually and not "enjoy a frisk" now and then. Nobody will be a penny the worse if he pronounces the most unjust verdict; he is not sentencing anyone to death. He will write his best and amuse his readers (and that primarily is what he is paid for) if he brings to his technical and cultural equipment some occasional flippancy or a willingness to laugh at himself.'* Of course, where regular critical articles on concert or opera are concerned, the critic is often hampered by the time there is available to him to consider his opinion as well as to write his notice with all the care it normally requires, while the space he is allowed is another problem. Newman had more time and opportunities to write at greater length, though he continually chafed at the space allowed him in the *Sunday Times*; for as will be seen in this book, he contributed a great deal to the weeklies. On the other hand, for many years he was critic to the *Manchester Guardian* and *Birmingham Post*, and in this capacity he was responsible for encouraging high standards in the provinces.

The reader who has not previously studied the writings of Ernest Newman would do well to have a nodding acquaintance

* Cardus: *Talking of Music*, p. 271.

with *A Musical Critic's Holiday*, in which, as I have already said, is the summing up of his art of musical criticism* and despite the fact that Beecham said, 'Critics, like politicians, are frequently accused of inconsistency when they change their opinions. . . . Ernest Newman has changed his about as much as any other man, for which praise rather than blame should be accorded him'.† Yet, we know that Newman very rarely faltered. Everybody knows that he was responsible for the recognition of Wagner, though probably fewer are aware how far he consistently championed Berlioz, Wolf, Sibelius,‡ and Elgar.

The Shaw–Newman controversy over Strauss is reprinted here from *The Nation* in its entirety for the first time – the earlier letters over *Elektra* when it was first produced in this country in 1911, and then the correspondence three years later when the two of them battled again over the merits of the composer himself.

A final word about the selection of material in this book. Throughout his long writing life Newman wrote on other subjects than music, especially in his early years, when he contributed a good many learned articles on philosophers and writers: later, when he was writing for the popular press, boxing and crime particularly engaged his attention, especially the former – he rarely missed a major contest if he could help it. It was intended to include a variety of such articles in this book, but with so much on music from which to make a choice, it is felt that this subject on which Newman has left such an influence, will be of more interest to readers. I have therefore chosen only a few extracts from his early writings with some further quotations which will be found in the last chapter of this book. As a young man he quickly showed his encyclopaedic knowledge. Thus he was interested in philosophy and he wrote upon Weissmann and at some considerable length on the then recently published *Journals of Amiel*. As a free-thinker, his earliest regular contributions

* A good many extracts from this book will be found in the last chapter.

† *A Mingled Chime*, p. 99 (Grey Arrow edition).

‡ Newman was honoured by the Finnish President for his work on Sibelius.

were to Bradlaugh's *National Reformer*, while his papers] on Ibsen and Turgenev are highly illuminating especially when one also considers Newman's youth and the time they were written. A few years later, he championed Conrad and Meredith, which proved that his critical perceptions were seldom in error. One appreciates that there is a definite orbit to Newman's work and that his criticisms are within his own inflexible circumference. He never compromises, and although his style is often difficult, he was emphatic in the assertion of his opinions.

A final word from Neville Cardus★: 'Only those who began to read and study Newman as young men can understand how much is owed to him in this country, for his work is enriching and fructifying an atmosphere and soil during an acrid time of provincial stuffiness and narrowness of vision. He was perhaps the first writer truly to Europeanize our music and our humane responses to music. He quickened our antennae, opened doors for us.'

Herbert Van Thal

★ Newman: in *Fanfare for Ernest Newman*. Ed. van Thal, p. 31.

I

CONFESSIONS OF A
MUSICAL CRITIC
1923

I

MUSICAL CRITICS, apparently, were not invented in Dante's day, or he would certainly have shown them having one of the worst times possible in the worst circle possible in hell. Nobody loves the musical critic; and when I come to think of it I can't see any reason why people should. He is, in the popular estimation, one of those objectionable fellows who profess to be able to tell you how to do everything without being able to do it himself. He could not write even a First symphony; but he can tell you what is wrong with the Ninth. He would not know a vocal cord if he saw it, and if you gave him one would probably show his ignorance by trying to tie a parcel up with it; but he can tell Caruso what is wrong with his 'production'. Pachmann, Kreisler, Cortot, Casals, Wood – he can put them all in their places.

And yet, somehow or other, these creatures are read; indeed, they have a bigger clientèle, when you think of it, than the people who call themselves 'artistes' (a spelling carefully adopted in many cases, one presumes, to indicate that they are not artists). I think it may be taken as an axiom that for every man or woman who goes to this concert or that, at least five hundred will read what some critic or other has to say about it. In a really civilized society, writers so widely read would be regarded as benefactors of the race; they would have wealth and honours showered upon them. As it is, they are treated as dogs, as pariahs, as criminals; and are mostly so badly paid that their continuing to exercise the functions of their profession can be attributed only to the reluctance of philanthropists to deprive the world of pearls of price, richly as the world deserves it.

Young men sometimes come to me and ask me how they can become musical critics. I invariably try to persuade them to give up the idea; there are at least fifty other forms of crime, I tell them, that are more pleasant and more profitable, that require less intelligence and less application, that have fewer working hours and longer holidays. The misguided young men generally persist in their inquiry, however; and then I have to tell them that I know nothing of how other men have become musical critics. I know a good many of them, but I cannot remember any of them ever talking about how he began.

When I come to think of it, this strikes me as being suspicious – almost sinister. It suggests that they are ashamed to be what they are, and are unwilling to let the world into the secret of their first fall. I think they are wrong in this; they ought to set forth, as a warning to the young, how they first came to tread the path of shame. It will be found, I am sure, that, in music as in morals, the first step on that path is so small a one that the unsuspecting person who takes it has not the slightest prevision of where it will ultimately land him. Many a critic is so only by accident - as, indeed, the cynical public may already have suspected. The young man may have been shaping nicely for an honourable and lucrative career in business, in politics, or in sport; then one fine day something lured him down a side path, and he went on and on pursuing the gleam till in the end he found himself changed, by some evil enchantment, into a musical critic.

That, at any rate, was my experience; and I propose now to tell the story of my ruin, not because I am so lost to shame as to be past blushing for it, but solely as a possible warning to others.

I shall be compelled to inflict a few autobiographical details upon the reader, and indeed to use the first person singular more than I like. I have no desire to talk about myself, except in the interests of science. A critic is a man who every day of his working life is confidently giving his opinions upon art and artists. His right to do so may well be challenged. 'Who set thee up as a ruler and a judge over us?' may legitimately be asked of him. If he is a fool, or at any rate not ideally wise, he may not be able to do much harm – not nearly as much as is popularly supposed, for readers soon take a critic's measure – but he can certainly inflict a good deal of unnecessary pain and arouse a good deal of un-necessary anger. At the best, most people hold, he can express only a personal point of view; what right has he to impose that point of view upon others?

For most professions a course of careful preparation is needed – nay, insisted on, in the interest of the public. What preparation does a critic get for such delicate and responsible work as judging? It is not enough that he shall be a musician. It is not merely as a practical musician that he is addressing the public; it is as a judge of music and musicians. To do the work efficiently he needs to be in the first place a very sensitive instrument, and in the second place to be able to play coolly upon that instrument as if it were something not inside but outside himself. It is not sufficient that he shall merely react in this or that way to this or that music. Anyone can do that; but his opinions, interesting as they may be as an expression of his own personality, do not necessarily amount to criticism in the proper sense of the word. A man, for instance, may quite honestly think Bach a dullard, but that opinion does not throw much light on Bach, however much light it may throw on him.

The plain man is at liberty to say 'I don't like Bach', just as he is at liberty to say 'I don't like apples'. The critic, however, is expected, and rightly, to express something more than a mere physiological or even psychological reaction. He is expected to be not a dogmatist, but a judge, and a just judge. But what training does he get in the art of judging–supposing there to be such an art? None whatever, except what training he can give himself in the course of the exercise of his profession. Granted that his judgments are simply an expression of himself, ought we not to know just what that self is, and how it has come to be what it is?

If we knew that, we might be able to account for many of his judgments with which we disagree, and so discount them.

The critic who is trying to see a composer as he really is learns as much as possible about him – what kind of man he was, especially what were the early influences he came under. Ought not the reader, if he wishes to understand why a critic thinks this or that, to know in particular what the influences were that have helped to give his mind its special cast? The conscientious critic, indeed, sooner or later, asks questions of this kind about himself; and I think he ought to tell the reader also something of what he has learned about himself, not out of egoism, not because he thinks himself of any interest to the world *qua* critic Brown or critic Jones or critic Robinson, but because he may be of interest to a few inquiring people *qua* critic, as a case for psychological study. It is in that spirit solely that I shall talk of myself.

II

The records of my family, so far as I have been able to delve into them, had never before been stained by a musical critic. So little thought had my parents of their child sinking so low that they did not even trouble to have me taught music. I have had only one music lesson in my life, and that lasted no more than half an hour. It was, I often think, my good fortune to have parents who did not take the slightest interest in my intellectual development; they left me free to get my own culture where and how I liked, or not to get any at all. Few students of art, and particularly of music, can have grown up so completely alone. Most of them, even if they do not pass through a conservatoire, have at any rate a teacher and fellow-student to talk to. I had one boyish friend, with whom I used to discuss literature, but my school education was of the usual type, with no special reference to art, and my association with my school-mates went no further than playing with them and fighting with them.

Search my memory how I will I cannot discover how or when I learned the rudiments of music. I suppose it was from some instruction book or other. But I fancy that, once having learned the notes, reading music was as simple a process with me as reading a book. At first everything was done quite unsystematically. I found myself playing the piano, after a fashion, without having learned anything of piano technique.

I have often wondered if one could draw up a balance sheet showing accurately the profit and loss of an education such as mine, an education without masters and without system. No doubt such a student benefits in some ways. He comes into contact with the great artists at first hand. He goes straight for the greatest things; it is on these that his taste is nourished. He enjoys every work of art he takes up, because he takes up only those he hopes to enjoy; and every work he enjoys sends him hotfoot after another.

With a master, even the most intelligent master (and very few masters are really intelligent), he is always being held back. His exuberance is curbed. He is told that he must learn to walk before he can run, and his early walks, under a master, condemn him to so much uninteresting country! He is kept at exercises that bore him, and at 'pieces' that may indeed be suited to the then stage of his technical development, but beyond which he may have travelled miles, intellectually and temperamentally. If he dislikes the drudgery with which it is associated, his first enthusiasm may be chilled.

It is surely better for him to learn to love music by approaching it from the wrong road than to hate it by approaching it from the right one. It is surely better for him to play *Tristan* abominably before he has learned to finger a scale properly, but yet to get at the heart of the opera in his own way, than to spend hours at the piano over a trifling Mozart sonata that he sees through in a couple of days, and so to conceive a prejudice against Mozart that may endure for years.

On the other hand, there is a good deal to be said for a systematic education, obvious as some of its disadvantages may be. A system sums up, however imperfectly, the combined experiences of many others who have travelled the same road before us, who have looked back after they have arrived, and have seen what, after all, was the shortest way, all things considered, from the

starting point to the goal, deceptively easy as one or two alternative routes seemed at the moment. None of us is so wise or so
clever that he can afford to condemn the slowly built up experience
of generations. The youth dislikes system because it means
discipline, and there is nothing youth chafes under so much as
discipline. In ordinary life, many a man may perhaps be all the
better for growing up wild; but not, perhaps, in art. Sooner or
later, if he is at all conscientious and self-critical, he will realize
that he, too, must go through the mill – not necessarily the
academic mill, but certainly some sort of mill. He will see that it
has taken humanity hundreds of years of painful effort to discover
a few stable truths, a few safe guiding principles, in art; he cannot,
unless he is absurdly vain, hope to discover for himself all that it
has taken generations to work out. Sooner or later he must go to
school.

III

This is what happened to me. I do not refer to piano-playing,
which I have never regarded as indispensable to a musician,
though even there I soon realized how impossible it is to learn to
play the piano by just sitting down and hitting the keys with a
score of *Parsifal* in front of you. I found I had to settle down and
do a little sensible practice in order to be able to play even
moderately badly. I may say, in parenthesis, that I never became
more than a bad pianist. For one thing, I always grudged even
the little time I spent in practising, for I felt that in the same time
I could be learning some more music. I never had any ambition to
play before others, and I was content to go on for a long time
with the moderate technique that enabled me to play what I
could of a work, my mind supplying, when I came to difficulty,
what my fingers would not do.

But it was not to piano-playing that I was referring when I
spoke of my realizing, one fine day, that I would have to study
music in the school way as well as in my own. I cannot remember
the time when I could not read music as one reads a book. I
suppose it was natural to me, for I had no lessons of any kind, and

I cannot trace any stages in the process of learning. It seems to me
that I was reading music, and playing it my own amateurish way,
from early childhood. For some reason or other, I was most
interested as a boy, in vocal music, and particularly in opera. I
lived in Liverpool at that time, and I used to get from one of the
public libraries some operatic scores in a series that I have never
come across since. I have often wondered who published them.
As well as I recollect, they belonged to the first half of the
nineteenth century, and had what I then thought were very
interesting prefaces. Like most young people, I was not particularly attracted to Mozart. He seemed cold to me, in my
ignorance – too simple, even superficial. I liked many of his
operatic arias, but as an opera composer, I thought Gluck greatly
his superior in those days, and I would have been prepared to cut
anyone's throat who thought otherwise.

Again, like most young people, I had unbounded faith in my
own judgment, and I used to wonder how the writers who fell
into ecstasies over Mozart could be so easily taken in. I suppose it
was because – once more like most young people – I was more
susceptible to ideas than to pure beauty.

I supposed I liked Gluck and Wagner and Schumann better
than Mozart or Schubert because the former seemed to me to be
dealing with a bigger order of humanity. Iphigenia, Tristan, the
girl in the *Woman's Life and Love* cycle, seemed to the ardent
humanitarian that I was in those unspoilt days, more truly human
than Cherubino or Masetto or the Hurdy Gurdy Man. I liked
Mozart and Schubert well enough in a way, but I put them with
Rossini and Auber and Bellini and the other pretty tune-makers,
though of course, somewhat in front of these.

IV

It is only as one gets older, I think, that one learns to appreciate
pure beauty in music, the beauty that begins and ends with itself,
that is all-sufficient to itself. This would account for something
that happens to us all in the long run – drawing nearer to Mozart
as we grow older. That, at any rate, has been my experience; I

have shed a good many of my early enthusiasms, both in poetry and in music, while my delight in Mozart has gone on increasing since I first came completely under his spell some fifteen or twenty years ago.

My earliest tastes were all for the strenuous, the highly-charged poetic, in music. It was always the slow movement that transported me into what was then, and for a long time afterwards, my favourite world – the world of Goethe's *Faust* and Words-worth's *Intimations of Immortality* ode, the world of brooding introspection and philosophic melancholy. I had no ears for the pure, simple beauty of a Mozart symphony; but I worked myself into frenzies of spiritual self-torture over the agonized adagio of Beethoven's great 'Hammerclavier' sonata.

We are curiously constituted. This adagio was for me, as a boy, the expression of the quintessence of human suffering: I always had a vision, when I played or read it, of Beethoven as a chained Prometheus, the eagle gnawing him. In the course of many years, when I had outgrown my youthful romanticism, this adagio and all the German music of which it is the type lost something of its power over me.

Artists who indulge themselves too much in images of suffering are like the people we meet with in ordinary life who insist on telling us their ailments at great length. We get a little tired of them both; we feel that it is something of the same kind of weakness, the same womanish craving for sympathy, that prompts the over-long story of the spiritual as of the bodily *malaise*. Paradoxically, it is those of us who are by nature the most sensitive to suffering and the most inclined to brood over it who come to resent most, in time, any excess of this kind of expression in artists.

I suppose the explanation is that some self-protective instinct within us warns us at last that it is as bad for us to keep the spiritual sores in us open as it is to keep our bodily sores; perhaps, at bottom it is the same perilous morbidity that makes us torture, and at the same time delight, ourselves with the bittersweet of Amfortas' terrible cry as makes it difficult for the sufferer from a skin disease to keep from scratching himself, though he knows it will be worse for him in the long run. There are sores of the soul as of the body; and one day it happens to all of us who have over-indulged ourselves in our youth in the morbidities of romanticism that we feel the need of a bracing mental and spiritual hygiene.

There came a time when I felt myself reacting against the introspection and self-torture of the German romanticists; and since the most intense expression of all this was, for me, the adagio of the Hammerclavier sonata, it was against that that I most consciously and most energetically revolted – very much in the way that, when we change our political party, it is against the leader of our old party that we turn our sharpest arrows. Not, of course, that the adagio ever came to be abhorrent to me, or that it does not still move me. But I can no longer give myself up to it and what it stands for as I used to do; and I think Beethoven would have been greater had he kept more control of himself in moments like this. Bach is greater because, with the very rarest of exceptions, he universalizes his sorrow.

Too often, with Beethoven and Liszt and Schumann and Chopin, we are over-conscious of the man himself. We see him straining under a load he cannot carry without an exhausting effort. In poignant things like the aria 'Have mercy, oh Lord', or the 'Eli, Eli, lama sabachthani' of the Matthew Passion, Bach does not strain in the least. We feel this suffering not as something merely personal to him, as we do in many of the overwrought moments of Beethoven and Chopin and Tchaikovsky, but as the suffering of the cosmos itself – not the tears of a fretted individual, but the tears that are in mortal things.

A good deal of the present-day revolt against Beethoven and Tchaikovsky is due to the revolt of a world that has been hardened by adversity against the men who indulge themselves in their weaknesses, who scratch their sores in secret instead of giving them to the sunlight and fresh air to heal.

When, a little while ago, I printed a letter I had had from a well-known Englishman of letters, in which he tried to account for his antipathy to anything in waltz rhythm by tracing it to some childish 'complex' or other – some occasion on which he may have suffered while a waltz was going on – another and more sceptical friend permitted himself a little genial humour at the expense of us both. But I see nothing improbable myself in the explanation. There must be many such complexes in all of us.

I am tempted to explain the extraordinary popularity of Scriabine among women by the curiously catlike quality of his music, in which one cannot say where eroticism ends and spirituality begins, or by his liberation of certain centuries-long suppressed complexes in them. I fancy they get something of the same kind of pleasure from Scriabine's soft curves and insinuating harmonies that they get from scents and the sheen of satins and the subtle electricity of furs. The critic who wants to understand himself must try to trace his own complexes, if only to rescue himself from them when they are likely to bar the way to his sympathetic understanding of every kind of music.

v

I spoke of the unsystematic nature of my first musical education, and of my realization, long before I was out of my teens, of the need of supplementing my haphazard study of music as an art by a study of music as a science.

I said I have had only one music lesson in my whole life, and that this lasted no more than half an hour. It must have been when I was about seventeen. At that time I was at the Liverpool College. As well as I remember, music was no part of the set educational course; indeed, it could not have been, or I should have had more than this one lesson. Yet I suppose music must have been taught in some way to someone or other, for there was a Mr. (perhaps Dr.) Richard Crowe there, who officiated at the organ in the college theatre on great occasions, and no doubt had other duties in the place.

I have no clear recollection of him except that he was a little man, that he was irreverently referred to by us boys as Dicky Crowe, and that we did not think much of him because he had nothing to do with our games. What his musical qualifications were I cannot say. To him I went one afternoon after school hours and had a short first lesson in harmony. I never repeated the

experiment, for the lesson was only a repetition of a disappointment and a disillusionment that I had already experienced in
private. When I had decided that it was time I learned something
of the science and the technique of the art, I bought one or two
text-books on harmony and counterpoint and settled down to
them with something of the emotion Lord Carnarvon must have
felt when he was breaking through the wall on the other side of
which was the tomb of King Tutankhamen, with all its long-
hidden treasures. Try to imagine what Lord Carnarvon would
feel like if, after getting into the last chamber, he found it as
empty as Madame Humbert's safe, and you will have a faint idea
of what I felt like when first I began the study of musical text-
books.

Remember that by this time I had dozens of scores in my head.
I knew most of them by heart – all the pianoforte sonatas and the
symphonies of Beethoven and the Forty-eight Preludes of Bach,
many of Mozart's piano sonatas and piano duets, practically the
whole of Wagner, Beethoven's *Fidelio*, all of Gluck's operas that
are obtainable in modern editions (*Orfeo, Armide, Paris and Helen,
Iphigenia in Aulis, Iphigenia in Tauris,* and *Alceste*), thirty or forty
other operas of all schools, including *Der Freischütz, Fra Diavolo,
William Tell, The Barber of Seville,* Paisiello's *Barber,* and Cimarosa's
Il Matrimonio Segreto, one or two of the oratorios and a few of the
clavier works of Handel, a few specimens of the older church
music, such as Palestrina's 'Pope Marcellus' Mass and 'Stabat
Mater', and the 'Stabat Mater' of Pergolesi (also the latter's little
opera *La Serva Padrona*), a few old English and Italian madrigals,
a good deal of Schubert, Schumann, Mendelssohn and Chopin
(I was very fond not only of Schumann's songs, but of his opera
Genoveva and the big ensemble works like *Faust* and *Manfred*),
and a heap of other music of all sorts, all periods, all schools.

For years I had been reading music daily, with the ardour with
which schoolgirls used to read novelettes, or schoolboys adventure
stories. When I was about twenty I had, in my simplicity, the idea
that it would be possible, in another year or two, to have learned
virtually all the music that really mattered. I rarely went to
concerts at that time. I never saw a musical journal, and I do not

suppose I knew that there was such a thing as musical criticism in the newspapers – in any case, newspapers hardly ever came my way in my schoolboy days.

The music I lived with was that of the classics, from Palestrina to Schumann. Of contemporary composers I knew next to nothing, with the exception of Wagner, who had seized upon my imagination from the first, and whose operas were my daily bread. I had no musical friends. I had an old history or two of music, that gave me at any rate the great names and showed the development of the chief schools. I had the catalogues of the popular editions of Peters and Litolff, and in my innocence I thought that all I had to do to know all about the real music that had ever been written was to work steadily through the chief works of the best-known men in these catalogues. I gave myself three or four years to complete this task, and thought the allowance ample. I did not then know how much interesting music lies off the beaten track. I did not know that contemporary composers were pouring out works as a fountain spouts water – what a race it was to try to catch up with them in later years! I did not then realize that of all students the student of music has the heaviest task.

A man whose job is literature may be interested in European literature as a whole, but what he really knows of it comes down in the long run to a close knowledge of the books of his own country, a pretty fair knowledge of the books of one foreign country, and a smattering of the literature of the others. But in music there is no language bar, and the musical periods of the various nations are part and parcel of each other. The student of music has to know the music of at least half a dozen countries as well as he knows the music of any one of them.

But however much I did not know of music in my early youth, at any rate I knew something of it, and what I knew had been learned at first hand. I had grown up in the art unhampered by theory. You can perhaps dimly imagine my puzzlement when, with all this music in my head – most of it first-rate – I began to work at the textbooks. I found myself being solemnly taught a number of things that I had learned for myself long ago – nay, I had not learned them, for they were natural and self-evident; one might as well speak of having learned to move the eyelids or to secrete bile.

Music was to me a living language: I spoke it and understood it as one speaks and understands one's native tongue, not so much learning it as unconsciously absorbing it out of the air around. To my amazement I found myself being taught in the text-books things that it seemed simply incredible to me that anyone should need to 'learn'. I was like a man who has read Shakespeare through with complete understanding and enjoyment, and then is expected to listen dutifully while an elementary school teacher solemnly tells him that an English verb must agree with its noun in number. 'Of course it does', he would reply. 'What else *could* it do? You might as well tell me that in order to walk I must put first one foot foremost, then the other. How else *could* I walk?'

VI

I began to describe the perplexities in which I found myself when, after a long saturation in music itself, I began to study the theory of music as set forth in the text-books.

My difficulty was twofold – I had to listen to things being explained to me that seemed so obvious and natural as not to need explanation; and I was always being told it was wrong to do something or other that I knew the great masters made no scruple about doing.

It took me a little time to realize that much of what was taught in the text-books as essential for the right practice of music had next to nothing to do with the art of composition.

If it were necessary to know all about – or even anything about – the theory of harmony in order to understand music, then concert-going would be restricted to a handful of trained theoreticians in each town. The plain lover of music no more knows the names of the chords he is listening to than the plain lover of poetry knows that this poem is in alexandrines, this in alcaics, this in sapphics. But just as, in the latter case, ignorance of the name of the metre is no bar to the enjoyment of the rhythm of the poem, so, in the former case, ignorance of the names of the chords is no bar to the understanding of what it is that the composer is saying through the chords.

The man in the seat next to me at *Parsifal* may not know a chord of the diminished seventh from an ichthyosaurus, or a minor ninth from a pterodactyl; but when Wagner stabs him with one of these chords his soul is hurt in the same way and to the same extent as mine is. He listens to Scriabine's *Prometheus* in blissful ignorance that the composer is here working on a new harmonic system of his own, building his chord out of fourths placed one on top of the other; but the man does not need to know anything of this to understand what Scriabine is talking to him about.

Indeed, in many cases the composer himself could not tell us the proper name of some of the new chords he is using. He only knows that he 'feels like that' – that he had something in him he wanted to say, and, without his volition, it said itself through these novel harmonies. He leaves it to the theoretician to name them.

Musical minds *think* in music as other minds do in prose or verse – music, to them, is a natural language. It has always been a difficulty to me to understand how people need to be *taught* music – it has always seemed to me as natural as speech. This may be, in part, because I grew up in the *practice* of music, where I spent some years before I went on to the theory of it.

When I found the text-books telling me that this was the way to resolve certain chords, or this the way to modulate from one key to another, I was astonished – not at the information, but at the fact that there were people interested in music who needed such information. It all seemed to me self-evident. But while a great deal of what the text-books told me struck me as superfluous, a great deal more struck me as nonsense.

I found myself being 'forbidden' to do things that I had seen the great composers frequently doing. I was told, indeed, that sometimes even the great composers were naughty boys, who did not keep to the rules, but that no good boy who wanted to get on would follow their bad example – unless and until he happened to become a great master himself, when, of course, he would be allowed to do what he liked, subject to the censure of the pedagogues.

It was all very puzzling. I could not help thinking that Wagner and Bach must have known more about composition than Macfarren or Rockstro or Prout. (I am not sticking strictly to chronology now. I fancy Prout's treatises did not appear till a few years after the period in my development that I am now describing. I cite him as a type; and my soul's conflicts with the textbooks lasted for many years.)

It shocked me to learn that hardly one of Bach's fugues was correctly written, and that so little did composers like Palestrina know about the 'rules' of counterpoint that Rockstro could hardly cite a single example from their works to illustrate the 'rules' but had to write examples of his own!

I was still young enough to have some respect for authority, and to believe what I saw in print. There must be something in what all these people say, I used to murmur to myself.

Sometimes I felt sorry for Bach and Palestrina and the rest of them, who, poor fellows, had been born too soon to profit by the instruction of such masters as Macfarren and Prout. At other times I would wonder what one of these theorists would do if he had an innovating genius to teach – a Wagner, say. Would he tell him, as he tells me, to observe the rules, or would he grant him that 'licence' which, it seems, only a master was allowed to take out? And at what age did a master qualify for a licence?

No doubt Beethoven and the rest of them began by observing the rules as little boys, and only ventured to flout them when they became masters. But would it not be as possible for one master to break a rule with safety at sixteen as for another to break it at sixty? Suppose, then, that Macfarren had a genius of sixteen for a pupil. Would he recognize his genius at that age?

It was all very well to wink at the peccadilloes of a composer whom the world for a hundred years had called a master; Macfarren could hardly say this or that passage should have been written otherwise without being laughed at. But might not some boy of sixteen talk as sound musical sense in defiance of the 'rules'

as, say, the mature Bach or Beethoven? If he did, how would
Macfarren handle him?

It was easy enough to spot a winner when the crowd was
applauding him after the race had been won; but could Macfarren
spot a winner in his own class, before the race began? I remember
how little perception Cherubini, when head of the Paris Conservatoire, had of the genius of the erratic young Berlioz; and I had
my doubts.

VII

I was soon made to realize, however, the need for a more solid
grounding in musical technique when I began to compose. Mr.
Squeers, in my opinion, has always been a much misunderstood
and unfairly disparaged man. His own spelling may not have
been above suspicion, but there is a good deal to be said for his
practical way of teaching spelling; when he said, 'W-i-n-d-e-r,
go and clean it', he was combining, and teaching his boys to
combine theory with practice.

Like all ardent young men with music in them, I had an itch for
composition. It was while I was under the staggering blow of my
first acquaintance with harmonic theory that I began. As I have
already told the reader, nearly half of what I read in the harmony
text-books seemed to me to be disputed by the practice of the
great masters, and nearly half the remainder seemed so obvious
that I could not understand why people should need to be told
such things; and as my reading, at this time, had mostly been
among harmonic rather than contrapuntal music, I had as yet no
idea of the difficulties of musical composition.

It appeared to me, indeed, quite as easy as writing poetry or
prose; you had something to say, and you just said it. There was,
of course, a good deal of difference between the things said by one
composer and those said by another; that simply meant, as in
poetry, that one composer was endowed by Providence with
better ideas than another.

At the age I was then, sixteen or seventeen, I naturally was quite
convinced that my own ideas were excellent. All I had to do, then,
was to put the thoughts on paper.

And that is where the trouble began. Then I realized that the understanding of an art was one thing, and the practice of it another. It is possible for any of us to lean back in his seat and explain why Carpentier is a good boxer, what harmony of forces goes to make that quick correlation between eye and brain and muscle. But to get a similar harmony of our own is quite another matter.

The best way to realize that such a harmony is necessary is to put on the gloves with a boxer; our conceit in ourselves will not survive the first short round. The best way to realize that swimming is an art is to fall into the water, or to go into it after something we very much want, and to scramble back to safety with difficulty, and without the thing we went in for.

When I tried to put my turbulent flood of musical ideas into notes, I soon saw the wisdom and the meaning of musical discipline. A little while ago, in the course of a removal from one house to another, I happened to come across some long-forgotten manuscripts of that period, settings of poems by Swinburne, Rossetti, Blake, Herbert and other poets. Some of the ideas were perhaps not hopelessly bad, but the technique! The clumsiness, the helplessness of it! I had the good sense to realize, even then, that this sort of thing would never do.

It was my first initiation into a truth that I have, I am afraid, often annoyed other young composers since by insisting on – that 'ideas' in music, in the sense of thematic invention, and more especially the invention of a theme to illustrate a poetic or pictorial idea, are the smallest and easiest part of musical composition. This may seem an extreme statement, but every experienced musician knows that it is no exaggeration.

Thousands of second-rate composers can invent quite good themes, but they cannot make good compositions out of them. On the other hand, many of the greatest of the world's works are made out of fragments of material that in and by themselves are nothing, or even, superficially considered, worse than nothing.

Composers like Liszt have a decided faculty for inventing expressive illustrative themes, but they never succeed in building

B

up a first-rate long work. Rimsky-Korsakov is another composer
with the gift of conceiving one enchanting tune after another;
but when he tries to write an overture or a symphonic movement
he can do little more than go on repeating his tunes.

Beethoven and Bach, on the other hand, often perform their
greatest marvels with bits of material that are in themselves quite
insignificant. If we did not know the Fifth Symphony, and saw
the two subjects of the first movement quoted in music type, we
would feel merely a sort of pitying contempt for the composer.
The first subject in particular would convey nothing to us; it is
not even a tune, as the second subject is. Yet out of these two
tiny fragments of wood and mud grows the gigantic tree of that
wonderful first movement.

Give Bach just three notes – say those of the opening phrase of
the third Brandenburg Concerto, which strictly speaking, are
only two notes (G, F sharp, G) – and he will go on spinning the
most delightful fabrics of tone out of them until the dinner-bell
rings.

Wagner was so bad an influence upon the young composers
who followed him, precisely because of his incomparable gift of
inventing significant themes. His powers in this respect have
perhaps not had full justice done to them; but anyone who
wants to realize it for himself has only to run over in his mind the
leading motives of the '*Ring*' alone. There must be well over a
hundred of them. Each of them hits off to a nicety the character
or the force or the object of which it is the symbol.

And many people are so absorbed in the pure expressiveness of
the themes as themes that they do not realize that Wagner is not
merely a great inventor, but, like Bach and Beethoven, a consummate architect and builder.

As later composers found to their cost, a musical drama
or a symphonic poem is not written when expressive themes
have been hit upon for the salient moments of the story. And there
are composers, such as Bach and Beethoven, who do not even
need striking themes in order to build up, somehow or other,
great palaces of sound that have the logic of a fine building and
the expressiveness of a fine poem.

VIII

I have said that my first studies in theoretical harmony taught me virtually nothing that I had not already learned practically at first hand from the great composers. Counterpoint, canon and fugue, however, are technical things that come to no man by the mere grace of God. As soon as I realized that the art of musical composition was not so simple a thing as the composing of poetry, and that a technique was necessary, I set myself to the acquiring of this technique. I may say at once that I very soon gave up the idea of shining as a composer. Whether the surrender was to be attributed to modesty or to vanity I cannot say – whether to the humble feeling that with so much splendid music in the world there was really no call for me or anyone else to write inferior music, or to the proud feeling that since I could not produce anything first-rate I would not appear before my fellow-men as a third- or fifth-rater. Anyhow, for a few years during which I composed I had the sense to keep my efforts to myself. Some of them were pretty ambitious; I particularly remember a big work – big I mean, in that it ran to some hundreds of pages of score – based on Shelley's 'Prometheus Unbound' – a sort of mystical blend of opera and symphony, inspired, I should now imagine, by Schumann's *Manfred*.

But I am anticipating somewhat. This and sundry other masterpieces occupied some five years of my time, and during those five years I was working hard at the technique of music. On second thoughts, no doubt it was a rational humility that made me ultimately give up composing, and never succumb later to the temptation to attempt anything more in that line. I saw that, however important my music might be to myself as a kind of emotional catharsis, it was very ordinary stuff compared with the real thing of the real composers. What I then felt about myself I now feel about a great many of the young composers of today. I am often accused of being 'unsympathetic' to these people and their works. I repel the charge indignantly. I am extremely sympathetic towards them. So far from discouraging them, I always encourage them to go on composing their songs and symphonies and concertos and operas. I assure them they will feel better when they get it out of their system. Writing music or poetry is to the average emotional young man merely the psychical equivalent of the Turkish bath. As this promotes a healthy action of the skin, composition promotes a healthy action of the soul. Hygiene demands the elimination of the spiritual no less than of the physical toxins; but the process, though highly beneficial to the subject, is not a matter of great interest to the rest of the world.

I am, then, anything but unsympathetic to the average composer; all I object to is his assumption that I ought to take a passionate interest in the average outpourings of his average soul. This I cannot do. Frankly, I have no use for average composers, or average artists of any kind. A musical friend once startled me by telling me I was a hero-worshipper. I jibbed at the description at first; but in a little while I saw that he understood me better than I understood myself. I reserve my enthusiasms for first-rate minds and first-rate things, and it is in the company of these, and these alone, that I would spend all my time if I were free to choose.

There is too much great music in the world that I do not know as intimately as I should like for me to be willing to give up any more time than I can help to music that has not even a flavour of greatness about it.

But though I soon, comparatively speaking, gave up the vain idea of being a composer, I worked hard at the study of musical technique for critical purposes. In this, as in everything else, I preferred to study alone. I hardly know what it is in my make-up that has always rendered it difficult for me to put myself in the hands of a 'master'. Perhaps it is an incurable native scepticism, the impossibility of believing that the whole truth, on any subject, is with any one man or any one school or any one party. It took very little study of musical theory for me to discover that the 'authorities' were often at variance; I would find, for instance, one pundit declaring positively that the second subject of the Beethoven sonata began in a certain bar, and another pundit declaring, with equal positiveness, that it began in quite another

bar. Little things of this kind aroused my suspicions, and confirmed my natural distrust of authority.

My way of study has always been to get as many books as
possible on the subject in hand, and make each of them supple-
ment the deficiencies, or show up the fallacies of the others. In
counterpoint, canon, fugue and form I worked steadily for several
years through text-books like those of Cherubini, Ouseley,
Rockstro, Prout, Richter, Jadassohn, Higgs, Bridge, Stainer,
Marx, and others; one of the works from which I derived great
benefit was August Reissmann's *Lehrbuch der musikalischen
Komposition*, in two large volumes – an excellent treatise for its
time (1866)*. Frederick Iliffe's useful analysis of Bach's '48' was
not published, I think, at that time; I fancy it appeared some time
in the eighteen-nineties. But I well remember the portentous
seriousness with which I went over Bach again under Iliffe's
guidance; only the other day, hunting for some lost papers, I
came across a big, sprawling volume I had manufactured for myself by interleaving Iliffe's book with the preludes and fugues
from a torn-up copy of Ernst Pauer's edition of Bach. But,
needless to say, my real teachers were not these theorists, but
Bach, Palestrina, Wagner, Beethoven, Mozart, and others of that
great family. I soon discovered how grey, as Goethe says, is all
theory. The essentials of musical theory and musical technique are
very simple, easily taught and easily learned. The applied technique of the masters is always an individual affair, and to the
study of this there is no end.

IX

When I began these garrulous Confessions, it was with the
laudable intention of trying to account for myself, both to
myself and to others. A critic is generally so occupied with
explaining other people that it does not occur to him that he may
stand in need of explanation himself, though it may be an agreeable part of his job to explain his colleagues, to account for this
one having such bad taste, say, where Schumann is concerned, or
for that one having written such egregious nonsense about

* Grove records three volumes (editor).

Brahms. It is true that the public, in its often justifiable irritation with us, explains us all in a rough-and-ready way; it puts our grumblings down to our livers. But that is really doing us an injustice.

The other day a very capable young artist described critics as 'mostly disappointed men, earning hardly enough to keep body and soul together'. I understand that great gratification was expressed in critical circles at this handsome recognition that critics *had* souls, which I have known some singers and fiddlers deny. As for critics being disappointed men, I am afraid we must all plead guilty. Our life is just one disappointment after another.

But the sin is not on our shoulders, but on the shoulders of those who disappoint us. In any case, our disappointments do not sour us. A more cheerful, kindly body of men I never met. Where else would you find people persistently passing off their sufferings with a joke! You do not find the man who has just writhed under the surgeon's knife regarding the surgeon and his knife as two of the funniest things on earth; but I have often seen two or three critics, after enduring at the hands of a singer's larynx, as the Irishmen might say, more excruciating pain than any knife could inflict (and, remember, we never have chloroform for *our* operations), turn to each other with a smile that was most expressive of their appreciation of the joke of such a person getting up in a public hall and calling herself a singer. Nor would the critics dream of saying anything unpleasant about her, in spite of her having paid for an advertisement.

I assure the reader that the picture generally painted of critics by disgruntled 'artists' is a false one; they have the patience of Job, the endurance of a horse, and the sweetness of an angel. They may not get their reward in this world; but if there is any justice in the scheme of things they will get it in the next; they will be sent to some place where the singers cease from troubling and the fiddlers are at rest.

No, it is not by our livers that we critics are to be explained; as a matter of fact, I think our livers are in particularly good fettle, owing to the fresh air and exercise we get sprinting from one hall to another. But, after all, it is writing about music, not about

performers, that is, or at least should be, the critic's business; and
since the oddities of critical judgment that we meet with every
day are to be accounted for by some idiosyncrasy of the critic, we
ought to know as much as possible about the mental make-up
and the bringing-up of the critic. Sometimes it is easy enough to
trace a critic's opinions to something that has happened to him –
when, for instance, we find a young man flagrantly unfair to
German music because he had a bad time during the war. But it
is in the earliest years of his life that a critic is really made, for
better or for worse, and when we get to middle age we cannot
help looking back and trying to see ourselves as if we were
someone else we were studying, trying to account for our present
attitude towards music in terms of our earliest influences and
associations.

We do this as a matter of course in the case of composers; we
find out where and how they lived in their early manhood, with
whom they studied, and so on. But a critic does not, like a
composer, go through a formal process of learning his business.
There are no schools in which he can study, no masters at whose
feet he can sit. He learns – if he ever learns at all – by practising at
other people's expense an art he has never been taught.

He begins with an unbounded, pathetic confidence in himself; he
ends with the most painful doubts about himself. I know that
there is a school that regards criticism as purely a personal matter,
the play of the critic's temperament upon a work of art, regardless
of questions and rightness or wrongness of judgment. But
rightness or wrongness of judgment assuredly enters into the
question. Criticism is not merely a personal coltish kicking up of
the heels in the meadows of art; it is an attempt to induce other
people to see the thing as we see it – which implies a belief that
one way of looking at the thing is essentially right, and the
opposite way, essentially wrong, that *Gerontius*, for instance, is a
greater work than *The Woman of Samaria*, not merely for Brown
or Jones, but for all who know anything about names.

'The whole man thinks', said George Henry Lewes truly.
Into each of our judgments upon music goes the whole man that
heredity, early training and life have made us.

Looking back on my own case, I can see that the solitariness of my earliest intellectual life has had its effects on me. It has made me, for one thing, a poor party man. Having got my first musical culture by myself, without schools, without masters, without even friends, I never formed any strong ties, either personal or clannish. When I see some of my most respected colleagues behaving indulgently, to say the least of it, towards poor work because it comes from a particular coterie, they seem to me merely a sort of trade unionist marching behind the banner of their union – a sad thing, perhaps, for artists to be doing. All the same, people, in this imperfect world, can only get certain big things done by acting together and sinking some of their purely personal predilections. It is my misfortune, no doubt, that I find it difficult to do this in matters of art. I dislike joining Societies, because I feel – absurdly enough, perhaps – that it hampers my freedom of judgment on details.

x

When I look back upon my adolescence it seems to me that one of the strongest influences in my life was my love of sculpture – especially Greek sculpture – and architecture. I sometimes attribute to my early experiences among these arts my later impatience with shapelessness of design or crudity of workmanship in music, for sculpture and architecture are the two arts in which any deficiency or excess of substance, any ungainliness of line, or any failure of harmony is most quickly noticed and most intolerable.

Yet the influence may have been the other way round. Perhaps we were always inclined to confuse cause and effect in matters of the spirit.

We put certain traits of the early Wagner, as man and as artist – his hectic living, for example, or his occasional lack of artistic refinement – to his having spent so many years as a boy and as a young man in the theatre or in the company of theatrical people.

The true explanation may be that he haunted theatrical society and adopted a theatrical career in the first place because his inborn instinct for the hectic and the overblown, both in life and in art, led him unconsciously to the theatre. We say that another composer's work owes its sexless quality to the fact that he was brought up among prim women and became a choir-boy at an early age, but it is equally probable that it was the passionless nature of his mental substance that sent him in the first place to the prim ladies and the choir stalls.

It is the old problem of which came first – the egg or the chicken? Does the 'influence' make the man, or does the boy instinctively and unconsciously select his own 'influence'? Perhaps the latter is the truer explanation. Probably none of us would ever have been moulded by life into our present mental shape if – to put it paradoxically – we had not been that shape from our birth, and would never have come under this formative influence or that had not the unconscious desire of the soul to realize itself along its own lines made us turn in the direction where the influence was to be found.

At the same time it is no doubt true that had we not come under the particular influence we should not have become so completely ourselves.

No doubt what I have sometimes thought was my early education in sculpture and architecture shaping some of my views on music was really only an inborn love for clarity and coherence and shapeliness seeking satisfaction in the outer as well as in the inner world. But all the same, the relative thorough-ness with which I pursued my studies in these arts, especially in sculpture, must have had a great influence on my later attitude towards music.

The point would be of no importance, or even interest, to anyone but myself were it not that it helps, perhaps, to explain some features of me as a musical critic that have earned me a good deal of no doubt well-deserved dislike.

I am not apologizing for myself; perhaps the offence is too deep for apology – I am trying to account for myself. It is often made a grievance against me that I am not sufficiently enthusiastic over the works of the average young composer. I must plead guilty. Average work of any kind does not interest me; and in the nature of things the bulk of the work produced in any given year can only be of average quality.

I quite realize that without a vast amount of musical activity that is practically worthless in itself the world can never get the one or two great men who stand for their epoch, but for my part I am content to wait until the great men appear.

I should be thoroughly satisfied to pass the whole of the next five or ten years without hearing a single bar of the just ordinarily good music that will be produced in such terrific quantity during that time. My tastes are modest and simple: give me the best of everything and you can keep the rest. Life is too short – and as one gets older it seems much too short – to waste any of it on things that do not matter. I would walk ten miles to see Cleopatra or Helen of Troy, but I protest against the notion that every plain Mary Ann or frumpish Elizabeth Jane I may pass in Tottenham Court Road is entitled to five minutes of my respectful gaze.

In a word, I am not greatly interested in imperfected things: there are already too many perfect or almost perfect things in the world that, to my sorrow, I shall die without having seen or heard. Anyway, I would rather give a day to brooding over some specimen of perfect beauty that I have known all my life than to give five minutes to some specimen of the average that happens to have been produced yesterday.

It may seem contradictory of me to say that while I have no interest whatsoever in the second-rate musical mind or second-rate musical work of today, I often find the second-rate in the past extremely interesting. But the contradiction is only a superficial one. At bottom my interest in the second-rate of the past comes from the same constitution of mind that makes me interested in only the first-rate of the present.

I cannot see, nor can any living soul see, what is going to be the form taken by music under the next great man's hands. Out of the present turmoil something will come, but it may be any one of fifty possible things. When it does come the particular little men and little works that led up to it will be of interest to the historian, and all the others of them will matter nothing.

Were I living a hundred years hence, I would no doubt be studying some of the little men of today in relation to the great man of 1950 with the same interest I now take in the study of, say, Lesueur in relation to Berlioz. Except in that relation Lesueur today has no life at all. It may be the good fortune of one or two of the little men of today to achieve a certain immortality in relation to some great genius of the next generation, but I shall not be here to study the connection.

XI

Leaving the long story of how I came to be the detestable thing I am, I propose to recount the steps by which I came to be the detested thing I am; in other words, how and why I drifted into the nefarious trade of musical criticism.

I was really intended for the Indian Civil Service. To this end, after leaving the Liverpool College, I went for a time to the Liverpool University – or, as I believe it was then called, the Victorian University. The principal then was Sir Oliver Lodge, who is probably unaware that he had the honour of teaching me all I know about electricity and physics, which is not much, I regret to say. That it is so little, however, is a reflection not on Sir Oliver but on myself; for I dodged as many of the science classes as I could and spent the time in the University library, mostly reading the Elizabethan poets and dramatists.

English literature and art, indeed, were the only things that interested me at the University. The lectures on both these subjects were fascinating. I still have the liveliest recollections of the joy I used to get from Professor A. C. Bradley and Professor (later Sir Walter) Raleigh, and I think Sir Martin Conway used also to lecture in my time. I remember also Professor Strong, the well-known Latinist – a rather bad-tempered man, I am afraid. I have forgotten his Latin classes, but I vividly remember his spleen one day when he discovered that some volume for which he had been vainly hunting in the library for a long time was in my possession.

Those were happy, irresponsible days. The future had no

worries for me. I had been given to understand that I was supposed to be preparing for the Indian Civil Service examination, but the information conveyed very little to me. I was quite content to let the Indian Civil Service wait indefinitely for the honour of receiving me, so long as I could go on reading books and studying music. I recognized myself recently in the account an old friend gave me of a little conversation with his youngest son on the subject of the choice of a career. The boy was of a charming, dreamy, artistic nature. His father thought it about time to waken him to a sense of the stern realities of life, so he asked him if he had thought at all about what he would like to be. (The eldest son had gone into the army, the second into the navy.) The boy said he hadn't thought about the matter yet, but was prepared to give it his careful consideration.

A few days after, his father asked him if he had settled what he would like to do in life. He said he had; he would like to read. His father thought it an excellent idea, and was delighted that after the display of military ardour on the part of the two older boys, the youngest son should so early display a preference for one of the learned professions. But he would like a little more definite information: reading for what – the church, the bar, medicine, or what? The boy hastened to correct this misapprehension; he didn't want to read for anything in particular; he just wanted to go through life reading, poetry for preference.

That had been my own case, even at a later age than his. I should have been quite happy reading, if only grown-up people would have left me alone and not pestered me with tiresome talk about examinations.

However, Providence intervened to save India from me. My health broke down a little while before the examination. My heart was badly strained, and my doctor told me that even if I got through the examination the medical examiners would not pass me for an Eastern climate. So that settled it; I gave up India without a pang. I had never really wanted to go there, because I felt I should be cut off from my two greatest joys in life, books and music.

Somehow or other, I got into a bank in Liverpool. There I

spent a good many years of my life, learning a little about banking, but more about music and literature. By one of those beautiful combinations of circumstance that make it simply impossible to doubt that there is a beneficent design in Nature, banks are always built near cafés. This enables bank clerks to economize time in passing from the serious business of life, which is reading or playing dominoes in a café, to the minor interests of passbooks and produce warrants and bills of lading.

From the first I had an instinct that for success in life it was necessary to form good habits. Guided by this sure instinct, I used to go every morning to a conveniently adjacent café to read. I was the better able to do this inasmuch as I was an exceptionally fast worker, and could always catch up the lost hour or so in the office before lunch time. So ingrained did this habit become in me that to this day I am unhappy if I do not get my coffee every morning at eleven – something like Mr. Barry Pain's gardener Edwards, who used to suspend his arduous duties every morning for what he called his elevenses. For some years my duties at the bank were 'out-telling', going round with bills for acceptance or payments, etc. The reader will see what scope this delightful occupation offered to any clerk with a taste for literature.

There were various devices, known only to the initiated, by which the time actually spent in going the round could be curtailed, while the time theoretically occupied by the round was multiplied, and by which the round could be made to run in the more desirable districts. By handing over to a junior colleague, for instance, some acceptance that would have taken me into the purlieus of the distant docks, and keeping for myself one that took me up Islington way, I could get half an hour in at the Walker Art Gallery or the Picton Reading Room. And, of course, one could always read as one walked; in Liverpool streets alone, in those years, I must have read hundreds of volumes.

Street-reading, though, has its perils. I remember that once, wrestling in spirit with Hegel, I banged my forehead against a lamp-post, and went about for the next fortnight looking like a unicorn. I had not thought much of the Hegelian philosophy before that, and I thought still less of it after.

XII

I am very often asked by young men how they can become musical critics. I almost invariably recommend them to give up the mad idea, for it is not a very pleasant life, and the same amount of energy and intelligence put into commerce, speculation, betting or practising the confidence trick on guileless American visitors would bring fifty times the pecuniary reward. I used to laugh at the doctrine of metempsychosis until I became a musical critic. Now I believe firmly in it, as I often used to tell my dear old dog when his conduct had not been quite irreproachable. I used to explain to him that I had probably been a dog in some previous existence, had led a life of sin and crime, and was now working out my punishment in concert rooms, listening to singers who cannot sing, and to fiddlers who cannot fiddle; and I warned him that if he was not a better dog he might be made a musical critic in his next incarnation.

Every time a young man asks me how he can make a start as a critic I look at him sadly. Here, I say to myself, is another poor soul whose conduct as a hyena or an armadillo did not come up to the standard demanded by the too exacting gods. They are plainly being driven by the Fates, for nothing will induce them to give up the idea. I paint the profession in the blackest colours, but they insist on seeing it in the rose-pink of their imagination. To them it is a blissful succession of free seats for concerts and operas, and liberty to pour out every day those words of wisdom upon art, for which, they are convinced, an expectant world has been waiting for generations. Poor fellows, they do not foresee the time when a batch of tickets draws from the critic more groans than a demand for income tax does, the time when he feels he would like to have a short heart-to-heart talk with Tubal Cain, or Orpheus, or whoever it was invented music, and tell him just what he thought of him.

But when the young man is quite resolved to become a musical critic, and only seeks me out to learn from me how he is to begin, I am reluctantly compelled to tell him that I do not know. All I can do is to tell him how I myself began. Perhaps that way is as good as any other, and better than most. It is this – to go on into business, practise writing as a sideline, and stay in business till your writing has brought you reputation enough to justify your trusting wholly to it for a living.

I need not say that, in spite of the fun I often had in the bank, I was not really happy in business. I could study music and literature – apart from the hour or two I might snatch from my duties inside the bank, in the manner I have already described – only in the early morning and late at night, which meant very hard work. Often I would read from six or so in the morning until about half-past eight, and then curse the fate that tore me from my book and drove me to the office. But I can see now that there was a rough kindness in the Fates' treatment of me. Not being under the necessity of earning my living by literature, I could afford to write, when I did write, on a subject of my own choosing, and to take as long as I liked over the preparation for it. I had somehow made the acquaintance of Mr. – now the Right Honourable – John M. Robertson, man of letters, philosopher, economist and politician, to whom I owe more than to any other living individual for help and sympathy and guidance in my early days. I used to write on literature and music for one or two journals under his editorship. They had only small circulations, but they were read by a few people who took an interest in ideas.

About 1895 Mr. Robertson was finishing a book on *Buckle and his Critics* that he had had on hand for some years. It occurred to him to publish it by subscription, and to this end he gave a copious summary of its contents in the *Free Review*. He knew that I had in manuscript a book on Gluck. This had begun as an essay some years before, and had grown into a book without my quite knowing how it had happened. Mr. Robertson generously suggested my giving him an outline of the work for publication along with that of *Buckle and his Critics*. This was done. A fair number of subscribers enrolled themselves. One, I remember, lived in Japan. There were not enough, however, to justify my undertaking the expense of publication. One morning, to my great surprise, I received a letter from Mr. Bertram Dobell, the well-known Charing Cross Road book-seller, the friend and publisher of James Thomson, and later the discoverer of Traherne. He had, it seems, read several of my essays and had liked them. The summary of *Gluck and the Opera* had taken his fancy, and he declared his willingness to publish the book. He did me a very great service, for I am certain that no other publisher in England at that time would have taken a work on such a subject. I had had a light on the state of affairs when the one big publisher to whom I had written about the book replied courteously that he would not even trouble me to send him the manuscript, as there was no sale for books on music in this country.

The only thing I have to regret in connection with this affair was that I inadvertently caused the death of Sir Charles Hallé. Mr. Dobell had had the summary of the book reprinted, and copies of this I sent to a number of prominent people in the musical world who, I thought in my innocence, would be delighted to put themselves down for, at any rate, one copy each, though I fondly hoped for more. Some of the replies I got were very curious. The most unexpected people subscribed, and the most expected people did not. One well-known musical critic, who was said to be very well-to-do, replied that he could not subscribe (the price, I think, was five shillings), but he would review the book if it were sent to the —— for that purpose. I well remember posting a copy of the circular to Sir Charles Hallé one afternoon. It must have reached him by the morning post next day, and before the afternoon he was dead. It was the first of many crimes with which my literary conscience is burdened.

XIII

I am often accused of being unsympathetic towards 'the young composer', whereas the truth is that I am unsympathetic only towards the young composer who has nothing of any moment to say. There is one person, however, for whom I always feel the greatest sympathy – the young student who, anxious to do original musical research, finds himself checked at every turn by the difficulty of getting the necessary material. This was my own case when I was writing *Gluck and the Opera*. (I may add that though the book was not published till I was about twenty-seven, it had been written some four or five years earlier.) Gluck affected me as powerfully in those days as Wagner and Brahms, Elgar and Wolf and others were to do in later years. Had I been free I would gladly have devoted my whole time to research in the Continental libraries. But not much research of that kind is possible to a young man who is cooped up in business all day for eleven and a half months of the year: it was impossible even for me to visit the British Museum.

I did the best I could under the circumstances. I had a fair amount of material at my disposal in the Picton Library, Liverpool, and I bought all the books and music I could. For biographical information I necessarily had to rely on the exhaustive volumes of such writers upon Gluck as Marx, Schmid,* Desnoiresterres† and Reissmann; but I made as independent a study as I could of the music and literature of the period – German, Italian, French and English – and I tried to see the aesthetic of the opera as it appeared to the men of the eighteenth century, and to define Gluck's relation to this aesthetic. I have not glanced at the book for twenty years or more, and shall probably never do so until I happen to write on Gluck again. But I chanced a little while ago upon a critique of it, which I am sure sums it up pretty accurately, by a German expert, Dr. Stephen Wortsmann,‡ in a book surveying the whole field of Gluck literature, published by the Gluckgemeinde – a Gluck Society founded a few years before the War, but now presumably extinct.

Dr. Wortsmann points out, quite rightly, my indebtedness to Marx and the others in the matter of biographical detail, but – this amuses me – he says that 'the imagination of the author has painted some episodes, particularly in Gluck's early life, in such lively colours that the uninitiated reader . . . will come to the conclusion that he is dealing with an extraordinarily wellequipped Gluck expert. For none of his conjectures, however, has Newman brought forward the least new evidence; he has only, by means of his own combinations, conjured up pictures

* Schmid's great work on Gluck was published in Leipzig in 1854.
† *Gluck et Piccini* (Paris 1875).
‡ Die deutsche Gluck-Literatur (Nuremberg 1914) (Ed.)

which, it cannot be denied, have a good deal of probability, against which, however, the reader must be warned, since mere hypotheses are stated much too positively.' Dr. Wortsmann thinks the second part of the book – dealing with Gluck as artist, and with the eighteenth-century theory of the opera – the better of the two.

I am sure if I were to re-read the book I should agree with him. I was so fired by my subject that I have not the least doubt I wrote about the incidents of Gluck's career as if I had personally been a witness of them. I was very young, very ardent, and Gluck-drunk. Gluck was more real to me than most of the people I rubbed shoulders with every day.

The book was generously received by the English reviewers, and Mr. Dobell suggested that I should do a book on Wagner, which he would publish. I gladly fell in with the suggestion. Here the material for the kind of book I then wanted to do was easily accessible even to a young student in a town so remote from civilization as Liverpool. *A Study of Wagner* was a biggish book of some four hundred pages. It took me, with only the evenings in which to work at it after the tiring day's labour in the bank, a good three years to write, and it was published by Mr. Dobell in 1899.

This was the second of the great services this good old man did to a young author whom he as yet did not know personally. His constant kindness and thoughtfulness I shall never forget. In his capacity as second-hand bookseller he frequently came across literature that he thought might be useful to me in my studies, and this he always sent to me. He produced both the Gluck and the Wagner in handsome style. They had a fair and steady sale, and I hope he did not lose much over them. These were the last books of mine that he published. I issued various volumes through other publishers during the next few years – books asked for by them, so that I could not have offered them to Mr. Dobell. Some thirteen or fourteen years after the *Study of Wagner* I worked at another big book on that composer, which was published, under the title of *Wagner as Man and Artist*, in 1914. I received a letter from Mr. Dobell, from whom I had not heard for many years, gently reproaching me for not having given him an opportunity to publish this book also. I was touched by the generous old man's continued interest in me and his willingness to risk his money on me, and could only explain that even had I thought of asking him to make any further sacrifice on my behalf (for of course he had not the business organization of the bigger publishers) I was not free in this particular case. Thereupon he asked me to do for him a volume of literary essays (Nietzsche, Amiel, Meredith, and other subjects upon which I had already written in various magazines), and to prepare a new edition of *Gluck and the Opera*, which was now out of print. Before I could fulfill either task Mr. Dobell died. I have never forgotten his many kindnesses to me; it was he who gave me my first real footing on the ladder.

XIV

I imagine there can be a few professions that are such a delight to the new hand and such a horror to the old hand as musical criticism. Someone in Dickens comments on the remarkable fact that no one ever sees a dead donkey. But there is a greater rarity even than this – a musical critic of twenty years' standing who is enthusiastic about concerts. So rare is this phenomenon, indeed, that I have never yet come upon it. I know no middle-aged critics who would not prefer a good dinner to a bad concert any day.

This weariness, this disillusion, does not, I think, take place in anything like the same proportion in the other learned professions, except, perhaps, the Church, of which I am not competent to speak from inside knowledge. I have often asked a doctor or a dentist, in whose hands I happened to be for a moment, if he did not get tired of his work. Each of them has assured me that his interest in it increased as he grew older. Even the burglar, I am sure, never conceives so profound a distaste for his profession that he has to brace himself, by a supreme effort of the will, before he can go out to 'crack' another crib. But then the burglar's business offers just that perpetual touch of new adventure that is lacking from the musical critic's. Send the same burglar out night after night to 'crack' the same crib, with the window-catch already slipped and everything else made ridiculously easy for him, and with nothing in the way of swag to show for his skill and toil at the end of it all but a brass farthing and a paste jewel or two, and it will not be long before he throws up pathetic hands to heaven and asks Providence why it made him a burglar.

That is the trouble with musical criticism as a profession, which means, of course, a great deal of concert reporting. It involves a fearful amount of the most appalling monotony on earth, and it involves physical as well as mental pain for the poor critics. The dentist or the surgeon may feel sorry for you when he is putting you through it, but his is a purely imaginative pain. But the average concert performer inflicts an actual positive, physical pain upon the critic. The plain man who reads this will know what it would feel like to have some unpleasantly rough fabric passed over his bare skin a thousand times an hour. He can perhaps dimly imagine, then, what a man with a sensitive musical ear suffers when a violinist or a singer plays or sings persistently out of tune during the greater part of an evening. There is, for the musical critic, only one more painful experience than to be hurt and irritated by this kind of thing, and that is not to be hurt or irritated by it. For in the latter case the horrified reflection occurs to him that he must be losing his ear, that his auditory nerve has become so brutalized by long ill-treatment that it no longer resents ugliness, much in the way that a man who has slipped away from virtue by slow stages may suddenly pull himself up one day and realize, to his horror, that he is doing something as a matter of course that a year ago he would have blushed to find himself even contemplating.

Let me not dwell further at the moment, however, on these more painful aspects of the musical critic's life. I may have occasion to recur to them later. Here I wish to speak rather of those first blissful years in which everything is so delightful and everything seems so easy. In later years doubts come to the critic. The magnanimous thought sometimes comes to him that he may be wrong; he finds in the air around him a hundred opinions upon this, that or the other, and, if he is a man of great intelligence, he will probably see that all these opinions cannot possibly be right, and that there is at least a probability that Providence has chosen someone other than himself as the receptacle for the first truth and the final wisdom of things. This is an awful feeling and, to do myself and my colleagues justice, the critic rarely gives way to it. But when he does, you may be sure that he is pretty old in the craft. The younger members of it never feel like that.

I speak from experience. I began newspaper criticism in, I think, 1905, when I was invited by the *Manchester Guardian* to succeed Arthur Johnstone – a cultured and brilliant man whose untimely death was a great loss to English musical criticism. Had it been suggested to me in those first bright days that I might have been wrong on any subject, I should probably have had serious doubts as to the sanity of the person making the suggestion. Precisely to what extent I may have made an ass of myself I cannot now say, for that would mean re-reading my articles of that time, and I have always been curiously shy of my own older work. But without enduring that painful ordeal, I fancy I can see my then self in one or two of my younger colleagues of today – brave, bright spirits who tweak the nose of an Elgar or a Hugo Wolf with as much unconcern as they would swat some too obtrusive fly on the window pane.

In those days I used to feel as, I suppose, these young friends of mine feel now – that there certainly was one right way among the hundred wrong ways of criticism, and that I, by the special grace of heaven, had been put upon it the first moment my tiny feet could toddle. As we get older, the problems of criticism become more and more perplexing; we see men for whose gifts and whose judgment we have the greatest respect thinking the direct opposite from us on a certain subject, and we are bound to ask ourselves why. In later years we spend a good deal of our time trying to understand not only a composer or a work, but also the critics who express such contradictory opinions upon him or it. But in youth we do not trouble much about these things. It is all very simple: if the other people differ from us they are wrong, and that is all there is to it. The possibility that it is we who may be wrong never occurs to us. Often now,

when I see a young critic confidently laying down the law on
some subject on which he can have had only a limited experience,
my mind runs on the words addressed by Cromwell to the
ministers of the Scotch Kirk after Dunbar: 'By your hard and
subtle words you have begotten prejudice in those who do too
much in matters of conscience (wherein every soul has to answer
for itself in God) depend upon you. Your own guilt is too much
for you to bear. . . . Is it therefore infallibly agreeable to the
word of God, all that you say? I beseech you in the bowels of
Christ, think it possible that you may be mistaken.'

xv

I spoke of the pains of the musical critic's life. But the life has
its pleasant side also, especially at first. Only a few weeks ago I
quoted elsewhere the remark of an old French musician to the
effect that in his youth he had enjoyed music as a mistress, while
now it was merely a wife. We all come to feel more or less like
that about our art or, at all events, about that portion of it that is
connected with our professional duties. Long experience has
convinced me that the only way to find enduring happiness in
music is to be an intelligent amateur of it – to retain it for ever, in
fact, as a mistress. There was a celebrated old French nobleman
of the eighteenth century who used to spend every evening of
his life in the salon of a middle-aged Parisian lady whose conversation had an especial charm for him. A friend suggested that as
he was so fond of the lady's society the obviously sensible thing
was to marry her. The old marquis held up his hands in horror.
'God forbid!' he said. 'Marry her? Where would I spend my
evenings?'

I always tell this story as a warning to those young men who
come to me to ask me how they can begin as musical critics. My
advice to them is put the awful thought away from them at
once, before it gets the mastery of them. I tell them to do anything rather than make music their profession – to go into
business and enjoy music in the evenings, to make commerce
their wife and keep music for a mistress. Let them take a leaf from

the book of our educationists. As everyone knows, the aim of the British educational system is not to teach the young Briton either art or science, but to make him proficient in sport. But the wise men who run the system know better than to let the boy see this. They know that that would be the surest way to put him off sport for the rest of his life. So they keep up the pretence that the only reason for his being at school is that he may learn the names of the rivers of England that flow into the North Sea, or how many angles of a triangle it takes to make two right angles: but they frown upon cricket as a trap laid by Satan for the immortal soul of the boy, with the natural result that the boy loves cricket and hates geography and Euclid. If he were compelled by the school regulations to play cricket for so many hours each day, to show instead of his books his gloves and pads whenever the master took it into his head to have an inspection, to learn by heart the batting and bowling averages for the last fifty years, and to work out on paper the angle at which a ball with a given trajectory would be likely to fly off a bat that meets it at a certain degree of inclination, the boy would come to hate the sight of the school cricket professional as he now hates the sight of the mathematics master, and we should find him risking a caning for playing truant to study the integral calculus in secret.

The ancient Spartans had also evidently hit upon the great truth that the best way to make a thing sought after is to frown upon it. In Sparta the young married men were kept apart from their wives and allowed to visit them only by stealth, severe penalties, I suppose, being inflicted on them if they were caught. For the young Spartan, in consequence, marriage remained a perpetual romance. For the critic music is a romance only when it has a touch of the clandestine about it. I shall never give a young man any other than my usual advice – to keep up his liking for music as the old Frenchman kept up his liking for the lady, by spending his evenings with her as a lover, not as a husband.

At first, to be sure, the life of the musical critic has all the fascination of an engagement and none of the ennui of marriage. Concert-going is a glorious adventure. His ear is as yet unwearied, his nerves fresh and quick to react. At almost every

concert he hears something or somebody for the first time, and
his brain plays upon the new experience with delight and a god-
like sense of intellectual power; the universe seems to be unrolling
itself before him simply that he may understand it. His pen is as
yet virgin – a virginity miraculously renewed with each fresh
experience. His first *Tristan*, his first *Eroica*, his first Pachmann,
draws the burning words from him without the least effort on
his part. He not only tastes a new vintage every day, he drinks
deep of it. A few years later he becomes the musical equivalent
of those melancholy men the professional 'tasters' of teas and
wines, who I am told, merely let the sample roll over their
tongues to get the savour and estimate the quality of it, but
never swallow any of it. They have long ago lost all stomach for
the beverage; their one concern now is not to let their palate
be corrupted any more than it is already.

But even the tea-taster is more fortunate than the critic. The
former, as he ruefully spits out the mouthful he has been compelled to sample professionally, simply says 'Good 'or 'Bad'. The
poor musical critic has to find fresh epithets each time for the
same work or the same performer for perhaps twenty or thirty
unhappy years. I have pondered long and deeply over this matter,
and I have come to the conclusion that there are only two ways
by which this martyrdom might be spared him. One is to abolish
the present system of expressing our opinions in words, and let us
express them by figures. I still hope to live to see the day, when,
instead of racking his brains to find yet another way (the two
hundred and fiftieth) of saying that Madame Larynxia was in
fairly good voice, apart from her bad vibrato and a tendency to
hit each note anywhere but in the centre, and that her Isolde would
not have been half bad but for the fact that she did not look the
part, could not act, and had evidently not the faintest idea what
Wagner was driving at, the critic will just 'mark' the lady in the
style of an adjudicator at a competition festival: Tone 13, Into-
nation 5, Phrasing 2, Rhythm 2, Interpretation and General Effect
24, and so on. It would save him trouble, the newspaper space,
and the reader time.

My alternative suggestion is that the newspapers should adopt the 'circuit' system that is, I believe, in vogue in Wesleyan and other churches. No critic would be allowed to remain more than three years in any town. At the end of that time he would be drafted elsewhere. The readers in each town would thus get a welcome change, while the critic, instead of having to be always thinking out new ways of saying the old things, as he has when he addresses the same circle of readers year after year, would be able to work off on, say, Newport Pagnell, all the phrases, the jokes and the epigrams he has elaborated in Ashby-De-la-Zouch, while the latter town, just beginning to weary of the too sustained brilliance of its own critic, would be toned up afresh by the coming of a new type of expert from Hayling Island.

Failing the general adoption of this system, we might have at any rate an occasional interchange of pulpits. Why should not newspapers now and then have a 'guest' critic, as an opera company has a 'guest' tenor?

II

ENGLISH MUSIC AND MUSICAL CRITICISM
1901
(From the *Contemporary Review*)

I

WITHIN THE last twelve months or so we have had two occasions – of which the daily and weekly press hardly took as much advantage as they might have done – of looking critically into the question of English music, past and present, and its prospects in the near future. The deaths of Sir Arthur Sullivan* and of her late Majesty both afforded excellent opportunities for such an examination of English music; for Sullivan, though now of diminishing importance if we look at his actual achievement, was historically useful as a basis for comparison of what went before and what is coming after him; and the termination of the late Queen's reign might have set us thinking to some purpose of the changes in the musical outlook of this country between 1837 and 1901. In neither case did the journalists light upon very much that was really illuminative. Sullivan was either super-ficially commended for writing decent little trivialities, or superficially cursed for not writing something better; but with one or two exceptions, the journalists quite failed to see how the position once held by Sullivan had altogether lost whatever merit it may have had at one time, owing to the new develop-ments of English music within the last ten, or even five years. Again, while every article on the late Queen referred to her fondness for music, no one was able to point to any real debt of English music to the Court during the last half-century – for the

* Sullivan died 1900.

43

patronage of such composers as Sir Robert Stewart* could hardly be pregnant with consequences, good or bad, to native genius. At the risk of tearing to tatters a theme that has now become somewhat threadbare, it seems necessary to point out how unduly dependent we still are upon the foreigner for our music and our musicians. Fortunately we are in a better position than fifteen or twenty years ago – not to speak of half a century ago. Much foreign music that was once greatly admired here has fallen into commendable disrepute. Only the outcasts of musical society – at each end of the social scale – now hanker after the worst products of Italian opera. Mendelssohn's influence and following are becoming smaller year after year. The passion for oratorio is dying – whether of repletion or of lack of nourishment, whether of too great a satisfaction of the appetite by the few good oratorios, or the too little satisfaction afforded by the many bad ones, is comparatively unimportant. The gratifying fact is that people generally are seeing the evil, the absurdity and the vulgarity of the three main forces that have till now retarded the development of English music. But while so many people, considered merely as individuals, have now a more open mind than at any previous epoch for the doings of our own men, there is comparatively little organized effort to bring about what we all desire – a community that, in case of need, can rely on itself for its own musicians, its own performers, its own conductors, and its own musical literature.

The unfortunate feature is that while the co-operation of the wealthier classes is more necessary here than in any other art, these classes lack interest in the nobler and more advanced forms of music. The composer, it must never be forgotten, stands at an enormous disadvantage compared with all other artists, as regards the first steps towards publicity. A painter can send his picture to an exhibition, or show it to as many friends as care to see it, or even put it in a shop-window and so bring it under the eyes of any passer-by. A sculptor has practically the same opportunities of appeal and of advertising. A poet or a prose writer, even

* Sir Robert Stewart, Irish organist, conductor and composer (1825–94).

if it is frequently difficult for him to get a book published, has always a crowd of magazines and papers more or less at his disposal for ordinarily good work. Further, in the case of poet, of painter, and of sculptor, their mode of speech, as well as the medium through which they speak, is on the ordinary level of men's every-day activities. To appreciate the best of poetry, of fiction, of painting, and of sculpture of course requires a certain training of the brain and the sense organs; but a man can go very far indeed in the enjoyment of all these forms of art without any technical tuition. Nor is it necessary to write poetry oneself to understand poetry, or to be a painter in order to appreciate pictures. There are many things in music, however, for which some amount of technical preparation is necessary before they can be properly understood; while we have even a fair knowledge of the actual products of the art one must either be able to play an instrument, or, in the case of orchestral music, to read a score with a clear comprehension of how it sounds. Thus the young musician, to whatever country he may belong, is handicapped from the start by this limiting of the circle of intelligent amateurs to which he can appeal. He has to encounter exceptional difficulties to which there is no parallel in the other arts, particularly if he writes in the larger forms of music. Once the poet's or the painter's work is in a condition to reach the ear or eye – once the poem is printed or the picture hung – there is nothing whatever to come between the artist and the public. No intermediary assistance is required by the latter. But the musician cannot bring to the public ear his symphony or his opera without the inter-vention of fifty or a hundred individuals. He is not his own interpreter; his work cannot be seen or heard without a number of middlemen. Nor can these middlemen present the work to the public without a certain amount of study and rehearsal, all of which has to be paid for. When I say that an ordinary rehearsal in this country costs £50 or £60, and that in the case of a new and difficult work the conductor has either to chance a bad perform-ance or run up a heavy expense for rehearsals, it will hardly be wondered at that our younger and poorer musicians so rarely get a hearing.

The musician, then, has peculiar and very serious obstacles in his path. Even if he works in the smaller fields, the same malignant spirits beset him. If he writes songs or piano pieces, for example, the publisher only cares for the second or third-rate work, because the vast majority of the people who buy it are necessarily, from the very nature of the case, only second or third-rate singers and players. And if he attempts to become known, say, by his songs, through the medium of the popular vocalists of the day, he finds himself checked, and his best work passed over, because the singer thinks, first, second, third and last, not of the song, nor of the composer, nor of his art in general, but simply of the popular applause. Under an accumulation of difficulties of this kind – and I have by no means mentioned them all – the young composer of much originality but little wealth very soon learns to curse the day he took to music. It is not every musician who can afford, like Glazunov, to print everything he writes; and perhaps, on the whole, it is as well that it should be so. But when one looks at the stuff that *is* performed and published in this country, and at the much better music that is neither published nor performed, one sees that the economic side of the question is really the most important side of all in the future of English music. No one who knows anything of what the younger men are doing, of the many fine things now hidden away in the desks of unknown men, can doubt that England is full of musical talent just now. We not only have more brains in the work than at any previous time during the last thirty years, but they are much better brains. On the other hand, we have only to observe the average concert audience to see how it yearly grows more willing to listen sympathetically and appreciatively to new English music. And, finally, in musical circles the burden of most of the conversation is that, although the new order of things has hardly been born as yet, the old order is decidedly dead. In a word, we have the men and the music crying out for the public, and the public prepared to welcome the music and the men. But there is no market. The sellers and the buyers have no opportunity to reach each other.

What, then, is the remedy? How are we to bring more and

better music to a hearing, and create a musical public as much interested in the latest work of Mr. Edward Elgar* as the poetical public is in the latest work of Mr. Stephen Phillips? I would suggest three courses, each of which would do something to make the bed of the English musician easier to him, would increase the output of music worth hearing, and would give our budding Wagners and Tchaikovskys a chance of survival, or – which is still more important – would make it possible for them to live, like any other artists, by the sale of their art. In the first place, let me point out how greatly English poetry has been benefited, during the last few years, by the action of one or two courageous publishers, who have dared to accept and print good work, and have made it profitable both to themselves and the poets. In literature, as in commerce, the fact that there is no market for a particular commodity is no reason why there should not be one. It is possible to *make* a market; if people do not want the article, they must be endowed with a new want. This is the breath of commerce; and that it may be made to vivify literature has been strikingly shown by the publishers to whom I refer. They very skilfully created in the reading public a want it had hitherto not felt; and, for the first time for many years in this country, there was a continuous output of high-class verse, and a public ready to buy and read it. Why should not something be done for music in the same manner? Why should not some enterprising publisher arise who will publish good English music in an attractive form and at a moderate price – music, that is, which the amateur can enjoy by himself in his own home? I may be confronted with what I have already said as to publishers preferring the inferior stuff because most amateurs are only second or third-rate singers and players. But good music is not necessarily very difficult; and the great need is that amateurs should have their standard of taste materially raised. This can only be done by familiarizing them with good work. I speak from practical experience and observation when I say that an average audience is as willing to listen to good music as to bad; that it will endure as readily a programme made up of Tchaikovsky, Liszt, Wagner and

* Elgar was knighted in 1904.

Dvořák as one made up of selections from the comic operas. To put it somewhat cynically, if the people do not know the difference between good and bad music they may as well be given the good; it is no worse for them and much better for everyone else. I have seen provincial audiences, recruited almost entirely from the man in the street, listen with the most rapturous attention at concert after concert, to complex modern music of which they had never previously heard a single bar. They may not have understood it all, but they certainly enjoyed it, and did their best to understand it. Good music clearly appeals to them just as much as bad music. There is therefore no danger in giving them the good, since the appetite for it seems to grow with what if feeds on. And I think the enterprising publisher to whom I look forward would soon find that it is possible to *make* a public for the better kinds of music. The average amateur at present buys second-rate songs and piano pieces because these are thrust down his throat in every music-shop he enters. Let the counter be piled with something better, and I think he will buy that just as readily, while the superior amateur, when he wanted some new music, would probably take home with him something by an Englishman, instead of the latest thing of Grieg or Sinding. I would also recommend our public vocalists to sing artistic songs instead of detestable shop ballads, did I not know too well how futile that recommendation would be. The amateur must be familiarized at first hand with better music of the kind he is used to buy; and this can only be done by an intelligent and music-loving publisher. I may be told that the venture would prove a failure, and the publisher be ruined. I reply that it has not been so in the case of the modern publishers of high-class poetry; and the poetical public is really not half as large or enthusiastic as the musical public.

In the second place, we need a decentralization of our English musical life. At present, London is almost the only city where the higher kinds of symphonic and operatic music can be persistently cultivated on a large scale. The result is, that nine out of ten of our younger composers have only London to look to for a performance. There is painful overcrowding, and the infantile death-rate is very high in consequence. 'Back to the country' should be our motto here, as in social and economic matters generally. A few of the large towns have their own orchestral societies, but we need fifty times the present number of these institutions. One of the seminal factors in the development of German music was the decentralized political system. In a country with innumerable little states and little capitals, each with its own orchestra and opera, there was a magnificent field for the young musician. He was not dependent upon metropolis for fame and publicity. He had the choice of a round score of orchestras. The area of life was wider, and it was possible for more germs to come to maturity. If each considerable English town had its own orchestra, which could be trained, in the course of a few years, to grapple with the most difficult modern music, we should multiply, a hundredfold the field of evolution. Of operas it is somewhat premature to speak. When such a country as this can do little more than support high-class opera in one city for a few weeks in each year, any schemes for the improvement of such a state of affairs must be more or less visionary. But as far as orchestral and the higher vocal music are concerned, the multiplication of orchestras would make it possible for a young composer to be heard some ten years earlier than the present system allows. Anyone who is convinced, as I am, that England is now ready and able to produce first-class music of its own, must realize how much fine talent is annually destroyed by our dreadful narrowing of the channel through which composers have to reach the public.

The third suggestion grows out of the preceding one. Literature in the past, and painting in the present, have owed a great deal to the wealthy patron. In our own day we have seen more than one artist's position secured by his pictures having the good luck to be bought largely by some prominent art lover. There is, of course, a stimulus in this case which is absent from music. The purchaser has a chance of acquiring the early work of a comparatively unknown man, who may one day become famous, and of finding his expenditure on the pictures a highly profitable commercial speculation. Unfortunately, the musician can hold

C

out his patron little inducement of this kind; no one who advances £50 towards the publishing of a young man's score is likely to find it come back to him, in later years, bringing a smiling five hundred per cent along with it. What the musical patron does for music will have to be done out of pure benevolence and love for the art. But if he is not hardened enough to despise a sentimental in comparison with a material reward, he could get a fair amount of pleasure, at the same time as a noble consciousness of having performed a supreme act of virtue, from a little judicious expenditure upon some promising young musician. This would only be the equivalent of what the artistic patron does for painting. A good price paid for a picture – either for the purchaser's own collection or for presentation to a public gallery – not only adds to a young artist's fame, but keeps him for the best part of a year. In the case of the sister art, the wealthy amateur's duty is not done when he has paid his five shillings to hear a new composer's work at a concert. It is his duty to see – if he likes the work – that the musician who wrote it shall get some more satisfying return for it than mere applause, and that he shall be put in a position to produce more work of the same kind. In other words, wealthy England should now do what indigent Italy and Germany did in the eighteenth century. We need a race of artistically-minded patrons, who will spend their money at least not less lavishly on music than they do on painting. If the rich man can afford to keep his chaplain and his butler, surely he can afford to keep his musical composer, who has not been used to any such luxuries as the other two, and would be found to be, in comparison, extremely economical. I am well aware that the system of patronage gives rise to many evils, and that under such a system the musician would sometimes have to cloak the more prominent elements of his personality. But that would only be a minor evil compared with the state we are now in. The composer would at all events get *some* of his music published and performed, which is more than he can hope for under the present system. Patronage, with its defects, worked wonders for Italian and German music in their infancy; and it would probably do for English music in ten years what it will take fifty to do without its help.

II

Here, then, are three plain, simple and practical proposals for raising English music. We want publishers to believe, and to act on the belief, that there is money to be made by issuing good as well as bad songs and marches and waltzes. We want orchestras all over the country, so that a composer will be able to send his score for perusal to twenty conductors, as an author can send his manuscript round to twenty publishers, or a painter can send his picture to twenty exhibitions. Finally, we want the wealthy amateur to select a musician or two, help him to study the best music, help him to publish his work, at a price that will not kill off the demand for it at the commencement, and help him to have his work produced somewhere or other. These proposals, I venture to repeat, are all plain, simple, and practical. They do not, of course, exhaust all the means by which English music can be improved. A better system of musical education, a change in the manner of conducting examinations, a restriction of the output of worthless degrees to mere pianists and organists, the burning of a few academies, the assassination of a few semi-moribund professors – along all these paths much good work might be done; and the man who will devote his life disinterested-ly to any one of them may find himself immortalized in English musical history. But the three main points on which I have laid stress are the most important, because they go to the root of the *economic* question. The musician must live to be able to write at all; and to write well he must not have his existence an absolute burden to him. I would not, of course, for a moment advocate making musicians' lives even tolerably happy. If we once begin to do that there is an end to all great music. No mathematician could calculate, for instance, what the world would have lost had Chopin had his cold bath every morning, followed by a vigorous use of the Indian clubs, or had Wagner been supplied with safe cures for dyspepsia and erysipelas. 'A reasonable quantity of fleas,' the American philosopher has told us, 'is good for a dog – keeps him from broodin' about bein' a dog'; and a reasonable amount of ill-health, disappointment and worry probably performs the same useful function in the physical and mental economy of the musician. But long-continued downright poverty is not good for any man who wishes to get out of his brain the best that is in it; and if there is any musical talent in England, it can only be brought out by making it possible for a composer to *live* by his music. Buckle long ago pointed out how the intellectual level of the Church is continually falling because able men can now find other and freer outlets for their ideas. If we want the emotional and intellectual level of music raised in England, we must be careful to make the musical career sufficiently attractive and sufficiently lucrative to the best men. At present, they struggle vainly for a few years, and then confess themselves beaten. Unless they can interest some wealthy man in them, or procure one of the public appointments open to men of the younger school in this country, there is nothing left for them but suicide, or the slower and more painful form of self-extinction known as 'taking pupils'.

Even the conservative reader will possibly agree with me thus far on the abstract principles at issue; but he may ask whether the concrete side of the case justifies him in disturbing his mind over the matter at all – whether, within the lives of the next generation or two, we are likely to have a school of English music that will compensate us for all our trouble and sacrifices. I venture to express my sincere conviction that most of us will live to see this English school in full vigour. To go no further back than five years, a remarkable change has come over the spirit and the outlook of young musical England. The men who were writing only fifteen years ago are still in no more than middle age, yet they are already hoary with antiquity in the artistic sense; while the little group that sprang into prominence some ten years ago, and won for a time the public ear by an unprecedented charm and daintiness of melody, is now trampled under foot by the stronger and hardier youngsters of the present day. A modern poet, with a taste for the cosmogonical epic, might write the history of English music during the last fifty years in a series of geological and biological pictures. We begin, about half a century ago, with a little better than sheer chaos; the musical state of that day was the primeval ooze, in which some tiny germs were struggling for life and air. Then came the epoch of the mammoth and mastodon, of the fabulous big men who had learned all that Germany could teach them, except to write interestingly. These were the great days of symphonies and cantatas and oratorios, and of fearful and wonderful musical criticism in the London Press. Some of the giant beasts of that day still survive, and are very useful for educational purposes, like the big skeletons in the museums. It is said that their superior height enables them to look down with contempt upon the smaller musical organisms that now run round them, and occasionally into them; but they feel the cold somewhat acutely. This epoch was succeeded by that of the little songbirds, who really sang very prettily indeed for a time, and of the artificial shepherds who did some quite charming tricks in the way of dancing. But their little throats soon became very tired, and their little ways began to pall on the public. They had, however, done one service to English music; they had substituted melody and grace for stodginess and boredom. Finally, there came the present school, who have done things of which their fellow-countrymen have no need to be ashamed. Men like Mr. Edward Elgar and Mr. Granville Bantock are of a type hitherto unknown in English music. They have a science that would turn the mammoths and the mastodons green with envy; but their technique is a native, not a foreign technique, and is used for native ends. Mr. Elgar worked his way up through a variety of experiments to full consciousness of himself in his now well-known *Variations on an Original Theme*, recognized at once by all competent observers as the most important piece of music till then produced by an Englishman. Mr. Bantock, after dallying for a long time with Oriental fantasies, producing some very beautiful music and some that was rather shattering to delicate persons – at last realized that he also was an Englishman, and brought out – at Antwerp – a work which, it is to be hoped, is the basis for a career of sustained organic energy. I refer to his fine variations on the theme 'H.F.B.',* which share with Mr. Elgar's variations the post of honour in modern English music.

* E. N. is referring to the Helena Variations dedicated to H.F.B. (Ed.)

If we had produced no other original composers than Mr. Elgar and Mr. Bantock we still need not despair of the future. But no one who goes about looking for signs of the new life can doubt that it is pulsating everywhere round him. No longer do our young men ape the manners of other days and other lands; even the once gigantic influence of Wagner does not affect them so seriously as it did the neophytes of ten or fifteen years ago, who have all paid the penalty of following too closely the tail of that perilous comet. The present generation may admire and study its Brahms or its Tchaikovsky, but it does not imitate them. Here, for the first time in modern English music, we light upon the one real sign of grace – that our best music bears no trace of the mere echoing of foreign composers. In almost every composition of the older school we could say, from moment to moment, 'This is Mendelssohn, this is Schuman, this is Wagner, this is Brahms'. No one is set upon the genealogical quest by the works of Mr. Bantock and Mr. Elgar to which I have just referred. In the symphonic poem '*The Skeleton in Armour*' of Mr. Josef Holbrooke – one of the most promising of the very young men – I think we have a work that will bring joy into the heart of every musical patriot. Nothing so rich and strong has ever before been written by an English musician of twenty. But it would puzzle anyone to find wherein Mr. Holbrooke has imitated any foreign composer, past or present. The music is purely English, absolutely native and self-governing. In the field of the song, again, work is now being done that stands out in the sharpest contrast from even the good songs of five or ten years ago. For the first time in this century we are producing a type of musician that can do for the best English poetry what the Germans have done for Heine and Goethe – he can set it to music worthy of the words. I will not speak of the dreadful efforts of some of the mammoths and the mastodons; but we have only to compare the setting of some of Tennyson's lyrics by a good musician of a vanishing type, like Mr. Arthur Somervell, with their setting by Mr. R. H. Walthew, or Mr. F. C. Nicholls, to see how rapidly we are developing. In a little and scarce volume of songs by Mr. Nicholls, written to words of Tennyson, we have the finest flower of this new spirit. To find such perfect things as 'Tears, idle tears', or 'The Swallow', or 'As through the land at eve we went', or 'Ask me no more' set to music that lifts us at once into the true atmosphere, satisfies our sense of sheer musical beauty and yet never falls for a moment below the poetic level of the verse – this alone is enough to convince us that the real dawn has come at last. I can speak only of the music it falls to my own lot to hear or read, and I do not doubt that there are other works, as fine as some of those I have named, whose acquaintance I have unfortunately not been able to make. But the very fact that the limited experience of one individual has supplied him with so many specimens of genuinely English music – and that first-rate music – makes the situation all the more hopeful. The germs of the new life must be fairly numerous. At all events, with Mr. Elgar, Mr. Bantock, and Mr. Holbrooke doing original work in the orchestra and in the oratorio-form, with Mr. Walthew and Mr. Nicholls creating a new type of English song, and with half-a-dozen other musicians doing things that never entered the consciousness of the previous generations, the outlook for a really English school is the brightest possible. The most emotional part of the life of the nation has been pent up for fifty years, through the lack of the right channel through which to pour itself. We are now, I think, in somewhat the same condition as the Russia of the last two or three decades. Inside our hearts and souls is a vast, unexplored territory of passion. Like the Russians, we begin to sing, and find the floodgates opened to the accumulated experiences of a hundred years. Past generations of Englishmen will become articulate in us, as the lives and deaths, the struggles and tortures, of generations of sorely-tried Russians find expression in the pity and anguish of Tchaikovsky. Already our younger men are treading paths that were mere impenetrable wilds to all our previous musicians. It will not be long before we shall have an English school that will incarnate the life and very being of our race and culture, that will speak to us as Wagner does to the German, or Tchaikovsky to the Russian, with a sense of intimacy that no nation can experience in the music of another nation, no matter how fine or universal it may be.

III

It is, perhaps, part of the logical evolution of things that our creative minds should, in the race to maturity, outstrip our critical minds, but it is not well to permit too great a gulf to be fixed between them. Unfortunately, there seems a danger at present of our critics failing to keep pace with our artists. The musicians are doing work that demands, and is justified in demanding, to be judged by the same standard as high-class German or Russian music; but the critics as a whole would be ill-advised to suggest a comparison between their work and that of our reputable literary critics. To put it concretely, while we are now producing composers whose work is as representative of modern English thought and feeling as the poetry of Tennyson or Browning or Mr. Stephen Phillips, or the fiction of Mr. Meredith, Mr. Hardy, and Mr. Moore, we have no musical critics who could stand in line with John Addington Symonds, Walter Pater, Mr. Archer, or Frederick Myers. Musical *literature*, indeed, scarcely exists as yet in this country. This is a defect that will need to be remedied before long, if we wish to create a public response to the best work our musicians can turn out. At present, with one or two exceptions, the musical writers produce nothing that can be read with even languid interest by any man who is accustomed to good critical literature.

One of the causes of this dearth of decent musical literature is the fact that most of the professional critics are tied to mere concert-reporting. There are signs that the public is becoming rather tired of the daily or weekly column that tells it, for the thousandth time, that Paderewski played or Albani sang at this, that, or the other concert in London. Not once in fifty times do the London men give us an article on *music* or a *musician*, apart from some concert or opera. The practical effects of the slavery to the concert hall or the operahouse are just what might have been foretold. A musical critic, of course, does not necessarily attend every concert he criticizes; but the number of those he actually does attend is sufficient to wear his faculties out in the course of a few years. The finer the man's brain, the more critical it is by

instinct, the more baneful is the bondage. But worse than this is
the demoralizing effect of sitting in judgment, day after day,
week after week, year after year, on all kinds of artists and
performers, for the benefit of a somewhat uncritical public that
has not been trained to look to first principles. The journalists fall
into the error of supposing that the slating or praising of mere
performers is the be-all and end-all of musical criticism, that they
themselves are such models of constancy and equilibration that
their verdicts upon performers and performances amount to very
much,* and that the really musical public cares two straws about
the matter. But as long as a journal engages a musical gentleman
just to report concerts and operas, so long will the standard of
English musical criticism remain at its present low level. It is as if
we had no higher notion – indeed no other notion – of poetical
criticism than reporting the performances of elocutionists.
Artists and singers are no doubt a necessary evil, and we need to be
kept abreast of what is going on in the world of music, but to
cultivate mere reporting at the expense of genuine criticism is to
transpose the real values of things. One or two musical critics do
make a gallant effort to lift the discussion of the art to a higher
plane; and one of them at least – Mr. Runciman of the *Saturday*

* Nothing is more boring than to read the interminable strictures
upon singers or players – he himself having the most touching belief
in his own standards of judgment, and the most pathetic ignorance
that there is such a thing as the personal equation. A little humorous
relief, however, may be had by the simple process of comparing one
thunderer with another. Look, for example, at these two specimens,
appearing the same day in different newspapers, *à propos* of a piano
recital by Mr. Harold Bauer: – CRITIC No. 1, 'Mr. Bauer was known
to London as an immature young pianist. *He is now a finished artist*, and
possesses a beautiful touch, an unerring rhythmical instinct, and a
peculiar force which should place him amongst the great pianists.'
CRITIC No. 2, 'The performance gave, on the whole, a good impression
of the young pianist's technical power. *He is still, however, a long way
from artistic maturity*.' Each of these pundits, I suppose, would be shocked
at the suggestion that you cannot measure musical performances as you
do cloth or timber, by a measure of length that never alters and is the
same for all men, for the simple reason that all the shortcomings of the
critic are necessarily found in his judgments.

Review – deserves to be in somewhat better company. Mr Runciman, unfortunately, does not always do himself justice; at all events one feels that he could, if he chose, produce better work than we sometimes get from his pen. It is quite certain that a man of the same gifts as Mr. Runciman, who happened to be a literary or artistic instead of a musical critic, would have been stimulated by his environment to take his work much more seriously, and would by now have produced half-a-dozen volumes of real literature. Mr. Runciman flings his talents away, conscious that he is addressing a relatively uncritical audience, just as the good little boy, playing with street arabs, permits himself the use of language he would hesitate to use in the more refined circle of his home. Mr. Runciman's case is, indeed, highly instructive. He is more sinned against than sinning, inasmuch as we are so glad to get really good, brainy, musical writing that we do not feel sufficiently murderous towards him when he perpetrates his worst eccentricities. But these will have to be weeded out of him before he gives us the best he is capable of. When he calls Robert Franz, for example, an intolerable dullard, or when he writes thus of César Franck – 'He was an industrious schoolmaster and nothing more; he had no invention nor any original impulses to drive him to invent; and nothing he wrote possesses any qualities beyond a certain mastery of the technique that has been evolved by the great and small composers preceding him, and a certain perfectly individual clumsiness in applying that technique' – when our best critic becomes so wildly uncritical as this, we have an unpleasant reminder that English musical criticism is really only in its infancy. For this is one of the marks of the immaturity of the science, this thorough-going condemnation of things in the heap, this bland and blissful disregard of the reasoned opinions of other competent men, this refusal to accept anything but one's own nerves at any chance moment as the measure of things musical. It is only in the early days that this clean-sweeping, carnivorous spirit reigns in criticism. In the course of time a critic comes to see that his is only one out of many possible ways of regarding an artist; and he hesitates to become dyslogistic about anything until he is as sure as much careful self-analysis can make him that his verdict is not the outcome of mere prejudice, or insufficient knowledge, or a momentary fatigue of the faculties. It is all very well to say that the critic should record the impressions of a work upon his temperament. That may be what all criticism resolves itself into ultimately, but the temperament is not a God-given, impeccable thing. It requires training and checking, like every other quality of the natural man; and it needs to remember that there are other temperaments in the world. Though the 'temperamental' critics will probably not agree with me, it is really much easier to wear the hair long and to scream out, with an air of sybilline conviction, that two and two make five, than to sit down and patiently work it out that two and two make four. The present appeal to 'temperament' in English musical criticism is too often the mere resort of critical innocence, the mere failure to understand what criticism has come to mean in the other arts and in literature. So long as criticism is undifferentiated as at present, from journalism, our musical writers are necessarily followers of that amateur organist of fiction who made up in expression for what he lacked in technique. But it is the absurd and antiquated system on which the 'musical column' of the ordinary paper is conducted – a system that dates from the times when singers and players were vain enough to think they had a right to the whole of the public ear – that accounts for the fact that so few of our most competent critics give us the best that is in them* They have not all round them, as the literary critics have, a mass of fine literature to serve as a criterion of their own work, and an ideal to strive after. The result is that the second and third-rate men never say anything worth printing, and the first-rate

* In the front ranks of the musical critics stands the gentleman who, for some time past, has written the excellent notices in the *Manchester Guardian*; indeed, only Mr. Runciman's articles can compare with his for all-round interest and stimulus, though he seems to me to give way at times to a temperamental asperity that is as uncritical as it is un-necessary. But he almost always gives us the impression of knowledge, sanity, and culture. It is characteristic of the low state of English musical criticism that a writer of his ability should be merely writing about concerts in a newspaper, instead of publishing lengthy and connected essays in book form. (Arthur Johnstone. (Ed.)).

men are content with that dubious sense of superiority felt by the one-eyed man in the kingdom of the blind.

Nor is this the only bad feature of the system that identifies musical criticism with concert-reporting. The criticism of music presents special difficulties that are unknown to any of the other arts. We can read a play or a story through in an hour or two, and then be quite able to discuss its main features. But to be able to speak with authority on a complex piece of music, like a Strauss symphonic poem or a Wagner opera, we need either to have heard it half-a-dozen times, – or to have devoted hour after hour to a study of the score. If a critic has heard the same symphony very often, even if he has never seen the score, he is perhaps in a position to pass an opinion upon it. But on a work with which he is only imperfectly acquainted, and which he hears only at rare intervals, the critic, as a rule, should be far more chary of expressing an opinion than he is at present. And when it comes to passing judgment not merely upon a particular work but upon the whole of a man's work, it is no exaggeration to say that not five men in England today are competent to undertake such a task. The reporter of a daily paper hears, for example, Tchaikovsky's second symphony for the first time, or the Pathetic symphony for the fiftieth time; and he straightway delivers himself in the most authoritative manner, of a column of criticism of Tchaikovsky's general virtues and defects. No literary critic who had half a conscience would attempt to write an article, say, on Zola, without having read Zola through at least once, and perhaps two or three times. But the musical critic sits down to criticize Tchaikovsky, or Brahms, or Berlioz, or Liszt, or Richard Strauss, without a real acquaintance with half of what the man has written. I am not exaggerating; it is a mere matter of time, and of pounds, shillings, and pence. Musical scores are so expensive that no one but a millionaire can afford to buy musicians' works in a mass. Unless a man is studying a particular composer for a particular purpose, he is not likely to be possessed of all his works. And if to this fact we join the further one, that a musical score demands more and closer attention than a poem or a novel, it will readily be seen that few critics can possibly know the whole of the music of even two or three of the big moderns. I venture to say that no three of our critics really know *all* the works of either Brahms, or Tchaikovsky, or Liszt, or Berlioz, and that not one of them knows all the works of the whole four.* This is evident, apart from *à priori* reasons, from the actual writings of our critics, where the positiveness of the judgment is often in inverse proportion to the right to form a judgment.

I need not labour the point any further. It need only be said that the critic has a quite simple and honest course out of his difficulty – to cease valuing his opinion more than Sainte-Beuve and Walter Pater would have valued theirs; to get away from the primitive notion that art-criticism consists only in feminine approbation or disapprobation, instead of in the impassive study of the products of the human brain; to admit that he does not know the whole of the works of the man he is criticizing; and to lean, in cases of doubt, to the side of charity. Let him, if he thinks Tchaikovsky feminine, believes that *somewhere*, among, say, the operas of Tchaikovsky which he has never heard, the composer may possibly show himself exceedingly virile. If he thinks a Liszt rhapsody vulgar and showy, he has every right to say so; but he has no right to give his readers the impression that refinement and nobility are nowhere to be found in Liszt's work. In a word, our critics will need to take their profession much more seriously than most of them do at present. The time is coming when an English school of music will appear before them for judgment, when they will have to separate carefully the wheat from the chaff. If the majority of them do not behave more seriously and more conscientiously in the presence of English music than they do towards foreign music, they will simply be obstacles in the way of the new school. Under the conditions of modern life, a new art-work is almost bound to move forward in two parallel columns. The creative men must have half the work of propaganda – and the rougher half – done for them by the friendly arm of criticism. The artist will bring forth the fruit and flower; but the soil and the atmosphere must, in part, at least, be made by

---

* To *hear* Liszt's *Faust* Symphony, for example, at a concert once every ten years, is not to *know* it, in the critical sense.

the critic. It is surely not a pleasant reflection that in the next ten years we may have a vigorous contemporary school of English music, hampered and impeded by a musical criticism fifty or sixty years behind the times.

THE MUSIC OF THE FUTURE, 1902

(From *The Speaker*)

MR. HERBERT SPENCER has recently been making a complaint that must have awakened a responsive chord in the breast of many a fellow-sufferer. Our philosopher has found, to his sorrow, that it is easier to let a strain of music into the brain than to turn it out; the tactless guest fails to understand when it has outstayed its welcome, and lingers on to irritate and depress the host who was foolish enough to open his doors to it. An experience of this kind must have fallen to the lot of all of us; our days and nights have been haunted by the incessant automatic reiteration of some piece of music that declines to quit our consciousness. Sometimes – most aggravating prank of all – it is the merest fragment of melody, whose beginning and whose end we cannot for the life of us remember; and we exhaust our grey matter in the vain attempt to find an answer to two questions, which, for the time being, concern our immortal soul more than all the problems of the over and the under world – (1) Who wrote this infernal strain? (2) In which of his infernal works does it occur? Perhaps it is something we have heard by chance, heard without even noticing that we have heard it, an unfamiliar phrase drunk in unconsciously at a concert, or from an organ in the street, or from a passing band, or born of any one of a thousand other contingencies. To attempt the tracking of *this* monster to its lair is the most exquisite penance of all; the labour of Sisyphus were luxurious ease to it. The curious thing is, that no other art but music afflicts its worshippers in this way. We do not find our consciousness haunted by a piece of architecture, a verse of poetry, a statue or a painting, to the extent to which a musical phrase will persist within us, never leaving the brain sometimes for days together, obtruding itself upon us, with almost ludicrous irresponsibility, even in some of the most serious moments of our life. There is a detachment of mental function here that is without a parallel elsewhere in the arts.

Yet this possibility of detachment has its compensations. It points, of course, to the fact that the musical manner of thinking is something more intensive, more esoteric, than any other mode of artistic cerebration – less dependent either for its beginning or its development upon anything coming from the external world. And herein lies the compensation of which I speak; for as this peculiarity of music enables the composer to work in comparative independence of the outer material world, so it permits our enjoying the rarest of his creations by means simply of the exercise of pure imagination. I put it to any lover of music whether his moments of supreme happiness have come when he has been actually listening to music or when he has been merely imagining it? Never, under the most favourable concatenation of circumstances, can we get an ideal performance of any work. Something is sure to be wrong – the orchestra or the singer will leave a little to be desired, the very sight of our fellow-beings in the same room with us is an affliction, or, even when everything else is in its favour, the performance may be spoiled for us by our own brain or body being out of tune for that particular thing at that particular moment. But you have only to think of the performances you can have beneath the dome of your skull in order to realize how infinitely superior they are to the best that can be given in any opera house or concert room. You can choose your own work; you can choose your own time and place for imagining it; you are not dependent upon any instrument, material or human; you can conceive it sung by the purest of voices, played by the most faultless of orchestras, phrased by the most perfect of artists. *This* is the way to enjoy music, not by the vulgar ear, but by the spirit. Walk through a sombre wood or by a great river by night, and let some of the immortal music of the world float through your brain – grave or gay, noble or gracious, sad or passionate – and you will then be one in spirit with the immortal soul who wrote it. Then, and only then, does the full meaning of his message really reach you.

I shall be told that not everyone can do this – that not everyone can let the inner ear replace the outer to the extent of being able to conceive not merely the form but the colour of a great orchestral work, without any assistance from actual sound. It is sufficient for my purpose that some of us *can* do this, if not with absolute fidelity – for that is well-nigh impossible – at all events sufficiently closely to let us surrender the actual performance without a sigh. If the majority of people cannot do it, that is their affair; I am in egoistic mood, and do not greatly care whether the common herd of men, who imbibe music through the fleshly ear, can or cannot ever climb the supernal heights whereon we, the elect, are proud to stand. Theirs, perhaps, is the day, but the morrow is ours. In the first place, at the present rate of progress in the art, it is only a matter of another decade or so for the best music to be almost unplayable – in the sense that composers are always aiming at bigger and richer effects, which can only be rightly rendered on the largest and most expert orchestras, after many rehearsals. This is possible only in towns that combine great wealth with an absorbing artistic curiosity – and such towns are exceedingly rare, in this country at all events. The time will thus come when ninty-nine per cent of the musical population will have no chance of hearing anything but the second-class work of the future. This is where the *élite* of the world of sound – people who imagine music instead of merely hearing it – will undoubtedly triumph. They can have a perfectly ideal perform-ance of any work they like by the simple process of learning the score by heart, and then letting the brain give its silent rendering of it – as they now do, say, with their favourite Beethoven symphony or Wagner overture. To say nothing of the joys of the present, surely it is worth while cultivating this faculty for the selfish pleasure it is going to give us in the future?

But further, this mode of rendering music will not only add to the enjoyment of the amateur, but will immensely enlarge the resources of the composer. Nowhere is the freedom of music from any dependence upon the real world shown more conclusively than here. You cannot, for example, if you want to remain intelligible, write prose or poetry and employ words that do not correspond with things; nor can you paint a picture with colours that do not exist – it is impossible, indeed, to conjure up before the inner eye any colour but the real ones that are familiar to the outer eye. But in the ideal world of inward music the composer will be hampered by no such limitations upon his fancy. I cannot imagine a material colour with which my experience has not presented me; but I *can* imagine a musical tone which no human ear has ever heard. So long as music is written to be merely played, so long will composers and auditors be limited by the mechanical imperfections of the orchestra; we cannot take the players above or below certain notes of the scale, nor can we get out of an instrument tones of equal value throughout the whole of its range. But this difficulty will vanish as soon as people begin to approach music through the spirit instead of through the flesh. A composer can then write what notes he likes, and although no horn or oboe or bassoon could be found to play them, we shall still be able to imagine what the notes would sound like on an ideal horn or oboe or bassoon. Thus at one stroke we shall free the composer from one of his greatest bugbears – the necessity of considering the capacity of mechanical instruments and the aptitude of the players. There will, of course, be an ever-present danger to guard against. As composers conceive orchestral colours that do not as yet exist, the instrument makers will set their brains at work to invent improvements that will permit the performer to realize the colour in actual sound. Nature, as in Mr. Whistler's story, will be always creeping up; and the composer must incessantly keep ahead of the possible. He must checkmate each move of the instrument maker by soaring into heights where mere actuality cannot breathe, until the happy day shall come when orchestral music shall no longer be played but only conceived. Not until the musician writes only for ideal instruments will he be able to paint, in all the fulness of its glory, that ideal world in which it is his privilege alone to live. At present he is in the position of trying to live. At present he is in the position of trying to render the illimitable in a medium limited by the ridiculous shortcomings of brass and wood and catgut.

III

SOME EARLY NON-MUSICAL WRITINGS

FROM *FORM IN THE NOVEL*, 1891

(University College Magazine, written under his original name, William Roberts)

THE NOVEL stands mid-way between Science and Art; on the one side it touches the poetical drama, on the other, the analytical domain of psychology, ethics, politics, sociology, and all that is included under the word 'philosophy'. The first comparison which is suggested, however, is with the drama. In each we have a concrete picture of life, with well-defined characters acting and re-acting upon each other, and being acted upon by their environment. Setting aside the difference in expression, the main difference between the novel and the drama lies in the preponderance of analytical interest in the one, and of imaginative interest in the other. While the drama stands mid-way between Music and Philosophy, the Novel stands mid-way between Philosophy and Poetry – using the word 'philosophy', of course, not in its ordinary technical sense, but as including any rational treatment of the world and of man. While the drama tends on the one side to concentrate into objective thought, on the other rarify into Music, the Novel endeavours on the one side to exist in the ideal world of poetry, on the other to view life with the realistic eye of science. The characters of the novelist are not quite so ideal as those of the dramatist, while at the same time sufficiently ideal to justify their existence in a work of Art; they are not subjected to the same cold, anatomical analysis as in the pages of the psychologist, while at the same time exhibiting

secret places of their minds, the complete unveiling of which is
denied to the dramatist. There is an ascending scale of ideality
from the novel, through the drama to the opera; and a motive, an
occurrence, or a situation, which occurs with perfect propriety
in one, would jar upon the imagination if introduced into another.
Hence every attempt is made, in the more ideal Arts, to eliminate
the familiar present. The drama usually deals with the men of
by-gone ages, because the appearance upon the stage of the life of
the present day would be so indelibly associated with conceptions,
the reverse of ideal, that the dramatist could not transport us
into the super-organic sphere of Art. When present day life is
introduced upon the stage, as in the social dramas of Ibsen, the play
loses in poetical power and gains in analytical. In the opera,
contemporary life never steps upon the stage; the passionate
ideality of music precludes the immediately real. In the novel we
stand upon a much lower plane: if, in supreme moments, our
heads touch heaven, our feet never leave the familiar earth. It is
in contemporary life that the great novelist finds the fullest field
for his powers.

Further, in the drama the author is non-existent; in the novel
he is omnipresent. While the atmosphere of the drama is homogeneous, that of the novel is heterogeneous. The characters of
the drama exist in their own sphere, and any elucidation of
motive, any expression of thought, or feeling, any criticism,
must come from the characters themselves. In the novel, besides
the world in which the characters live and move and have their
being, there is the further world in which the author lives, and
the light of the latter is being constantly projected upon the
former. The novel, in fact, is a prose drama plus another personality – that of the author. Obviously this enlarges the sphere
of the novel. Shakespeare, in his unfolding of a character, can
make use only of the thoughts of the character himself or of
another personage of the drama; George Eliot, besides giving us
the concrete embodiment of an idea, and its action and re-action
in society, gives us also a side-light upon it from her own nature.
She supplements the concrete by the abstract, the particular by
the universal.

Like considerations meet us when we look at the different media of expression in the novel and the drama. Verse, in its broadest sense as including rhythmical speech of any kind, is of a more imaginative nature than prose, while rhythmical utterance in its highest form, as revealed in Music, is still more imaginative. Hence the creative powers of the artist are modified by the medium through which they find speech. In the musical drama we have characters of supreme ideality; such a character as Lohengrin, for instance, would be an impossibility, even in Poetry. The flood of light in which Wagner bathes the character is of a kind too impalpable to be transmitted through a coarser ether; in our insight into Lohengrin's nature we see with spirit – eyes alone, turned inward with an introspective power that is denied to any artist working in a more concrete material. The distance between the characters of a novel and those of a poetical drama is less than that between the characters of the drama and those of the opera, because there is not the same wide difference in the media of speech, but a plainly perceptible gulf does exist between them. While the idea undoubtedly determines the form, it is not too much to say that, in some degree, the form also determines the idea; and given a particular medium of artistic expression, that which is uttered through it will inevitably travel along certain lines of force, and as inevitably avoid others. Examining, then, the speech of poetry and the speech of prose, we find that while, as both expressing rational concepts, they meet on common ground, there is a residuum of force in each which tends away from this common centre. While the inner essence of words in poetry tends towards the imaginative sphere of music, the inner essence of words in prose tends towards the analytical sphere of science. In the one case the definite intellectual significance is submerged in the indefinitely imaginative; in the other, the imaginative tends to become lost in the intellectual. In any actual work, of course, these two elements are combined; but still there exists the distinction, which, in its most pronounced form, is the basis of the variety of character in the novel and the drama. While in the former the mind of the artist is pre-eminently analytical, in the latter it is pre-eminently imaginative. Such a character as Lohengrin is impossible in poetry, such a character as Desdemona is impossible in the novel. The sphere of the latter is partly imaginative, partly philosophical, with a slight bias towards the latter.

Having thus tentatively marked out the nature of the novel in its single parts, let us look at it for a moment as a whole. Here we may endeavour to confirm inductively the conclusion reached above deductively. What we wish to establish is this – that the novel depends upon a faculty of creation partly imaginative, partly analytical, and that as the human mind increases in analytical power, the novel correspondingly gains in breadth and depth.

Evolution is defined as 'a progression from an indefinite, incoherent homogeneity to a definite, coherent heterogeneity, consequent on the integration of matter and the dissipation of motion'. As applied to the development of Art, this may be understood as a progression from that which is formless, indefinite, unreal, to that which is symmetrical, definite, and real, attended by a differentiation of parts, together with an increased dependence of each part upon all the rest, and a wider union of diverse elements. leading to a more direct and living effect. All early Art is static, all mature Art dynamic. The difference between a mass by Palestrina and an opera by Wagner, between a story by Malory and one by George Eliot, is the difference between Art that achieves its purpose in accordance with Euclid's definition of a straight line as the shortest distance between two points, and the Art that from time to time leaves the direct route to enter upon others, but at last achieves its purpose more truly, more symmetrically, and more convincingly. This difference may be seen at a glance by comparing any piece of early Art, whether in Poetry, Painting, Music, the Dance, or Fiction, with a later product of the same genus. 'The tales of primitive times,' says Mr. Herbert Spencer, 'like those with which the story-tellers of the East still daily amuse their listeners, are made up of successive occurrences that are not only in themselves unnatural, but have no natural connection; they are but so many separate adventures put together without necessary sequence. But in a good modern work of imagination, the events are the proper products of the characters working under given conditions and cannot at will be changed in their order or kind without injuring or destroying the general effect. Further, the characters themselves, which in early fictions play their respective parts without showing how their minds are modified by one another or by the events, are now presented to us as held together by complex moral relations, and as acting and re-acting upon one another's natures.'*

What is the principle involved in all these changes of Art? It is this – that the minds of early artists are comparatively simple and homogeneous, those of later artists complex and heterogeneous. While the former deal with few facts, diverge very little from the straight path, and pay more attention to the parts than to the whole, the latter deal with many diverse orders of facts, make wide circuits from the uniform path, and combine irregularity of parts with a greater concentration of the whole. This principle may be observed by anyone who will listen to a child's comments on a picture. All its attention is directed first on one point, then on another; there is a total absence of the power to combine all these detached representations into one synthetic representation. With a growth in synthetic power, many diverse ideas are gathered into one; and in the history of the nations, the novel has developed simultaneously with the development of this power to entertain many ideas, and to realize them as all bearing upon one central idea – to look beyond the immediate idea itself to ideas as yet existing only potentially.

While this holds true of the novel as a whole, it also holds true of each of its parts. Concurrently with an advance in that representative faculty which shows itself in a wider and more complex plot, there is an advance in that representative faculty which shows itself in a deeper insight into individual character. The *Morte D'Arthur* differs from *Daniel Deronda* both in its depth of insight into individual character, and in its breadth of combination among the characters as a whole. The novel, in its development, grows laterally as well as vertically – a similar phenomenon meeting us in Music, where the growth of melody,

* *First Principles*, pp. 326–7.

the horizontal, is accompanied by a growth in harmony, the vertical.

While this simultaneous growth in synthetic and analytic power shows itself both in the drama and the novel, it is in the latter that its results are important. The poetic insight into character differs from the novelistic in being more imaginative, and less dependent upon objective circumstances. In that intense flood of emotion which, by its nervous discharge throughout the ganglia of the entire system, concentrates the experience of years into a moment – a phenomenon which in its lowest form is ordinary excitement, and in its highest is music – the poet sees all life in epitome. His reading of character is more subjective than that of the novelist. The latter interprets humanity more through the environment than does the dramatist. In fact, poetry with an undue preponderance of analysis almost ceases to be poetry, as the *Sordello* of Browning, which almost approaches the novel. And in dramatic art, *Hamlet* is more of the nature of the novel than *Romeo and Juliet* or *Cymbeline*. While growth in synthetic power leads, on the one hand, into art like that of Victor Hugo, of Goethe, of Wagner, it leads, on the other hand, into thought such as that of Kant, of Spencer, or of Comte. In this latter form, it touches upon that particular faculty of the mind concerned in novel production.

We have seen then, that for the production of a novel there is required a mind partly imaginative, partly analytical, that the novelist must have something of the poet's insight into character, but must deal with his men and women upon a lower and less ideal plane; and that, beyond the faculty of insight into individual character, he must have the faculty of synthesis. One other point claims a few words of treatment.

We have been told that the novel should be carried on chiefly by means of conversations, and that the nearer it approaches the conversational and recedes from the descriptive the more perfect does it become. If this were so, there would apparently be no necessity for the novel at all; everything performed by it could be equally well performed by another form of Art – the prose drama. But the novel, as we have endeavoured to show, is something less than the drama in ideality, and something more than the drama in range and purpose. It is of a more intimate and more contemporary nature than the drama, and this mainly because it admits of interests and forces other than human. In a word, it is in the treatment of the environment that the novel surpasses the drama. It is precisely here that the novelist holds himself aloof from the purely imaginative realm of the dramatist. He directs upon the thoughts and actions of men a glance that goes beyond them and their immediate circle of human interests; he shows the life of humanity as bound up with the life of nature. It is unnecessary to demonstrate here how in this, as in so many other matters, the novel is the peculiar production of our later ages, where science, art, and social life have thrown us more into contact with the outer world, and shown the organic and the inorganic worlds in close inter-relation. Here it is sufficient to point out that it is this conception of the union between human forces and forces other than human that differentiates the novelist from all other artists, and that makes his work more interesting, more vital, and more contemporary.

We set out with a definition of Form as the objectivation of the psychical, the rendering concrete and assimilable of a purely mental hierarchy of facts and relations, and we have endeavoured to show, briefly, that the novel, viewed from its subjective side, as a concentrated picture of life in the mind of the novelist, has in it certain latent qualities, sources of origin and motives; that these latent qualities, in becoming concrete, seek a mode of expression which, in the nature of the words employed, in the conceptions of character revealed, and in the union of all single representations into one synthetic representation, is the true objective correlate of the inward idea itself; and that in this mode of expression alone can the novel, as a specific manner of looking at life, find its adequate revelation. It is not implied, of course, that every piece of literature usually designated a novel must comply with these conditions. But of the true novel – that is, a study of man in relation to other men and other things – these conditions do hold. The genuine novel, in fact, should be a problem in spiritual dynamics, in which the forces A, B, and C, are living men and women, with varying momenta, setting out from different points, aiming at different goals. In their passage across the earth they meet, and then proceed, in deflected paths, and with diminished velocities, to goals newly determined for them. In the beginning of the book the novelist presents us with the human forces and the lines along which they act; he shows us their meeting and their contest; and in his final pages he gives us the resolution of all the forces.

A NOTE ON GEORGE MEREDITH, 1903

(From the *Weekly Critical Review*)

AMONG THE many fine criticisms scattered about in Oscar Wilde's dialogue *The Decay of Lying*, there is one on George Meredith, which though illuminative like all Wilde's judgments, somewhat misses, I think, the real cause of one of our grievances against the novelist. We are all agreed in disliking certain elements in his style; what we do not agree about, is why Mr. Meredith's style ever came to have such irritating blemishes. 'Ah! Meredith!' says Vivian in the dialogue. 'Who can define him? His style is chaos illumined by flashes of lightning. As a writer he has mastered everything but language. . . . Whatever he is, he is not a realist. Or rather I would say that he is a child of realism who is not on speaking terms with his father. By deliberate choice he had made himself a romanticist. He has refused to bow the knee to Baal, and after all, even if the man's fine spirit did not revolt against the noisy assertions of realism, his style would be quite sufficient of itself to keep life at a respectful distance.'

With the last dictum we will all agree. We might have had some difficulty in extracting Mr. Meredith's philosophy of fiction from the novels themselves; but he has expounded his principles pretty fully in one manifesto or another; and there are some of us who rather prefer his philosophy to his fiction. Like Mr. Hardy, he sometimes gives us the impression of an acute observer and brilliant critic who has wandered into the novel-form by mistake. 'The Savour of Truth, the right use of the senses, Reality's infinite sweetness – to quote his own words – are not by any means writ large over most of his works: nor is his the fiction which is the summary of actual life, the within and without of us . . . philosophy's elect handmaiden.' He sees life through too much of a mirage for that. His invariably pre-posterous patronage of the poor and humble in his fiction, his habit of treating them with humorous condescension, his failure to see the lives of all these people as they themselves see it – this alone would show his limitations as the philosopher of reality in fiction. It is not, I suppose, that he cannot see these and other phenomena of human life sanely, but that he cannot make vital fiction of what he sees and knows. For this reason, perhaps, his poetry often gives us the impression of being more essential, more inevitable, than his prose; and even in his fiction his finest moments are those in which the pure imagination has been left free to soar into its own ideal atmosphere.

It may not seem very illuminative to say that he is too imagina-tive to be a convincing realist even in his own sense of the word. Nevertheless, an examination of some of the mental qualities underlying his style may throw a little fresh light on the formula. When I say that it is Mr. Meredith's imagination that makes his treatment of life unconvincing, I mean that he is so much the slave of a verbal faculty that is always getting unmanageable at the slightest suggestion from his fancy, as to be incapable of producing life as he has seen it. The imaginative mind fastens upon each impression as it appears, and gives it out again coloured by the reflection upon it of light from other impressions. But this faculty of spontaneous co-ordination needs to be held in check by a higher nervous centre; and in Mr. Meredith this superior control is decidedly lacking. Not only is his verbal faculty extremely opulent in itself, but it is always liable to be over-charged by the influx of irrelevant suggestions from his imagina-tion, that groups together, in one lightning flash, things that are sometimes only distantly related. Hence both the final obscurity of the idea and the oddity of its expression. The nervous hastening of the dissevered images to meet, may produce merely the effect of a mild mannerism, or it may be wild enough to set the reader raging furiously. Mr. Meredith's ladies, for instance, never walk, they always swim. Mrs. Doria swims to Richard Feverel; Mrs. Mount swims 'wave-like to the sofa'. Here the novelist's imagination has been seduced a step further by the 'swim'. The addition of the absurd 'wave-like' is clearly due to the irresponsible association suggested by the swimming. These however, are not very distressing aberrations of style, though objurgation is surely pardonable over such confused concepts as Hippias Feverel's 'somnolent door', or the fish that comes to 'the gasping surface', or Caroline sitting 'with her hands joined in pale dejection', or Dahlia 'eyeing' Edward 'a faint sweetness'. The worst comes when he is not merely correlating one or two images but indulging in a lengthy simile or series of similes. Take, as an example, the opening page of *The Egoist*: 'Who, says the notable humorist, in allusion to this book, 'who can studiously travel through sheets of leaves now capable of a stretch from the Lizard to the least few pulmonary strips and shreds of leagues dancing on their toes for cold, explorers tell us, and catching breath by good luck, like dogs at bones about a table, on the edge of the Pole?' Note the beginning of the sentence and the end of it. Mr. Meredith started out with the intention of emphasizing the length of the book to which he is referring. The book is so long that the leaves would stretch from the Lizard to the Pole, he meant to say. But having once thought of the Pole, his un-controllable imagination flies off on its own account, fastens on the idea of cold that is associated with the Pole, enlarges on this, drags in two or three comparisons and similes, complicates the notion of cold by the adjective 'pulmonary' – meaningless as he uses it – and finally makes the thing that has been said instead of 'the Pole' so long and so involved, that the dazed reader either wonders what on earth all this has to do with the 'sheets of leaves' with which he started, or staggers blindly under the weight of the end of the sentence and forgets all about the beginning. When Mr. Meredith wishes to convey to us an idea of a woman in the days before she became man-like, he tells us,

'Yet was there an opening day when nothing of us moustached her.'

When she does become somewhat masculine, we are 'amazed', as well we may be – 'by the flowering up of that hard rough jaw from the tender blooming promise of a petticoat'. And so we reach the distorted, tormented style of *One of our Conquerors* and the latest works, where we have such charming experiments with our tongue as this: 'The word "Impostor" has smacked her on both cheeks from her own mouth;' or this: 'She called on bell-motion of the head to toll forth the utter night-cap negative,' by which Mr. Meredith only means to say that the lady shook her head emphatically. A long course of this kind of thing would almost prompt us to characterize Mr. Meredith, in his own chastened and elegant phrase, as 'a fantastical planguncula, enlivened by the wanton tempers of a nursery chit'. Where the 'derangement of epitaphs' does not go far as in some of the passages I have quoted, the effect of Mr. Meredith's style may be admired even in spite of a certain flavour of the artificial. In *One of our Conquerors* we are told that 'Skepsey toned his assent to the diminishing thinness where a suspicion of the negative begins to wind upon a distant horn'. Here not only are the images all congruous, one growing naturally out of the other, but the total impression is clear and homogeneous.

Why, then, could Mr. Meredith not have kept the imaginative qualities of his style within proper bounds? Why need he ever have degenerated into this froth of inexpressive verbalism, these painful and far-fetched similes, this indirectness, this lack of unity between the purpose with which he begins a sentence, and the image with which he ends it? Partly, as I have said, because the imaginative faculty in him, though vivid and far-darting in some respects, is in others flaccid and ill-co-ordinated – it lacks control of a higher vision, and tends to run riot on its own account – and partly because, contrary to Oscar Wilde's opinion, he has mastered language so completely that the tongue is not only the perfect minister of the brain, but even at times an independent sovereign. We have one of the worst manifestations of this verbal opulence in the empty cackle of certain of Mr.

Meredith's great ladies. Here the temptation to talk for the mere pleasure of talking has proved irresistible to him, with the effect we all know to our sorrow. On the other hand, wherever he happens to hit upon a character whose very essence is volubility, as in the case of Roy in *Harry Richmond*, we have the best side of his verbal gift. Even the crusty old Squire becomes positively superb when Mr. Meredith has a chance to let himself speak through him; and for sheer magnificence of eruption there are few things in literature to compare with the final scene between Roy and Squire Beltham, where the old man pours out his scalding invective like a stream of lava. Truly it is not mastery of language that Mr. Meredith lacks, as Oscar Wilde thought. If in his latest works, and particularly in his latest poetry, he has become increasingly obscure, it is not because the mere means of expression have failed him. The verbal faculty in him still is, as it always has been, equal to any task the brain can set it. It seems to me more reasonable to suppose that it is just this faculty which leads him astray. We all know from our own experience how a word can suggest a mood and a phrase, how a tone or a chord can suggest a piece of music. In Mr. Meredith we have this phenomenon in a quite abnormal degree. The organs of thought are sometimes absolutely unable to keep pace with the images that start up from the organs of speech. What goes on in the phrase and the paragraph is only the counterpart of what goes on in the novel as a whole. With this verbal sense continually reacting on too exuberant imagination, and stimulating it to all kinds of irresponsible fantasias, it is inevitable that his fiction should often fall short of the ideal reality after which he aspires.

MR. MEREDITH AND THE COMIC
SPIRIT, 1903

(From the *Weekly Critical Review*)

IT WOULD greatly lessen the labour of the critic if all writers of fiction, drama, and music were compelled by law to produce at least one book explanatory of their philosophy and their objects. Notice how helpful Wagner's prose works are to any one who wants to understand the man and his music, and imagine, if you can, the world discussing Wagner with no other material before it than the music dramas themselves, and you will realize how necessary it is that every artist should occasionally enter the field of self-defensive exposition. A complete treatise by Shakespeare on the drama, or one by Beethoven on the symphony, might possibly be of no more final critical value than the multitudinous efforts of Wagner's pen; but think of the light it would throw upon the practice of its author, and of the enormous assistance it would be to the critic! Looked at in this way, Mr. George Meredith's comparatively little known *Essay on Comedy and the Uses of the Comic Spirit* has an interest quite apart from the one its author intended it to have. It may not tell us much about the Comic Spirit, but it incidentally tells us a good deal about Mr. Meredith.

It is notoriously hard to make valid distinctions in psychology among phenomena that lie very close to one another, and whose edges here and there overlap. Satire, Irony, Humour and the Comic are all tenants of the same house, and it is not easy to say where the rule of one ends and that of the others begins. Between the first two and the last two the dividing line is fairly obvious on the whole; but in the marking off of the Humorous from the Comic each of us apparently goes upon a system of his own. Here is Mr. Meredith's system. 'You may estimate your capacity for Comic perception by being able to detect the ridicule of them you love, without loving them less: and more by being able to see yourself somewhat ridiculous in dear eyes, and accepting the correction their image of you proposes. . . If you detect the ridicule, and your kindliness is chilled by it, you are slipping into the grasp of Satire. If instead of falling foul of the ridiculous person with a satiric rod, to make him writhe and shriek aloud, you prefer to sting him under a semi-caress, by which he shall in his anguish be rendered dubious whether indeed anything has hurt him, you are an engine of Irony. If you laugh all round him, tumble him, roll him about, deal him a smack, and drop a tear on him, own his likeness to you and yours to your neighbour, spare him as little as you shun, pity him as much as you expose, it is a spirit of Humour that is moving you. The Comic, which is the perceptive, is the governing spirit, awakening and giving aim to these powers of laughter, but it is not to be confounded with them: it enfolds a thinner form of them differing from satire in not sharply driving into the quivering sensibilities, and from humour in not comforting them and tucking them up, or indicating a broader than the range of this bustling world to them.'

In Comedy, in fact, according to Mr. Meredith, the brain is always uppermost: 'It laughs through the mind, for the mind directs it; and it might be called the humour of the mind. . . . The test of true Comedy is that it shall awaken thoughtful laughter.' The distinctions are excellent; and if that between the Humorous and the Comic is not absolutely convincing, it is only because we are in the region where an objectively true distinction is an impossibility. But let us accept Mr. Meredith's definition, and let us further subscribe to his dogma that one test of the civilization of a country is 'the flourishing of the Comic idea and Comedy'; and then let us take the specimens he himself puts before us as genuine samples of the Comic.

'At a dinner-party,' he says 'one of the guests, who happens to have enrolled himself in a Burial Company, politely entreats the others to inscribe their names as shareholders, expatiating on the advantages accruing them in the event of their very possible speedy death, the salubrity of the site, the aptitude of the soil for a quick consumption of their remains, etc.; and they drink sadness from the incongruous man, and conceive indigestion, not seeing him in a sharply defined light, that would bid them taste the comic of him.' That is, they take him seriously instead of humorously. But who would take him seriously, even at a British dinner-table? Surely all but the very dullest of us would see the comedy in such a situation as this; it is not particularly delicate or elusive comedy in any case, and for Mr. Meredith either (1) to fancy that the average man could not detect it, or (2) to believe that its detection implies a gift for 'thoughtful laughter', is to give us a hint that his own comic perceptions are a little singular. So with his next example of the general failure to see the comic in ordinary life. 'It is mentioned that a newly elected member of our parliament celebrates his arrival at eminence by the publication of a book on cab-fares, dedicated to a beloved female relative deceased, and the comment on it (by the diners) is the word "Indeed".' Again the wonder is not so much at the mental processes of the diners as those of Mr. Meredith. Even the Comic Spirit, one thinks, if he were hovering over the table at that particular moment, would scarcely condescend to stretch the corners of his mouth, be it ever so imperceptibly, over so thin a suggestion of the Comic as lies in this.

Take the third case: 'A certain French Duke Pasquier died, some years back, at a very advanced age. . . . An argument arose, and was warmly sustained, upon the excessive selfishness of those who, in a world of trouble and calls to action, husband their strength for the sake of living on. Can it be possible, the argument ran, for a truly generous heart to continue beating up to the age of a hundred? . . . Now, imagine a master of the Comic treating this theme, and particularly the argument on it. Imagine an Aristophanic comedy of 'The Centenarian', with choric praises of heroical early death, and the same of a stubborn vitality, and the poet laughing at the chorus; and the grand question for contention in dialogue, as to the exact age when a man should die, to the identical minute, that he may preserve the respect of his fellows, followed by a systematic attempt to make an accurate measurement in parallel lines, with a tough ropeyarn by one party, and a string of yawns by the other, of the veteran's power of enduring life and our capacity for enduring him, with tremendous pulling on both sides.' Does it really argue an insensibility to Comedy – 'which', as Mr. Meredith says, 'is the genius of thoughtful laughter' – if one finds oneself unable to grow enthusiastic over this idea and the comedy which, it is suggested, might be built out of it?

The interesting point of the matter is that a good deal of the Comic in Mr. Meredith's own novels is perilously like the Comic in these somewhat bloodless specimens. It is not without reason that he is forever lauding women, and claiming that Comedy

D

only thrives in societies where the women are on the equality with the men. It is not precisely clear how he arrives at this proposition, if we take the Comic in its broadest meaning. But if we understand it in his own somewhat limited sense the connection becomes obvious. His own perceptions of the Comic are those of the women; they are feminine both in their strength and their weakness, in their subtle refinement and their occasional bordering on the puerile. In the three examples I have cited of what Mr. Meredith regards as peculiarly Comic, in a number of the epigrams in *Richard Feverel*, in page after page of the conversations of its society ladies, we see a kind of delusion as to what is really comic or humorous – a brain of extraordinary delicacy standing aloof from the current of the things, and seeing much in it that rouses philosophic laughter, and yet rarely being able to tune its laugh deep enough. It is rarely male laughter, or if it is, it is the thin laughter of a valetudinarian or the cachinnation of an old man. He has, of course, another humour than this – rich, happy, full-chested, redolent at once of earth and spirit. But he is a being compact of contradictions; and nowhere is this more evident than in the contrast between his masculine and his feminine laughter. The strange thing is that, while almost all the critical portions of his Essay on Comedy – which are informed with sane feeling and ripe judgment – are the product of his masculine moods, the more speculative parts, and the illustrations by which he supports them, too plainly belong to that side of him wherein he is most like some of the grand dames of his own creation – forever straining after the humorous and never attaining it. To the outsider, indeed, there is at times nothing so comic as Mr. Meredith's own evident admiration for these distressing ladies. He has told us that the Comic Spirit is overhead, observing us incessantly. 'Man's future upon earth does not attract it; their honesty and shapeliness in the present does; and whenever they wax out of proportion, overblown, affected, pretentious, bombastical, hypocritical, pedantic, fantastically delicate; whenever it sees them self-deceived or hoodwinked, given to run riot in idolatries, drifting into vanities, congregating in absurdities, planning short-sightedly, plotting dementedly . . . the Spirit overhead will look humanely malign and cast an oblique light on them, followed by volleys of silvery laughter. That is the Comic Spirit.' Well he must have looked 'humanely malign' upon a goodly number of the novelist's own feminine essays in the Comic, which can hardly be traced to 'the genius of thoughtful laughter'. Fortunately this aspect of him is not the complete Meredith; and it is his own more genuine humour that has taught us to look tolerantly on him and his characters whenever they call too vociferously for those 'volleys of silvery laughter' that are the sign of the Comic Spirit.

THE NOVELIST AND THE MUSICIAN, 1903

(From the *Weekly Critical Review*)

WHEN TOLSTOI wrote that egregious tract *The Kreutzer Sonata*, he gave expression to the views of many a half-informed psychologist on the subject of the connection between music and sex. He was not very convincing; indeed, he traced much more accurately, the influence of the feminine jealousy upon love and marriage than the influence of music. But he was listened to because a great many worthy people feel dimly that the roots of music and of sex-feeling are closely intertwined, if not, indeed, merely one. Tolstoi was somewhat unfortunate in his choice of musical examples, for the Kreutzer Sonata would hardly be looked upon by most musicians as the kind of work that would goad people to a life of crime. 'Ought it to be played,' says the Russian novelist in tones of horror, 'in drawing rooms, in the midst of ladies in low-necked dresses, or at concerts, where the piece is finished, applauded, and then followed by another piece? Such works should only be played on certain important occasions, and in cases only where it is necessary that certain actions be provoked in correspondence with the music. But to provoke an energy which corresponds neither with the time nor the place, and which expands itself in nothing, cannot but have injurious effects.' The hero of the work must indeed have been an extremely excitable young man, to have been so painfully disturbed by a piece of classical commonplace like the Kreutzer Sonata; and he must have been stirred to his very depths when, later in the evening, his wife and the violinist played together 'a passionate piece by (I forget what composer) a piece so passionate that it reached the point of pornography', which, with all due respect to the great Russian, is pure nonsense. Music as music, can never positively suggest the pornographic; suggestion only comes in with words, as in the song, or with words combined with action, as in opera – say the garden scene in *Tristan*. Play the whole of the love-duet in *Tristan* to a man ignorant of the story, and keep from him all knowledge of the words and all sight of the action, and he would not detect in it one thousandth part of the sex-suggestion that we are conscious of in the theatre. It is amazing that novelists should harp for ever upon the supposed suggestiveness of music, when it is unspeakably feeble in this respect compared with either poetry, prose, or painting.

One easily sees, of course, the reason why the musician is so often made the victim of pretentious pseudo-psychological fiction. The author of *The Green Carnation* makes one of his characters remark how curious it is that while the sinner takes no interest at all in the doings of the saint, the saint is always very much interested in the doings of the sinner. For saint read the general unaesthetic public, and for sinner read the artist – especially the musician – and you have the key to the mystery. The artist looks down upon the common herd; but the common herd looks up to the artist with admiration for his talent and envy of his emancipated moral sense. What makes people read so greedily any revelation of artistic life – particularly if the revelation is at all scandalous – is at bottom the same feeling of half curiosity, half awe, that sends the average man loafing round the stage door at a pantomime. A musical novel that had not something spicy in it would be more or less a fraud; and to do our novelists justice, they have rarely erred in this respect. Whether their fiction will stand any critical examination into its psychological veracity is another question.

Take Mr. George Moore, for example, whose *Evelyn Innes* and *Sister Teresa* were hailed as most fascinating contributions to the vexed problem of the connection between music, sex and religion. The subject of nuns and convents is one which I must yield to Mr. Moore in knowledge, but I appeal to anyone who knows anything of music to say whether Mr. Moore has thrown any new light either on it or its relation to sex. That Mr. Moore is extremely susceptible to music I have no doubt. There are some particularly beautiful passages in *Evelyn Innes* in which he describes the effect of music and singing. But these are purely literary effects, the felicitous achievements in descriptions of a man with a gift for analysing his own sensations. Mr. Moore, one feels, could have described a sunset or a cab accident with equal veracity. What one cannot feel is that Mr. Moore has the really musical brain or temperament, or that he really has any insight into the psychology of the musician. Apart from mere descriptions of musical sensation, nothing that Mr. Moore says concerning music betrays any special knowledge of it. Just as he makes Owen Asher, in Paris, talk literary shop to Evelyn, stringing together a lot of platitudes about Balzac, so he makes Mr. Innes talk musical shop. 'From the twelfth to the fifteenth century,' he remarks to Owen Asher, 'writers did not consider their music as moderns do. Now we watch the effect of a chord, a combination of notes heard at the same moment, the top note of which is the tune, but the older writers used their skill in divining musical phrases which could be followed simultaneously, each one going logically its own way irrespective of some temporary clashing. They considered their music horizontally, as the parts went on; we consider it vertically, each chord producing its impression in turn. To them all the parts were of equal importance. Their music was a purely decorative interweaving of melodies. Now we have a tune with accompanying parts.' Well, all this is one of the merest commonplaces of the text-books. There has never yet been a student of counterpoint who has not been told, in precisely the same words, that we consider our music vertically, whereas the ancients considered theirs horizontally.

This would hold true, indeed, of a later date than the fifteenth

century. But the guileless Asher is so struck by these platitudes
that he turns round to Evelyn, awe-struck, with the remark:
'What a wonderful knowledge of music your father has, Miss
Innes!', which makes one sorry for him. In *Sister Teresa*, again,
Evelyn 'took a score by Brahms from the heap. "In Haendel
there are beautiful proportions", she said, 'it is beautiful, like
eighteenth-century architecture, but here I can discover neither
proportions nor design.' Evelyn's musical education must have
been somewhat neglected, in spite of her advantages in possessing
a father with a wonderful knowledge of music. Most people can
see proportion and design in Brahms if they can see nothing else;
some people can see nothing else. But Evelyn also remembered
that César Franck's music affected her in much the same way.

Her father ought not to have allowed her to call him 'Caesar
Francks'. But perhaps he was too much occupied with the
horizontal music of the twelfth century to notice little things like
this.

'Shrugging her shoulders, she said "When I listen I always
hear something beautiful, only I don't listen." ' This is much too
cryptic for the average intelligence, like the epigram of M.
Daveau in Mr. Moore's *Mildred Lawson*, when he was asked if he
liked classical music. – 'There is no music except classical music.'
Mr. Moore is not quite so bad as the lady novelist – I think it was
Mrs. Alexander – who described her hero as leaning across the
table and talking in a thorough-bass; nor as the late Mr. Hamerton,
who once spoke of the choristers chanting the Dead March in
Saul; nor as Mr. George Augustus Sala, who said that he had
looked through several biographical dictionaries and found there
were about a dozen musicians named Kreutzer, but could not
discover which of them had written Kreutzer's sonata. But he
comes perilously near, at times, to creating the impression of the
stumbling amateur in a field that is not his own.

This, however, is a minor grievance. The most serious flaw in
the two books is that while Mr. Moore's one object is to show
the intimate connection between music, sex, and religion, his
work in this respect lacks all vraisemblance. For him, as for
Evelyn, the sentiment seems to hold good that the human

animal finds in the opposite sex the greater part of his and her mental life; and he fathers on Owen Asher the superficial theory that 'the arts arose out of sex; that when man ceased to capture women he cut a reed and blew a tune to win her, and that it was not until he had won her that he began to take an interest in the tune for its own sake'. This is absurd enough as a reading of life; but it is extremely primitive as a piece of musical psychology. Supposing it were as true as it is really false, however, Mr. Moore's whole conception and portraiture of a musical character are still altogether imperfect. For nowhere, from cover to cover of the two books, is it shown that the rise, progress, decline and fall of Evelyn's soul are in any way due to the fact of her being a musician. A genuine study of the musical temperament would leave no doubt to the influence of music upon a given character's thoughts and life; he would be what he was because he was a musician, because, in the great crises of his life, his actions were consciously or unconsciously shaped by the fact that he looked at the world through the eyes of a musician. In *Consuelo*, for example, even such a character as the Anzoleto of the first hundred pages is plainly a musical being before everything else; and when Porpora dissects him one feels that he is laying bare for us an eternal musical type. Cut the music out of a character like this, and the whole portrait would fall to pieces. But cut the music out of *Evelyn Innes* and *Sister Teresa*, and the story would flow on almost unaffected, for the simple reason that everything that happens to Evelyn is quite independent of the fact that she is a musician. We feel indeed that her life might have been different had she not been an opera singer; but we also feel that her life might have taken precisely the same course had she adopted some profession quite apart from music, so long as it brought her into plentiful contact with men.

Looked at in this way, Mr. Moore's books are not studies of a musician at all. In *Consuelo*, in Balzac's fine *Gambara*, in Mr. Stanley Makower's *Mirror of Music*, we see that the characters are what they are precisely because they are musical. One feels about Evelyn that she is what she is not because she is musical, but merely because she is sexual. There was no need to make her a

musician; Mr. Moore's scheme would have worked equally well
if he had made her a poetess or a painter, so long as he made her
similarly sensual. It is sex that controls Evelyn's life, not music.
She is simply an erotic woman with a perpetual tendency to
incandescence. Allowing for the social distinctions, the descriptions of her sensations and adventures would hold equally true
of the debauched dressmaker or the lascivious laundress. There is
still room for a modern study of the musical temperament, the
kind of thing Mr. Joseph Conrad would do if he were a musician.
It must be written from the inside, not from the outside, by a man
who really knows how an artist's life of thought and feeling and
action is shaped for him by the musical constitution of his brain
and nerves. Mr. Moore at any rate, to say nothing of the minor
story-tellers, gives us a picture falling far short of this; it bears the
same relation to the real thing as the popular notion of stage life
bears to the actuality. The one attempt at imaginative recon-
struction is just as fantastic as the other.

THE ANIMAL IN FICTION, 1903

(From the *Weekly Critical Review*)

THE DECLINE and fall of Mr. Kipling's talent as exhibited in his
latest book of *Just So Stories* sets one thinking again of the qualities
of his earlier fiction, and especially of that portion of his fiction
that deals with animals. The *Just So Stories* are indeed a disappointment, with the solitary exception of that perfectly
delicious story of 'The Cat that Walked'. This is Mr. Kipling in
his best manner, with all his irritating faults kept in the back-
ground, and all his better qualities in the happiest equipoise.
But the rest of the stories are mere bungling. One wonders for
what kind of reader he can have meant them. They certainly do
not appeal to the adult who knows what a good animal story
ought to be; and one can imagine the bewilderment of the
child-mind at a good half of Mr. Kipling's flashiest points. For

the stories as a whole – and this is their great defect – are flashy, tawdry, full of abortive strain after all kinds of effects that do not 'come off'. This, of course, is quite in keeping with everything Mr. Kipling has done. Now and again he has achieved considerable verisimilitude in his fiction; one or two of his short stories would put him almost by the side of Maupassant. But as a whole his work is flawed by his constant tendency to pose, to talk big, to assume an air of patronizing omniscience, to lay down the law on all topics, from animals to soldiers, from babies to international politics. In the latter sphere alone, things have not gone altogether well with England since Mr. Kipling appointed himself adviser-in-chief to the Anglo-Saxon race. He does not understand more than a little of human nature; nor – popular opinion notwithstanding – does he understand more than a little corner of animal nature.

I am well aware that the two *Jungle Books* gave him a reputation among the unthinking as a great master of animal fiction, just as his *Soldiers Three* and his *Barrack-Room Ballads* were taken to be photographs of the soldier as he really is. Perhaps, on the whole, the soldier-studies, though even there 'The Absent-minded Beggar' showed how Mr. Kipling's vision had becomed thickened as time went on. The earlier stories had some touches of humanism, some sense of the music – cheap and vulgar though it may often be – that is in the soldier as in the rest of us; but 'The Absent-minded Beggar', set in the congenial surroundings of the *Daily Mail*, revealed the organ-grinder pure and simple. The Jungle stories, again, were never convincing for more than a moment or two at a time. They were neither pure realities nor pure fantasies. There was, of course, as in all Mr. Kipling's work, an assumption of a far profounder acquaintance with the subject than the mere layman could ever hope to obtain; but even the mere layman could see that this assumption was not justified by the result. Some of the notes rang so falsely that the least delicate ear could detect that the instrument was out of tune. Thus at the very commencement of the first story, Mr. Kipling tells us that 'the Law of the Jungle . . . forbids every beast to eat Man except when he is killing to show his children how to kill'.

The real reason for this, he goes on to say, 'is that Man-killing means, sooner or later, the arrival of white men on elephants, with guns, and hundreds of brown men with gongs and rockets and torches. Then everybody in the jungle suffers'. This is possible. It may or may not be the real animal psychology, but it is not starkly unreal. But then Mr. Kipling adds, 'The reason the beasts give among themselves is that Man is the weakest and most defenceless of all living things, and it is unsportsman-like to touch him' – one sees at once that this is bad psychology and bad art. In the attempt to show that he has penetrated into the inner-most recesses of the consciousness of the Jungle, Mr. Kipling has simply become clumsily absurd.

This fatal invraisemblance runs through almost all the stories. Compare any of them with the superb animal stories of Mr. Ernest Seton Thompson, or the equally faithful studies of animals in such a book as Mr. W. J. Long's *School of the Woods*, and you will see how flashy, how theatrical, how untrue, are almost all Mr. Kipling's stories. The complaint is not that they are not real – like Mr. Seton Thompson's *Biography of a Grizzly*, for example – but they are not consistently fanciful. We do not sniff at the fairy tale because it is not a realistic novel; but what we do have a right to expect is that it shall be consistent within its one sphere. Mr. Kipling's story of 'The Cat that Walked' is pure fantasy, but it is real within the limits of the fantastic. The majority of his other animal stories are not in any respect; they have neither the reality of life nor that of art. One seldom feels that he has really understood any animal, that he had taken suffi-cient pains to find out how a particular animal would express his views on the world if he could utter them in language. The great value of Mr. Seton Thompson's stories is that not one of them could be told of any other animal than the one round which it is written; you could not tell the bear story of the wolf, nor the partridge story of the rabbit. Here each animal has its own world of thought and feeling and instinct, its own character, its own individuality. But in the Jungle Books you could, for three-fourths of the time, substitute one animal for another without at all interfering with the general course of the stories.

Two or three of the animals are consistent studies, shaped, as it were, from the life; but the majority of them are pasteboard figures. They are simply the clumsily jerked puppets of a bad dramatist.

To see the point more clearly, look at Mr. Kipling when he achieves a real delineation and again when he simply swaggers melodramatically. Take first 'Quiquern', the story of the two Esquimaux dogs who were lost for some time, in a period of great scarcity of food. The two dogs were ultimately discovered, fat, well-looking, and quite restored to their proper minds; but coupled to each other in an extraordinary fashion. When the black leader ran off, you remember, his harness was still on him. He must have met Kotuko the dog and played or fought with him, for his shoulder-loop had caught in the plaited-copper wire of Kotuko's collar, and had drawn tight, so that neither dog could get at the trace to gnaw it apart, but each was fastened side-long to his neighbour's neck. They are separated, after having lived together for some weeks, and having been forced by their common bond and common necessities to hunt round for food together. As soon as they have properly greeted their master, 'these two, who had been forced to sleep and eat and hunt together for the past few weeks, flew at each other's throat, and there was a beautiful battle in the snow-house'. Now this, one feels, is truthful; this is real dog. It is just what dogs would do, and what would be done by no animal but dogs. The little stroke is both good fun and good psychology. But whatever fun there may be in Mr. Kipling's treatment of some of the other animals, there is certainly very little psychology. His crocodile, his panther are all seen from the outside, not from the inside. The limits of the preposterous are reached in the tiger, Shere Khan – a fragment of pure transpontine melodrama. He is the villain of the piece; it is our old friend, the heavy tragedian, transplanted in to the animal world; he scowls incessantly, cringes before the strong and bullies the weak, receives every now and then a knockdown blow from the nice good hero, and generally comports himself as impossibly as his human counterpart. His thoughts are altogether evil, his intentions wholly

vile – he might be one of Mr. Kipling's pro-Boer aversions – and
when he is finally done to death the gallery cheers with virtuous
delight, just as it does when the stage villain is run over by the
very railway train before which he tried to throw the heroine.
And the one thing, like the other, is written for the gallery. It is
all hopelessly theatrical, hopelessly unconvincing either as as
painting of life or a pure effort of the imagination. In fact, Mr.
Kipling fails here, just as he fails in his human fiction, because of
that fatal tendency in him to assume a knowledge he does not
possess. It is a necessity of his artistic nature that he shall patronize
something or somebody; and the result is that, except at its best,
his work has always this nauseating oracular tone. It came out
clearly in *The Light that Failed*, particularly in the scene where the
palpably unreal war-correspondents talked shop with an impossible swagger. It comes out in his treatment of the soldier, who,
Mr. Kipling sees, as indeed he sees everything, though a glass that
distorts the real picture. For him the sociological problem of the
soldier begins and ends with a few platitudes and a great deal of
rant; he is capable, as we know, of lauding in bad verse the dirty
work of the soldier at the same time that he bespatters with
contumely the saner heads who would fain save the nations from
the necessity of putting men to such work. All this comes from
Mr. Kipling not seeing things face to face, but through the
medium of a disordered temperament and ill-trained intelligence.
It is thus that he does his best, from a safe distant, to goad two
nations into bloody war, and then (see *The Times* of 27th February
last) offers artificial verses, reeking with the vinous platitudes of
the philosopher in the street, as his contribution to the work of
making grass grow again in the wilderness he did his best to
spread. He goes through life slapping the universe on the back.
First of all he took under his wing the Indian army; then it was
that pathetic myth Tommy Atkins; then it was the foreign and
colonial policy of Imperialism; now it is the enemy whose name
at one time was anathema to him.

He so rarely does good work, work that will last, because of
this habit of confusing the inside and the outside of every question
and the other habit of ascending the tripod upon every possible

occasion. Finally, when he comes to write about the animal, he is as unconvincing as usual because he will look down at the animal, or over his head, instead of trying to see into him. Just as he pats Tommy Atkins on the shoulder, and signifies to the mob his lofty approbation of its insensate foreign hatreds, so does he patronize the python and condescend to the hippopotamus. One need not have been in the jungle to see the lack both of truth and of artistry that this attitude must lead to. We have the final result of it in the *Just So Stories*, where all is pose, all swagger, all bounce. If the animals could talk, one asks oneself, would their conduct and their witticisms savour invariably of the music hall? Then one thinks of the real humour, the real observations, the real feeling, the real understanding of Mr. Seton Thompson's animal stories, and one sees that Mr. Kipling has only been playing the low comedian in the nursery. But after all has he not played that rôle on other and larger stages than this?

IV

CONTRIBUTIONS TO THE *BIRMINGHAM POST*

THE PRIMA DONNA IN PRINT,* 1911

SOME DAY a book will have to be written on the psychology of the prima donna; and the author of it will have to find the solution of one problem that becomes more insistent with each book that is written by, or by authority of, a singer – how is it that these people, who are so interesting and occasionally so subtle in their art are so utterly uninteresting and inexpressibly simple the moment they take a pen in their hand? The lives of most of them could apparently be compressed into a single sentence: they were born, they learned to sing, they sang, they made money and bought diamonds, they got Royalties to write in their autograph albums, and they died. Are certain great singers intellectually uninteresting by a law of Nature, or does their life make them so, or do they only pretend to be so? Intellectually uninteresting Madame Albani's book certainly is. Its tediousness is equalled only by its artlessness. For those who care about such things there are any number of details of the operas and oratorios Madame Albani sang in in this year or that, the presents that were made to her, the flowers that were hurled at her, the poems that were written about her, the great audiences that gathered to hear her, what the newspapers of thirty or forty years ago said about her, and so on and so on. For those who do not care a brass farthing for all this historical débris, what is there?

* *Forty Years of Song.* By Emma Albani. (Mills & Boon.) 10*s.* 6*d.* net.

What, indeed! Madame Albani must have met hundreds of remarkable people in her time. Upon not one of them has she an original or even an ordinarily perspicacious reflection to make. She meets Brahms, for example, in Vienna, and can only record that 'his room was full of old furniture and precious things, and he had a very high desk at which he always wrote standing'. A sharp child could have noticed as much. These singers seem to move about in a world peopled only with amiable shadows and simulacra. Are they deficient by the visitation of God in the faculty of observation and criticism, or is the faculty slowly killed in them by their 'successes' and the adulation that these bring with them? Some half-dozen honeyed adjectives suffice for them to characterize everyone whom they have met. Royal personages are, of course, always 'most gracious'; lesser people – but still great people in comparison with the ordinary run of us – are always 'most kind'.

The prima donna seems to swim in a sea of happiness; the public admires her, everyone is very courteous to her, the great of this world give her diamonds and lend her their houses for the summer, and, crowning joy of all, monarchs and princesses write their names with their very own hands in her autograph book! This may seem incredible to a sceptical reader; but the number of facsimiles of the awe-inspiring documents that Madame Albani reproduces in her book puts it beyond dispute by anyone honestly open to conviction. Madame Albani has had so many experiences of this kind that she can even isolate them from the events of common concert and operatic life and lump them into one dazzling chapter with the golden title 'Singing Before Royalty' – much as some rich diamond broker in Amsterdam will toy negligently with a handful of jewels each of them worth a prince's ransom. Even greater monarchs than those of Europe have not disdained to show Madame Albani honour. Did not that acute critic of singing, King Kalakua of the Sandwich Islands, compliment her, and was she not, as might be expected 'very gratified by his kindness,' and did he not decorate her with the Sandwich Islands Order of Merit? There can have been nothing quite equal in pathos to this touching scene since the historic day when Tartarin of Tarascon and the African King rubbed noses together and swore eternal fidelity to each other. The heart of the bored reviewer goes out to his Serene Majesty King Kalakua and to the Chinese Ambassador who went to sleep and snored audibly, to the scandal of everyone, at a concert at Buckingham Palace; they seem the only real, natural human beings in all these mel- lifluous saccharine pages. The book reveals a sweet and rather simple nature, and will no doubt give pleasure to some of Madame Albani's personal friends; but as a piece of literature it does not count. The authoress has nothing helpful to say even about singing – nothing but the old clichés about using, not abusing, the voice, and taking care of your tissues between concerts; and though she mentions that she has read books and seen pictures and enjoyed scenery, she has nothing even mildly interesting to say on any one of these topics. Madame Albani would have been better advised to have left with us simply a memory of her as one of the finest singers of her day. As it is she tells us nothing about herself that we did not know already, except a number of things that most of us do not think worth knowing.

THE GIRL OF THE GOLDEN WEST, 1911

(First English Performance)

AT COVENT GARDEN tonight Puccini's new opera, *The Girl of the Golden West*, was given for the first time in England.★ It is mostly rather poor Puccini, though there is charm in some of the music, and the mingling of sentimentality and melodrama in the story will probably endear it to a certain section of the operatic public. The plot will be familiar to a number of people from the drama by David Belasco, on which the opera is founded, and to others from a condensed version of the play that went the round of the music halls some time ago. The music hall, indeed, is the proper place for it, for romantic balderdash of this kind is not to be taken

★ 30th May, 1911

too seriously. In a mining camp in California in the days of the gold fever (about 1850) there is a certain Minnie, who, by her beauty and her virtue, has enslaved the hearts of all the miners. She keeps a tavern known as the 'Polka', where these rough fellows gather nightly for the card-playing, singing, quarrelling, and occasional pistol-shooting that presumably form the evening recreations of all miners – at all events, of all stage miners. We see them hard at it in the first act of the opera. Of course, one of them cheats at cards, and, of course, the others want to shoot him at sight. He is merely condemned, however, to wear the two of spades pinned to his chest for the rest of his life, and to be shot if he removes it – a touch of melodrama that would delight the heart of any boy scout.

Of course, the miners have another row after that, and, of course, Minnie enters at the nick of time and pacifies them. Of course, they are all in love with her, and each hopes that she will marry him. Everything, it will be seen, is running on the most approved shilling-shocker lines. Of course there is a bill displayed in the tavern, offering a reward for the head of a certain Ramarrez, the head of a gang of daring gold thieves. Of course Ramarrez enters, disguised, and calling himself Dick Johnson. He has really come after the barrel, in which the miners keep their gold, and which they leave in charge of Minnie when they go out. (Everyone knows that this is what all proper miners do). But he and Minnie recognize each other. They had met under romantic circumstances some time before, and, of course, fallen in love. Of course Johnson repents him of his felonious purpose when he is left alone with Minnie, and instead of making off with the gold, he yields to her charm, and promises to visit her later on in her cabin, which is a little way removed from the tavern.

In the second act, which takes place in this cabin, they, of course, have a love scene. Minnie gives up her bed to Johnson. When he has retired behind the curtain Rance, the Sheriff enters. He is even more in love than the rest of them with Minnie, but she has repulsed him and greatly irritated him by her obvious preference for Johnson. Of course, Rance tells her that her handsome young dandy of a Johnson is really Ramarrez; he has obtained this information from that gentleman's mistress, Nina Micheltorena – for Ramarrez is regrettably pluralistic in his attachments. After Rance's departure, Minnie, of course, rounds on Johnson, who, of course, explains that he has been driven into a life of larceny by circumstances over which he had no control. Like the hero of fiction he is, he goes out into the darkness and is promptly shot by Rance, who has had his suspicions, and has been hanging round the cabin to see what would turn up. Desperately wounded, Johnson staggers back into the cabin, whereupon, of course, Minnie passes a bill of indemnity in his favour and loves him as much as ever. She assists him up a ladder into the loft, where she bids him hide. Rance, of course, rushes in, after having allowed an interval to elapse, for all this ladder-climbing to go on, and demands his prey. Minnie has almost fooled him into going, when, of course, he happens to stand beneath the very place in the loft where Johnson happens to be, and, of course, a drop of the wounded man's blood happens to fall upon his hand.

Of course he has poor Johnson down in next to no time, meaning either to shoot him or to take him to be hung by what Mr. Mark Sheridan would call 'the b-hoys'. Minnie, of course, challenges Rance to a game of cards. If he wins, he is to have both her and Johnson; if he loses, he is to go away and keep his mouth shut. Of course, the first round is won by Minnie, and the second by Rance; it would never do to let either of them win two out of three straight off. Then, just as things are beginning to look black for Johnson, Minnie, with the guile of her sex, pretends to faint, makes Rance jump up and get her a restorative, and while he is away substitutes for the cards in her hand a much better set which she has had the foresight to place in her stocking. The baffled Rance goes out looking very glum, and a nice 'curtain' is made by Minnie throwing her arms round the neck of Johnson, who had fainted some time before.

In the third act Johnson is captured by the b-hoys, and realistic preparations are made for lynching him. Of course, Minnie comes in just in time to forestall the swinging and the revolver peppering, and, of course, succeeds in so working upon the affections of these rude sons of toil that, Rance's rage notwithstanding, they give her Johnson, with whom of course, she goes away to begin a new life elsewhere. Altogether it is a subject that would bring tears to the eyes of the most hardened scullery wench.

And as the story is, so is the music; it is largely a blend of naïve sentimentality and raw melodrama. Of the old Puccini, the man of talent who wrote *Tosca*, *La Bohème*, and *Madame Butterfly*, there is hardly a trace until the final scene, where Minnie's music reaches a height of refined expression that contrasts markedly with the crudity of the earlier music. For crude it mostly is, as we listen, for example, to the melody of the duet between Minnie and Ramarrez in the second act – a tune fit only for the barrel organs – we wonder what has become of the Puccini who used to weave such delicate spells round us. Hardly anywhere does he succeed in achieving the least continuity of style; the score seems to live from hand to mouth. To discuss it in detail is impossible; it has not sufficient individuality for that. It is mostly a stream of facile, disconnected commonplace, with a few exciting moments. The first two acts are rather dull; the third, with its galloping horses and yelling men, and all the paraphernalia of a lynching, is effective in a kind of raw operatic way. But the whole work gives one the impression of a lapse into the spirit of the stupid old Italian opera, with the stupidities slightly disguised in modern dress.

Mlle. Destinn turned all her intelligence on to the part of Minnie, with the sole result of making us wish she had something more worthy of her to sing. Her voice is a little too white to be a fully expressive dramatic instrument, and tonight she looked rather too matronly for the part; but one could never be in any doubt as to her brains or her musical feeling. M. Gilly was admirable as the sinister, saturnine Rance. The Johnson of Signor Bassi was disappointing; he seems to be an ineffective actor with a poor voice. The other parts were all capably done, and the opera was well staged. Signor Campanini, the conductor, and the orchestra were excellent. There was a fair amount of enthusiasm, and Puccini had to appear after each act; but a good deal of the applause came from one part of the house, and it is hard to say how much of it was meant for Mlle. Destinn. An unprejudiced observer, used to these first-night demonstrations and knowing how to discount them, could have little hesitation in saying that the opera fell very flat.

MOZART AND STRAUSS, 1911

TODAY'S PROGRAMME* at the London Festival was originally made to suit Richard Strauss, who was expected to conduct the concert. As he excels in Mozart, a symphony and a concerto by that composer were put down for performance, the remainder of the programme being devoted to Strauss himself. He has been too unwell to come to England, however, so that the conducting of today's concert fell to Sir Henry Wood. Truth to tell, a good many of us found Mozart a little meagre after the strong fare we have had lately. The pianoforte concerto, excellently played as it was by Mr. Harold Bauer and the orchestra, seemed emptier than usual; and Heaven knows how empty some of these instrumental works of Mozart can be! The G Minor Symphony has more *Eingeweide* in it, but, even here, one sometimes felt that we were merely listening to the nursery prattle of a bright child. It would be a good thing if the critics were now and then to try to see an old work precisely as it would strike them if it were a new one. How interesting it would be, for example, if someone were to apply the same critical rigour to these two works of Mozart as was done in today's papers to the three new compositions produced at last night's concert! It seems to be infinitely more difficult to make a great reputation in music now than it was a hundred and fifty years ago. Mozart is a myth, a legend; and the average musician no more thinks of revising the traditional notion of him than a savage thinks of questioning the divinity of Mumbo-Jumbo. So everybody today tried to look very interested, very knowing, and very happy – everybody, that is, except a few of

* 26th May

my critical colleagues, who turned the Queen's Hall into a dormitory for a time.

It is the correct thing of course, to lament the passing of Mozart – or at all events of a good deal of his work – and to cry that something has gone out of music that will never return. It may be so; but, on the other hand, a great deal has come in that Mozart never dreamt of; and modern music has gained infinitely more than it has lost. One needed only to pass to the Strauss *Burleske* for piano and orchestra to realize this. It is very early Strauss; but already there is a difference between this and the Mozart concerto comparable to that between a grown man and a pretty child. The later works in the programme – the *Also Sprach Zarathustra* and the selection from *Salome* – of course accentuated this difference in stature and intelligence. The splendid orchestral playing in these two works made every point of them tell. They, no doubt, annoyed some people considerably; others of us they filled with a kind of awe before the enormous possibilities of psychological expression that music has developed during the last half-century. In the Mozart symphony and concerto – to hark back to these once more for the purpose of comparison – one seemed to be little more than playing with life, or even playing at playing at it; some of it told us no more of ourselves than the pattern on the wall paper does. In the *Zarathustra* and *Salome* we are dissected alive. It is not merely portraiture, such as we get, for example, in Wagner; it is an absolute laying bare of the very nerves and their most secret processes. I was particularly struck with this today in the *Salome* selections, partly, no doubt, because there was no stage action to distract us. I have never realized before the full wonder of this music – the 'Dance of the Seven Veils' and the final scene – its appalling truth to life, its pitiless revelation of what madness of sensation the nervous modern brain and body are capable. Music, perhaps, will soon be the one art in which a man can show us to ourselves as we really are, without fear of censor or of police. The Pathetic Symphony sometimes preaches an anarchism that would send anyone to Siberia who ventured to put it into speech. In this *Salome* music there is more told us of the horror of our bodies and souls than in all the ravings of saints or satyrs, or in all the manuals of pathology. And the proof that it is great art is the sense of joyousness it gives us – that sense of clarified understanding of life that it is the business of all tragic art to give. Like all great art, again, it floods us with pity. How anyone can feel revolted at this final scene of *Salome* I cannot imagine. To me, in spite of its horror, it is supremely pity-moving. But be that as it may, he must be a dullard who is not shaken to his bones by the drastic truth of it. Today it was not only magnificently played by Sir Henry Wood and the orchestra, but magnificently sung by Madame Aïno Ackté, the young Finnish soprano, who took the part of Salome at the first English performance of the opera last year. It was an experience one would be sorry to have missed. Madame Ackté, who is evidently an extraordinary personality, stopped just short of the line that divides platform acting from that of the theatre; but, on the right side of the line, she gave us a Salome so complete that one still wonders at the consummate art of it. Her voice was superb in its power and in the delicacy of its inflections. Incidentally, one got some new ideas upon the theory and practice of theatrical make-up. No facial expression that I have ever seen upon the stage was comparable in its variety and suggestiveness to that of Madame Ackté today; there was simply nothing like it in any performance of the opera in the theatre. Her face, no doubt, is an exceptionally mobile and expressive one; but certainly the greater part of the effect today came from the fact that the natural lines and tints of the cheek and mouth and eyes were not overlaid and impeded by stage cosmetics, through which it must surely be as hard for the thought to leap to instantaneous life in the lines of the face as it would be for a violinist to play sensitively with gloves on.

Altogether, once the Mozart was off the board, it was a great afternoon. Sir Henry Wood gave an extraordinarily lucid and impressive performance of the *Zarathustra*; the solitary mistake in it was toning down the opening of the *Science* fugue so excessively that for a few bars it was almost inaudible. In the *Burleske*, Mr. Bauer, besides playing with great technical brilliance, gave admirable point to the somewhat hard and audacious humour of the work.

VERDI, 1913

So FAR as performances of his music are concerned, the centenary
of the birth of Verdi, on Friday last, passed practically without
recognition in England. This country, indeed, with its deplorable
inefficiency in almost all matters musical, is worse equipped than
any other under the sun for celebrating centenaries adequately;
one is tempted to say that England visits its spite on the heads of
great musicians for refusing to be born here by refusing them
commemoration honours after they are dead. It is characteristic of
this oratorio-ridden land that the only work of Verdi's that is at
all well known here is the Requiem. The ordinary Englishman,
indeed, knows singularly little of Verdi, and nothing at all of the
greater Verdi. We get an occasional performance of the operas of
his middle period – *Rigoletto* (1851), *Il Trovatore* (1853), *La
Traviata* (1853), and *Un Ballo in Maschera* (1859); but these no
more represent the real Verdi than the *Flying Dutchman* and
Tannhäuser represent the real Wagner. Even *Aïda* (1871), which is
decidedly popular, does not show him at anything like his best.
The true Verdi lover is even a little annoyed by it at times; he does
not mind the roughly effective and slightly comic methods and
the stereotyped Italian tricks of the earlier operas, for he knows
that a cub cannot walk or tumble in any way but that of a cub,
and *Trovatore* and the rest of them are just the awkward but
fascinating sprawlings of a cub of an uncommonly vigorous
breed. But in *Aïda* Verdi has lost a good deal of his old manner
without having fully acquired his newer one; and the opera, to
my thinking, falls between two stools. Yet, when all is said, had
Verdi's career closed with *Aïda* we should have been struck by the
length of the road he had travelled since the *Nabucco* of 1842. (He
had written a couple of operas before that, but they are not
generally known or accessible. The *Nabucco* is still extremely
interesting.) Verdi himself, indeed, then nearing his sixtieth year,
regarded *Aïda* as the end of his activities; he retired to his estate,
living all day, as he says in one of his letters, 'in the fields and the
woods, among the peasants and animals, especially the little four-
footed ones, who are the best of all'.

But he had another thirty years of life before him, to be filled with a slow crescendo of astonishing achievement. In 1874 he gave the world the beautiful Manzoni Requiem. Thirteen years later he made everyone marvel at his *Otello*, an opera of great intellectual power, in which his musical genius has taken a flight for which not even *Aïda* and the Requiem had prepared us. And in 1893 came the most dazzling wonder of all – the *Falstaff*. The wonder was not that after writing lurid tragedies all his life he should turn to comedy in his old age, for that is in the natural order of things. Here in England we often rail at our young composers for being so tragically minded, and exhort them to leave the problems of the cosmos alone for a while and write a little comic music. But after all, perhaps, nature is handling them in the right way. There is comedy and comedy, of course; comic music of the ordinary stage type any decent musician could write blindfold. But for the richer sort of comedy, in which the smile is more searching than the laugh, and the humour and the humanity lie even deeper than tears, a man needs to wait till he has at any rate a toe or two in the grave. Garrick used to say that anyone could act in tragedy, but that to do comedy well was the very devil. And so our young men are, no doubt, doing the right thing in going about swathed in sackcloth and powdered with ashes. In this dismal garb they will gradually get rid of their tiresome growing pains; and in thirty years or so the best of them will be sitting in slippered ease and chuckling in their music over the fun of life. Wagner had his first idea of the *Meistersinger* when he was thirty-two, but wise and kindly nature kept him from writing the opera until he was nearly fifty.

It was in accordance with the nature of things, then, that Verdi should purge him of his tragic bile before he could give himself up to pure joy in sunlight and laughter; but the amazing, almost incredible thing is that at nearly eighty years of age he should still be so rich in physical and mental vigour as to be able to carry through without a single lapse so gay and sunny a work as *Falstaff* – an opera that is a pure delight from first to last. It and the *Meistersinger* stand in a class by themselves – though I myself would be inclined to grant admittance to this circle to Hugo

Wolf's beautiful opera *The Corregidor*. *Falstaff*, of course, is much lighter in texture than the *Meistersinger*, and for that reason would probably make a better model for the comic opera of the future. There is no real need, perhaps, for the music of comedy to be so fat and polyphonic as Wagner makes it. That Titan of necessity used the instrument that had come to his hand from those of his great forerunners – an instrument that was never a light one, and that has become heavier and heavier by successive accretions of technique, till in the hands of men like Strauss and Roger it is almost comically unwieldy. Verdi, like the Latins in general, was satisfied with a lighter and swifter style of expression; and this clarity we have at its rarest in the incomparable *Falstaff*.

Apart from the delicacy of its texture, and the virtual avoidance of the leading motive system, there is little in the opera that is specifically Italian. Our folk-song enthusiasts will have it that in some undefined and indefinable way the music of each country should be recognizably 'national', whereas the truth is that the greater the music is the less distinctively is it French or German or Italian or anything else. *Falstaff* is not nearly so 'Italian' in style as, say, *Il Trovatore*; a German or an Englishman might have written it had he had Verdi's grace and wit. As he grew older, indeed, Verdi seems to have recognized the fallacy of 'nationalism' in art, and to have seen that nothing mattered but the personality of the artist. 'I wish,' he writes to a correspondent in 1875, 'that a young composer, when he sits at his desk, would not bother his head about being a melodist, or a harmonist, or an idealist or a music-of-the-futureist, or what the devil all these pedantries are called. Melody and harmony in the hands of an artist are only a tool for the making of music; and a day will come when people will no longer talk of melody, of harmony, of a German school and an Italian school, of the past and the present, and so on; and then perhaps we shall enter into the kingdom of art.' This reminds us of Hugo Wolf's dictum that what the composer has to do is to write not German music or French music or Russian music, but simply music. If Verdi seems pronouncedly 'Italian' in the Requiem, it is because northern Protestantism and southern Catholicism have come to hold divergent opinions as to the essence and the forms of religion. In the greatest Verdi of all, the Verdi of *Otello* and *Falstaff*, the typical Italian stigmata are barely visible. When, I wonder, will these two works become part of the ordinary English repertory? Even on the Continent they are not given quite as often as one would expect. *Otello*, written originally for Tamagno, is a little cruel to the average tenor; while both this opera and *Falstaff* call for performers who are subtle actors as well as fine singers. In England, therefore, we shall still, in all probability, have to derive our knowledge of the later Verdi from the Requiem alone.

DER ROSENKAVALIER, 1913

WHEN PLAYED precisely as it is written, the *Rosenkavalier* is about four hours long and rather broad. The man in the street might add, with a wink and a grin, that it is also a bit thick. But even in Germany, I believe, it is not given now precisely in accordance with the stage directions in the score, and at Covent Garden last night the action and situations of the opera were still further toned down. As it was originally planned, neither Hugo von Hofmannsthal (the librettist) nor Strauss could be absolved from the charge of making a skilful use of indelicate situations for the benefit of the box office. The play, as a play, is a good one only in the sense that it is better than the usual stuff that is thought good enough for opera; but much of what is good in it is not new, and and much of what is new in it is not good. The scene is laid in the Vienna of the eighteenth century. The first act shows a boy of seventeen, Octavian, in the bedroom of his middle-aged mistress the Princess von Werdenberg, whose husband is away hunting. The time is apparently next morning. In the original, the Princess is supposed to be reclining in bed in a night gown; in the censored version she sits in a chair in what might be either a dressing gown or an opera cloak. In time a cousin of the Princess arrives – a certain middle-aged, coarse-mannered, coarse-minded Baron Ochs von

Lerchenau. He has come to marry one Sophia, the young daughter of a parvenu merchant, Herr von Faninal. He has never seen the lady, but neither her father nor Ochs takes love into his calculations. The former's one desire is to marry his daughter into nobility; Ochs' only wish is to add another pearl to his already long list of feminine acquisitions. Octavian, unable to escape from the room, has had to disguise himself in women's clothing; the Princess passes him off as her maidservant, Mariandel. With the pretty Mariandel, of course, Ochs at once falls in love. His immediate object, however, is to find a Rose-bearer – a young gentleman of good family who used to take a silver rose from bridegroom to bride. The Princess recommends to him one Rofrano, who is, of course, Octavian. This transaction arranged, the Princess holds her levee; the apartment fills with a curious crowd of suitors, beggars, musicians, etc., and after the exit of the Baron and the crowd there is a touching scene between the Princess and Octavian. He swears eternal fidelity, but she prophesies that sooner or later he will leave her for a younger and prettier woman. In the second act Octavian brings the rose to Sophia, and the pair at once fall in love with each other. Ochs angers both Sophia and Octavian by the brutal coarseness of his wooing, and the boy wounds the burly braggart in the arm. At the end of the act he is lying alone on his chair slightly fuddled with wine, when a letter is brought him from the supposed Mariandel, making the appointment for the tête-à-tête he had asked for in the Princess's room. He is in high glee, but refuses to reward the bearer of the letter – an Italian adventuress Amina – who forthwith vows vengeance. The scene of the third act is a room in an Inn – part supper-room and part bedroom. Octavian appears in woman's clothes and she and her accomplices fool the Baron to the top of his bent: conspirators concealed under trap-doors and in cupboards pop out their heads at times and make him believe his brain is going, and Amina and a number of children pass themselves off as an abandoned family of his. First the commissary of Police arrives, then the Princess. It ends with the Baron retiring in confusion, and the Princess sacrificing her own happiness for that of the young lovers.

It is a mixed piece of work, sometimes interesting, sometimes very stupid and thick fingered. The Baron is an amalgam of Tony Lumpkin, Bob Acres, Count Almaviva and Don Juan, but with everything in him Teutonically coarsened to the texture of a sausage. Octavian is a modern Cherubino, and the Princess a modern Countess Almaviva. The primitive humour of the last act is very tiresome. The scene at the Princess's levee is like a succession of music hall 'turns'; and there is a touch of pantomime, again, in each of the episodes in which a little negro servant of the princess takes part. And as the play, so the music. It is a bewildering packet of all-sorts. One might sum it all up as being one-third worthy of Richard Strauss, one-third worthy of Johann Strauss and Lehár, and the remainder only worthy of the waste paper basket. A great deal of it is in that vein of clever bluffing that Strauss has become far too addicted to of late. For a good hour and a half of the time he is simply chattering away without anything definite to say; with his harmonic cleverness and his consummate orchestral technique he can 'spoof' the unsuspecting listener into believing something really musical is going on when it is not.

The music given to Sophia is mostly quite uninteresting. The waltzes are the salvation of the opera; but these, in a sense, are a ready made article, a kind of pre-digested food. It is not at all difficult to write a taking waltz; and there must be at least five hundred men in Europe today capable of writing waltz tunes as good as those of nine-tenths of Strauss. Just as, after Bach and Brahms, it is possible to make quite a decent show with the transmitted musical technique, even if you have no very striking ideas of your own, so it is possible for any good musician to make an excellent show with some variety or other of the captivating waltz-dishes that have already been served up for us time without number by Viennese operetta writers. If only we could hear a Johann Strauss or Lehár waltz scored for the Richard Strauss orchestra, I fancy we should not be able to make such distinction between it and one of Richard Strauss's. The 'Rosenkavalier' waltzes, however are, it must be admitted, very jolly things of their kind. A visible and audible purr of contentment went through the audience each time they sang out; if the whole opera could have been couched in this idiom it would have made a very pleasant after-dinner entertainment. But the work achieves no unity of style; it is by turns Richard Wagner, Richard Strauss the earlier, Richard Strauss the later, Johann Strauss, and Mozart. He has not been able to weave a new and homogeneous comedy idiom for himself as Wagner did in the *Meistersinger*.

And yet, on the whole, nobody but Strauss could have written the work; and in its greater moments it is inexpressibly fine. The two towering things in it are the affecting scene between the Princess and Octavian at the end of the first act – in which the music breathes the very subtlest essence of wisdom, tenderness, and a life's philosophy – and the trio for the three women's voices at the finish of the opera. This has been growing on me continuously for more than eighteen months; but last night it sounded more glorious and more masterly than I could have anticipated. The obvious comparison is with the famous quintet in the *Meistersinger*; and Strauss more than holds his own in the comparison. Such warmth of blood, such boldness of flight, and such power of endurance are beyond the scope of any other living musician.

The entrance of the Rosenkavalier in the second act is also a dazzling piece of work, though I have come to like the dissonant harmonies less and less; they are too obviously manufactured. One came away wishing that Strauss would now separate himself from the theatre, that has done him so much harm as well as good during his ten years' association with it, and concentrate upon some purely orchestral work that would call out all the best that is in him, and the form of which would force him to think concentratedly, because there would be no stage action to keep us uncritically occupied while he was merely cleverly marking time in the orchestra. He may yet do a work of this kind. If he ever does, it will be a masterpiece.

SCHÖNBERG'S FIVE ORCHESTRAL PIECES, 1914

ARNOLD SCHÖNBERG – one of the advanced composers of our day who make people like Richard Strauss seem quite old-fashioned – made his first appearance in London at a Queen's Hall concert on Saturday afternoon, when he conducted a performance of his *Five Orchestral Pieces*. It may be remembered that when these works were played at a Queen's Hall promenade concert in September 1912, they seemed so destitute of meaning and so full of discords that the audience laughed audibly all through the performance, and hissed vigorously at the end – which is a very unusual thing for an English audience to do, even when it is not pleased. The management was evidently apprehensive that something of the same sort might happen again on Saturday and hurt Schönberg's feelings, for in the programme there appeared the following diplomatically worded note: 'Herr Arnold Schönberg has promised his co-operation at today's concert on condition that during the performance of his Orchestral Pieces perfect silence is maintained.' In other words, 'Don't shoot the composer; he is doing his best.' It was hardly to be expected that the audience would in any case be so rude to Schönberg to his face as it had been behind his back; but as events turned out, although there was a faint hiss or titter now and then, the music was actually applauded with some warmth. The applause was evidently not merely a matter of good nature and politeness to Schönberg himself; for though he was greeted cordially when he came on the platform, smiling and looking very much alive and alert, the first of the Five Pieces was received practically in silence, the applause commencing after the second piece and increasing to the end. It was not universal, of course, and in volume was nothing like what was lavished on Tchaikovsky's Circus – and sawdust – piano concerto in B flat minor and its performer; but it was fully evident that the audience, though often puzzled, was decidedly impressed.

It was clear, indeed, that we were now really hearing the music for the first time. Perhaps it had been better rehearsed; and of

course the composer knew, as no one else could know, exactly
how it ought to be made to sound. Certainly I cannot imagine a
greater difference between two performances of music, and the
effects of them, than there was between Saturday's performance
of this Schönberg work and that fifteen months ago. Only the
composer, I imagine, can show them to us as they are really meant
to be. They have a new orchestral feeling and technique, to
which the score is only an imperfect guide. A note prefixed by
Schönberg to one of the movements – to the effect that the
conductor is not to concern himself with bringing out this or
that voice, that seems to him important, or to soften what seems
to him discords, for all this is allowed for in the orchestration,
and all the conductor has to do is to see that each player employs
the precise degree of force indicated in his part – I thought at first
a little affected. But the music, when properly given, justifies
what Schönberg says of it. The various timbres are blended in the
most cunning way imaginable. Discords that on paper look
unendurable and meaningless are tinted in such a way that one feels
only a vague and often most alluring effect of atmosphere and
distance. This is not absolutely new, of course, in orchestral
music, but Schönberg's vision of the things to be done in this
line, and his skill in doing them, go beyond those of any other
composer I know. The third piece is quite remarkable in this
respect; it does not contain a single phrase that can be called a
'theme' in the ordinary significance of that term, and is a sort of
shimmering, gently heaving sea of tone. It is impressionism pure
and simple, and impressionism is bound to bulk more and more
largely in the music of the future. It will be a little hard for us to
adapt ourselves to it at first, for the very vagueness of the picture
in the composer's mind, and the absence from the music of all
literary or materialistically pictorial sign-posts, often destroy all
the connecting links we have been accustomed to between the
composer's imagination and ours. Others of these Five Orchestral
Pieces are not impressionistic in the same way as No. 3, though
what at present seems their lack of definite thematic working and
clear outline is apt to make us sum them all up under the same
term. There is thematic repetition in the First, but here, too, the

main effect comes from the harmonic and orchestral colour and the sense of driving energy conveyed by the rhythmic motion.

But always we come back to the harmonic problem. What distinguishes all Schönberg's music since the Three Piano Pieces of Op. 11 from his earlier work is the apparently deliberate throwing over of the century-old distinction between consonance and dissonance. Hitherto, though we have become more tolerant each decade of discords that our predecessors would have winced under, they have justified themselves to us by standing in some sort of logical relation to a central idea of consonance. Schönberg upsets all this. He treats dissonance as a tonal language, complete and satisfying in itself, owing no allegiance, or even lip-service to consonance, either at the beginning, in the middle, or at the end of the work. It is amazing how far we can already go with him, how strangely beautiful and moving much of this music is, that, judged by the eye alone, is a mere jumble of discordant parts. But it is frankly impossible for the most advanced musician to see a coherent idea running through a great deal of this music. I do not say the coherent idea is not there, but simply that at present its coherence and its veracity are not always evident. Time alone can show whether it is our harmonic sense that thinks too slowly, or Schönberg's harmonic sense that thinks a little too rapidly for the rest of the world.

E

V

THE NEWMAN-SHAW
CONTROVERSY CONCERNING
STRAUSS
1910 AND 1914

From the *Nation*

*T*HE BEECHAM SEASON *at Covent Garden in* 1910 *was one of the most exciting in the history of music. The repertoire was chosen from Delius'* A Village Romeo and Juliet, Ivanhoe (*Sullivan*) Tristan and Isolde, *Ethel Smyth's* The Wreckers, Carmen, Hansel and Gretel, L'Enfant Prodigue, *and* Elektra. *And it was the last named that caused more discussion than any opera for years, and with the exception of the death of King Edward was the event of the year. Nothing had been heard of the 'greatest living composer' for the last five years when his* Sinfonia Domestica *had been performed and was a comparative failure.*

'Strauss's share of this work,' wrote Beecham, 'taken as a whole, is his most *characteristic achievement. Here he has the fullest opportunity of working that vein of grotesque and weird fantasy of which he remains the greatest master in music. On the side of pathos and tenderness he rises to a fairly satisfactory height and in spite of inequalities of style realizes a unity which is lacking in his other stage works. The almost entire absence of charm and romance makes it unique, and if it is reported truly that Gluck in his austerity thought more of his muses than the Graces, then Strauss might here be fairly said to have shown a preference for the tunes. The public was undoubtedly impressed and startled, and to satisfy the demand for the future performances I was obliged to extend my Season'.*

* Beecham: *A Mingled Chime*, p. 129.

115

As to the opening performance the excitement of musical London
rose to fever-pitch; fantastic prices were offered for seats, and a packed
audience, that included the King and Queen and other members of the
royal family, and many leading musicians greeted the performance with
immense enthusiasm. The amount of space devoted by the press to the
performance both on the following day (a Sunday) and on the Monday
morning, was greater than ever before. Rarely had there been such wonderful notices of an operatic event in London, in which all elements, singing
and playing, combined to make a completely unified whole. The Elektra
of Edyth Walker was 'a triumph of well-calculated restraint, as well as
of bodily endurance,' wrote* The Times; *'Nothing could have surpassed
the almost superhuman energy of this richly endowed artist, whether as
singer or actress,' said the* Telegraph; *while the* Observer *commented
that 'incredible as it may seem to those who know the score, it was
possible for Mme Walker, never a hair's breadth from the centre of the
note, to vocalize perfectly the most trying and strenuous passages'. The
Klytemnestra of Mildenburg earned similar praise,* The Times *suggesting
that her interpretation was 'so vivid a picture of decadence that while she
was on the stage it was possible to forget all about the music'. Frances
Rose, an American soprano, was Chrysothemis and Hermann Weide-
mann, the Viennese baritone, Orest. The orchestral playing under
Beecham was thought to be the finest heard in the Opera House since
Nikisch had last conducted there; and at the end of the evening the
ovations continued for minutes on end, and Beecham was presented with
a laurel wreath.†*

I

Judging from the tone of a number of last Monday's articles,
our musical critics, as a whole, are still a little doubtful as to the
propriety of saying what they must really feel about Strauss. They
cannot possibly like a great part of what they hear, but at the back
of their heads is the thought that, as Wagner was abused by the
critics of his own day for extravagances that time has shown to be
no extravagances at all, so time may show that Strauss was right

* Saturday, 19th February, 1910.
† Rosenthal: *Two Centuries of Opera at Covent Garden,* p.346.

in *his* extravagances, and that the critics who objected to them were wrong. So a number of the prudent gentlemen stay the flood of ridicule that is almost on their lips, and, instead, talk darkly of the future showing what it will show, and utter other safe commonplaces. All the while there is no real comparison between the Wagnerian case and the Straussian. All new music, from the mere fact that it is new, is apt to be misunderstood, and an idiom may seem wild or incoherent merely because we are not yet accustomed to it. But because the human ear has sometimes disliked a new thing and afterwards liked it, it does not follow that it will some day like everything that today it cordially dislikes. There are other things to be considered, and one of these is the fact that nowadays we are much better placed than our fathers were for judging new music accurately. They had, for the most part, to listen to it without the slightest previous knowledge of it, and to express an opinion upon it probably after one hearing of the work. In these days we can generally study the score of the work long before we hear it. To talk of hearing *Elektra* for the first time on Saturday last is nonsensical. The vocal score has been at our service for twelve months or more, and it was open to any critic to have it by heart before he went into Covent Garden on Saturday. A piano arrangement, it is true, does not tell us all about a complex modern work; but it tells us a great deal, and with that knowledge we can listen to a first performance on the stage in a better state of preparation than the Wagnerian critics could do at a tenth performance. All this critical timidity, then, is not very creditable. Anyone who had taken the trouble to study the score of *Elektra* could easily gather from Saturday's performance whether the parts he had marked out as requiring elucidation sounded as bad as he had expected them to do, or better. And, after the performance, he should be quite able to relieve posterity of the trouble of making up his mind for him on nine points out of ten. Anyhow, it would be better to make the attempt.

All but the Strauss fanatics will admit that, though he is undoubtedly the greatest living musician, there is a strong strain of foolishness and ugliness in him, that he is lacking in the sensitive feeling for the balance of a large work that some other great

artists have, and that consequently there is not one large work of
his, from *Don Quixote* onward, that is not marred by some folly
or some foolery. If it were not for this strain of coarseness and
thoughtlessness in him, he would never have taken up so crude a
perversion of the old Greek story as that of Hugo von Hofmannsthal. One does not in the least object to a modern poet looking at
ancient figures through modern eyes, so long as he can see them
convincingly and make them live for us. But to make a play a study
of human madness, and then to lay such excessive stress upon the
merely physical concomitants of madness, is to ask us to tune our
notions of dramatic terror and horror down to too low a pitch.
Strauss, of course, revels in this physical, and therefore more
superficial, side of the madness, with the result that, instead of
impressing us, he generally either bores us or amuses us. We have
only to look at a pathological study of human morbidity such as
Dostoievsky gives us in *Crime and Punishment*, so fine, so un-
obtrusively true to life, and then listen to the vulgar din by which
Strauss tries to convey to us that a woman's brain is distraught, to
realize the difference between a man of genius and one who, for
the moment, has become merely a man of talent. For the real
complaint against the excited music in *Elektra* is that it mostly does
not excite you at all; you are rather sorry, in fact, that the composer should take so much trouble to be a failure. For he is so
violent that, as a rule, you cannot believe in the least in his
violence. He has the besetting Teutonic sin of over-statement, of
being unable to see that the half is often greater than the whole;
and all this blacking of his face and waving of his arms, and
howling 'bolly-golly black-man – boo!' at us leaves us quite
unmoved, except to smile and wish he wouldn't do it. One
could easily name a hundred passages in ancient and modern
music that thrill us far more horribly, and with far simpler
means, than all the clatter that breaks out when Orestes, for
example, is murdering Aegistheus. The mere recollection of the
stories of ghosts in the churchyard, or of his own fears when, as a
child, he was left alone in a dark room, might have told Strauss
that horror and the creeping of the flesh are not necessarily
associated with noise and fury. His orchestra doth protest too much.

Nor do we need to wait for posterity to tell us that much of the music is as abominably ugly as it is noisy. Here a good deal of the talk about complexity is wide of the mark. The real term for it is incoherence, discontinuity of thinking. 'The three angles of a triangle are equal to two right angles' sounds absurdly simple, but really represents a good deal of complex cerebral working; so does the G minor fugue of Bach. But 'the man in the moon is the daughter of Aunt Martha's tom-cat,' though it sounds very complex is incoherent nonsense; and so is a good deal of *Elektra*. Unfortunately, while we have obvious ways of testing the sense or nonsense of the remark about the man in the moon, it is not so easy to test the sense or nonsense of a passage of music; and so a good deal of quite confused thinking gets the credit for being hyper-subtle thinking. What awestruck worshippers call complexity in *Elektra* would often be more correctly described as impudence at its best and incompetence at its worst. As for the more normally lyrical pages in *Elektra*, there are very few of them worthy even of a smaller musician than Strauss. The first solo of Chrysothemis, for example, is merely agreeable commonplace; the theme of triumph in the finale is so cheap that it must have been picked up on the rubbish-heap of Italian or French opera. Nothing marks so clearly the degeneration of the musician in Strauss from what he was fifteen years ago than the average melodic writing in *Elektra*.

What saves the opera is, first of all, the wonderful beauty of parts of the scene between Elektra and Orestes, especially when, ceasing to be a maniac and becoming a normal woman, she pours out her soul in love for her brother. There is grandeur again – spasmodic, of course, but none the less unescapable – at a hundred points in the score. It may last merely a moment or two, and then flicker off into ugliness or commonplace, but while it is there we are mastered by it. Elektra's cry of 'Agamemnon', whenever it occurs, always holds us in this way. Strauss in *Elektra*, indeed, is like a huge volcano spluttering forth a vast amount of dirt and murk, through which every now and then, when the fuming ceases and a breath of clear air blows away the smoke, we see the grand and strong original outlines of the mountain. And when

Strauss puts forth his whole mental strength, it is indeed overwhelming. We may detest the score as a whole for its violence
and frequent ugliness, but the fine things in it are of the kind that
no other man, past or present, could have written – the monologue
of Elektra just mentioned, for example, or the wailing themes
that dominate the section preceding it, or the tense, fateful gloom
of the finish of the opera. The result of it all is to give far more
pain to Strauss's admirers than it can possibly do to those who have
always disliked him. In spite of the pathetic way in which he
wastes himself, playing now the fool, now the swashbuckler,
now the trickster, you cannot be in doubt that you are listening
to a man who is head and shoulders above all other living composers. One still clings to the hope that the future has in store for
us a purified Strauss, clothed and in his right mind, who will help
us to forget the present Strauss – a saddening mixture of genius,
ranter, child and charlatan. As it is, one would hardly venture to
prophesy more than a few short years of life for *Elektra*, for the
public will not long continue to spend an hour and three-quarters
in the theatre for about half an hour's enjoyment.

II

Sir, – May I, as an old critic of music, and as a member of the
public who has not yet heard *Elektra*, make an appeal to Mr.
Ernest Newman to give us something about that work a little less
ridiculous and idiotic than his article in your last issue? I am sorry
to use disparaging and apparently uncivil epithets as 'ridiculous
and idiotic'; but what else am I to call an article which informs us,
first, that Strauss does not know the difference between music and
'abominable ugliness and noise'; and, second, that he is the greatest
living musician of the greatest school of music the world has
produced? I submit that this is ridiculous, inasmuch as it makes us
laugh at Mr. Newman, and idiotic because it unhesitatingly places
the judgment of the writer above that of one whom he admits to
be a greater authority than himself, thus assuming absolute
knowledge in the matter. This is precisely what 'idiotic' means.
Pray do not let me be misunderstood as objecting to Mr.

Newman describing how *Elektra* affected him. He has not, perhaps, as much right to say that it seemed ugly and nonsensical to him (noise, applied to music, can only mean nonsense, because in any other sense, all music is noise) as Haydn had to say similar things of Beethoven's music, because Haydn was himself an eminent composer; still, he is perfectly in order in telling us honestly how ill *Elektra* pleased him, and not pretending he liked it lest his opinion should come to be regarded later on as we now regard his early opinion of Wagner. But he should by this time have been cured by experience and reflection of the trick that makes English criticism so dull and insolent – the trick, namely of asserting that everything that does not please him is wrong, not only technically but ethically. Mr. Newman, confessing that he did not enjoy, and could not see the sense of a good deal of *Elektra*, is a respectable, if pathetic, figure; but Mr. Newman treating Strauss as a moral and musical delinquent, is – well, will Mr. Newman himself supply the missing word, for really I cannot find one that is both adequate and considerate?

When my *Candida* was performed for the first time in Paris, the late Catulle Mendès was one of its critics. It affected him very much as *Elektra* affected Mr. Newman. But he did not immediately proceed, English fashion, to demonstrate that I am a perverse and probably impotent imbecile (London criticism has not stopped short of this), and to imply that if I had submitted my play to his revision he could have shown me how to make it perfect. He wrote to this effect: 'I have seen this play. I am aware of the author's reputation, and of the fact that reputations are not to be had for nothing. I find that the play has a certain air of being a remarkable work and of having something in it which I cannot precisely seize; but I do not like it, and I cannot pretend that it gave me any sensation except one of being incommoded.' Now that is what I call thoughtful and well-bred criticism, in contradistinction to ridiculous and idiotic criticism as practised in England. Mr. Newman has no right to say that *Elektra* is absolutely and objectionably ugly, because it is not ugly to Strauss and to his admirers. He has no right to say that it is incoherent nonsense, because such a statement implies that Strauss is mad, and that

Hofmannsthal and Mr. Beecham, with the artists who are execut-
ing the music, and the managers who are producing it, are insulting the public by offering them the antics of a lunatic as serious
art. He has no right to imply that he knows more about Strauss's
business technically than Strauss himself. These restrictions are no
hardship to him; for nobody wants him to say any of these
things: they are not criticism; they are not good manners nor
good sense; and they take up the space that is available in the
Nation for criticism proper; and criticism proper can be as severe
as the critic likes to make it. There is no reason why Mr. Newman
should not say with all possible emphasis – if he is unlucky
enough to be able to say truly – that he finds Strauss's music
disagreeable and cacophonous; that he is unable to follow its
harmonic syntax; that the composer's mannerisms worry him;
and that, for his taste, there is too much restless detail, and that the
music is over-scored (too many notes, as the Emperor said to
Mozart). He may, if he likes, go on to denounce the attractiveness
of Strauss's music as a public danger, like the attraction of
morphia; and to diagnose the cases of Strauss and Hofmannsthal
as psychopathic or neurasthenic, or whatever the appropriate
scientific slang may be, and descant generally on the degeneracy
of the age in the manner of Dr. Nordau. Such diagnoses, when
supported by an appeal to the symptoms made with real critical
power and ingenuity, might be interesting and worth discussing.
But this lazy petulance which has disgraced English journalism in
the forms of anti-Wagnerism, anti-Ibsenism, and, long before
that, anti-Handelism (now remembered only by Fielding's
contemptuous reference to it in *Tom Jones*); this infatuated
attempt of writers of modest local standing to talk *de haut en bas* to
men of European reputation, and to dismiss them as intrusive
lunatics, is an intolerable thing, an exploded thing, a foolish thing,
a parochial boorish thing, a thing that should be dropped by all
good critics and discouraged by all good editors as bad form, bad
manners, bad sense, bad journalism, bad politics, and bad religion.
Though Mr. Newman is not the only offender, I purposely
select his article as the occasion of a much needed protest, because
his writings on music are distinguished enough to make him

worth powder and shot. I can stand almost anything from Mr. Newman except his posing as Strauss's governess; and I hope he has sufficient sense of humour to see the absurdity of it himself, now that he has provoked a quite friendly colleague to this yell of remonstrance.

Yours,

G. Bernard Shaw.

10 Adelphi Terrace, W.C.
1st March, 1910.

III

Sir, – A lady once asked Mr. Shaw to dine with her. Mr. Shaw's answer was, 'Certainly not: what have I done to provoke this attack on my well-known morals?' or words to that effect. The lady's telegram in reply was as effective as it was quiet: 'Know nothing about your morals, but hope they are better than your manners.' I, too, hope so; for Mr. Shaw's manners, judging from this letter of his, are getting almost as bad as his logic. If I were to respond to his 'appeal' to me in a spirit similar to his own, I should appeal to him not to talk so dogmatically and offensively of things he knows nothing about – for he confesses that he has not yet heard *Elektra* – and to control his bad temper and his vanity to a degree that will save him from too gross a parody of the case he is attacking – one does not expect, of course, too much from the man who has written about Shakespeare and other people as Mr. Shaw has done. I nowhere said that Strauss did not know the difference between abominable ugliness and noise, or that he is 'the greatest living musician of the greatest school of music the world has produced'. Mr. Shaw plainly does not know the difference between what he reads and what he dreams. To say that a man at times writes ugly music does not imply that at other times he cannot write beautiful music; and to say that Strauss's large and wonderful previous output, plus the wonderful passages of *Elektra*, prove him to be the greatest of living composers (the 'greatest school of music, etc., etc.,' is the product of Mr. Shaw's own hectic imagination) is not inconsistent with the opinion that in recent years Strauss has sometimes done vulgar and stupid and ugly things. I hope this is clear, even to Mr. Shaw.

I shall be happy to discuss *Elektra* with Mr. Shaw when he knows something about it; and to discuss the general problem of aesthetic judgment with him when be shows some appreciation of the real difficulties of it. For a man who is always at such pains to inform the world that he is cleverer than most people, he really talks very foolishly – if I may be permitted to copy his own style of adverb. It is wrong for me to object to some of Strauss's music, even after careful study of it; but it is quite right of Mr. Shaw to say I am wrong, while confessing that he himself has not heard *Elektra*! But Mr. Shaw's logic was always peculiar. Look at some of the delightful deductions he draws from my article. I said that there was a lot of incoherent and discontinuous thinking in the opera. From this plain ground the industrious Mr. Shaw raises the following wonderful crop, which he puts to my credit: (1) Strauss is mad, (2) *Elektra* is the antics of a lunatic, (3) Mr. Beecham and the singers and the orchestra are insulting the public by performing it. Prodigious logician! How does he do it? Mr. Shaw's ingenious theory is that I don't like some of Strauss's music because I can't follow it – his 'harmonic syntax', for example. My objection to passages of this kind is not that they are opaque to my poor mind, but too transparent; and general objection, as a musician, to some of Strauss's later themes and his combinations of them is that they are so ridiculously easy to write. But perhaps I am taking Mr. Shaw and his outburst too seriously. I quite agree with him that his letter – so rich in knowledge, so admirable in reasoning, so perfect in taste, so urbane in style! – should teach the musical critics something even if only in the way that the language and the antics of the drunken helots were held to be useful for teaching the Spartan youths the advantages of sobriety.

Yours etc.

Ernest Newman.

12th March.

IV

Sir, – It is our good fortune to have produced in Professor Gilbert Murray a writer and scholar able to raise the Electra of Euripides from the dead and make it a living possession for us. Thanks to him, we know the poem as if it were an English one. But nothing Professor Murray can do can ever make us feel quite as the Electra of Euripides felt about her mother's neglect to bury her father properly after murdering him. A heroine who feels that to commit murder, even husband murder, is a thing that might happen to anybody, but that to deny the victim a proper funeral is an outrage so unspeakable that it becomes her plain filial duty to murder her mother in expiation, is outside that touch of nature that makes all the ages akin: she is really too early-Victorian. To us she is more unnatural than Clytemnestra of Aegistheus; and, in the end, we pity them and secretly shrink from their slayers. What Hofmannsthal and Strauss have done is to take Clytemnestra and Aegistheus, and by identifying them with everything that is evil and cruel, with all that needs must hate the highest when it sees it, with hideous domination and coercion of the higher by the baser, with the murderous rage in which the lust for a lifetime of orgiastic pleasure turns on its slaves in the torture of its disappointment and the sleepless horror and misery of its neurasthenia, to so rouse in us an overwhelming flood of wrath against it and ruthless resolution to destroy it, that Electra's vengeance becomes holy to us; and we come to understand how even the gentlest of us could wield the axe of Orestes or twist our firm fingers in the black hair of Clytemnestra to drag back her head and leave her throat open to the stroke.

That was a task hardly possible to an ancient Greek, and not easy even to us who are face to face with the America of the Thaw case, and the European plutocracy of which that case was only a trifling symptom. And that is the task which Hofmannsthal and Strauss have achieved. Not even in the third scene of *Das Rheingold*, or in the Klingsor scenes in *Parsifal*, is there such an atmosphere of malignant and cancerous evil as we get here. And that the power with which it is done is not the power of the evil

itself, but of the passion that detests and must and finally can destroy that evil, is what makes the work great, and makes us rejoice in its horror.

Whoever understands this, however vaguely, will understand Strauss's music, and why on Saturday night the crowded house burst into frenzied shoutings, not merely of applause, but of strenuous assent and affirmation, as the curtain fell. That the power of conceiving it should occur in the same individual as the technical skill and natural faculty needed to achieve its complete and overwhelming expression in music, is a stroke of the rarest good fortune that can befall a generation of men. I have often said, when asked to state the case against the fools and money changers who are trying to drive us into a war with Germany, that the case consists of the single word, Beethoven. Today, I should say with equal confidence, Strauss. That we should make war on Strauss and the heroic warfare and aspiration that he represents is treason to humanity. In this music drama Strauss has done for us just what he has done for his own countrymen: he has said for us, with an utterly satisfying force, what all the noblest powers of life within us are clamouring to have said, in protest against and defiance of the omnipresent villainies of our civilization; and this is the highest achievement of the highest art.

It was interesting to compare our conductor, the gallant Beecham, bringing out the points in Strauss's orchestration, until sometimes the music sounded like a concerto for six drums, with Strauss himself bringing out the meaning and achieving the purpose of his score so that we forgot that there was an orchestra there at all, and could hear nothing but the conflict and storm of passion. Human emotion is a complex thing: there are moments when our feeling is so deep and our ecstasy so exalted that the primeval monsters from whom we are evolved wake within us and utter the strange tormented cries of their ancient struggles with the Life Force. All this is in *Elektra*; and under the baton of Strauss the voices of these epochs are kept as distinct in their unity as the parts in a Bach motet. Such colossal counterpoint is a counterpoint of all the ages; not even Beethoven in his last great Mass comprehended so much. The feat is beyond all verbal description: it must be heard and felt; and even then, it seems, you must watch and pray, lest your God should forget you, and leave you to hear only 'abominable ugliness and noise', and, on remonstrance, lead you to explain handsomely that Strauss is 'vulgar, and stupid, and ugly' only 'sometimes', and that this art of his is so 'ridiculously easy' that nothing but your own self-respect prevents you from achieving a European reputation by condescending to practise it.

So much has been said of the triumphs of our English singers in *Elektra* that I owe it to Germany to profess my admiration of the noble beauty and power of Frau Fassbender's Elektra. Even if Strauss's work were the wretched thing poor Mr. Newman mistook it for, it would still be worth a visit to Covent Garden to see her wonderful death dance, which was the climax of one of the most perfect examples yet seen in London of how, by beautiful and eloquent gesture, movement, and bearing, a fine artist can make not only her voice, but her body, as much a part of a great music drama as any instrument in the score. The other German artists, notably Frau Bahr-Mildenburg, showed great power and accomplishment; but they have received fuller acknowledgment, whereas we should not have gathered from the reports that Frau Fassbender's performance was so extraordinary as it actually was. A deaf man could have watched her with as little sense of privation as a blind man could have listened to her. To those of us who are neither deaf nor blind nor anti-Straussian critics (which is the same thing), she was a superb Elektra.

Whatever may be the merits of the article which gave rise to the present correspondence, it is beyond question that it left the readers of the *Nation* without the smallest hint that the occasion was one of any special importance, or that it was at all worth their while to spend time and money in supporting Mr. Beecham's splendid enterprise, and being present on what was, in fact, a historic moment in the history of art in England, such as may not occur again within our lifetime. Many persons may have been, and possibly were, prevented by that article from seizing their opportunity, not because Mr. Newman does not happen to like Strauss's music, but because he belittled the situation by so

miscalculating its importance that he did not think it worth even
the effort of criticizing it, and dismissed it in a notice in which
nothing was studied except his deliberate contemptuous insolence
to the composer. It would have been an additional insult to
Strauss to have waited to hear *Elektra* before protesting, on the
plainest grounds of international courtesy and artistic good faith,
against such treatment of the man who shares with Rodin the
enthusiastic gratitude and admiration of the European republic,
one and indivisible, of those who understand the highest art.
But now that I have heard *Elektra*, I have a new duty to the
readers of the *Nation*, and that is to take upon me the work Mr.
Newman should have done, and put them in possession of the
facts.

And now, Ernest, '*Triff noch einmal*'! Yours etc.

G. Bernard Shaw.

17th March, 1910.

V

Sir, – Mr. Shaw's second letter makes argument with him more
possible than the first did. He himself aptly described that as a
yell; and discussion with Mr. Shaw while he is merely yelling is
too much like arguing with a locomotive whistle in full blast.
But now that Mr. Shaw's manner has lost something of its blend
of the patronizing pedagogue and the swaggering bully, we can
get more directly to the real matter in hand.

My offence, it seems, is a triple one. (1) I wrote an article upon
Elektra in my own way and from my own standpoint, instead of
first finding out the way and the standpoint of Mr. Shaw, and
writing accordingly. This, I own, was unpardonable, and I
apologize for it. (2) I took a wrong view of Strauss and *Elektra*.
(3) In expressing this view, I necessarily made use of language
that was not always complimentary to Strauss. Let us first look
at No. 2.

Mr. Shaw has now heard *Elektra*, and he pronounces it very
good. I know that this authoritative announcement ought to be
enough; but I am still so perverse as to maintain that parts of

Elektra are very ugly, and other parts of it a failure. I repeat that there are abundant signs in it of the development of the bad elements that have spoiled so much of Strauss's work during the last few years – ugly, slap-dash vocal writing, which he attempts to carry through by means of orchestral bravado, a crude pictorial-ism, ineffective violence simulating strength, a general coarsen-ing of the tissue of the music, a steady deterioration in invention, especially on the melody side. Mr. Shaw performs an enthusiastic fantasia upon von Hofmannsthal's drama, which, to my mind and the mind of many others, is – beauty of diction apart – a most un-pleasant specimen of that crudity and physical violence that a cert-ain school of modern German artists mistake for intellectual and emotional power. In setting this violence to music, Strauss tries to out-Herod Herod. I should not blame him so much for this, if the things were only well done. In *Salome* the subject is a trifle un-pleasant, but Strauss has given us a marvellous study of the diseased woman's mind. My complaint against *Elektra* is that he frequently fobs us off with the merest make-believe. The music (I am speaking, of course, of the bad parts of it now) does not itself cut to the roots of the characters as that of *Salome* does; Strauss tries to bluff us partly by the tumult of his orchestration and partly by the easy pathos of the theatre. I have no objection to Mr. Shaw being bluffed in this way; but I am not going to be bluffed myself by means so transparent. Mr. Shaw, in his des-perate attempt to justify the ways of Shaw to men, actually tells us that 'on Saturday night the crowded house burst into frenzied shoutings, not merely of applause, but of strenuous assent and affirmation, as the curtain fell'. The spectacle of Mr. Shaw bringing up the opinion of a British audience on a point of art as a support for his own is delicious. Oh, Bernard, Bernard, has it come to this? May not that applause be accounted for in another way? One curious feature of these *Elektra* performances has been that while many advanced musicians, real admirers of Strauss, have been chilled by the work, the general public has been enthusiastic over it. I take this to be due, roughly speaking, to two causes. Some people have been swept off their feet by the first excitement of the thing; others have been astonished and delighted to find that, so far from the Strauss idiom being so advanced and recondite as they had been led to believe, many of the tunes, such as that of Chrysothemis and that of the final triumph, are of the most friendly and accommodating commonplace. I ask Mr. Shaw to look at the latter theme, on p. 238 of the score, and tell me honestly whether it is not banality itself. It is fit only for third-rate French or Italian opera; you can hear the same kind of tune on the band in the park any Saturday. And, thinking that a theme of this kind is utterly unworthy of Strauss, I have every right to say so. I have a right, again, to speak of the 'impudence' of the attempt to bamboozle me into the belief that great music is going on in the orchestra when I know that it is only the big drum banging, or some trick of orchestration sending a shudder under my skin. I have a right to speak of 'incompetence' when a composer makes a tremendous show of rising to the supremest heights of a situation, and, in spite of all his mouthing and his violence, falls as far below it as Strauss does in the ineffective noise that accompanies Elektra's digging-up of the axe, or the murder of Aegisthus. (*Technical* incompetence I never urged against Strauss, as Mr. Shaw seems to think.) I have a right to say that pages such as 36–40, or 53–56 (there are many others like them) are an unblushing evasion of the problem of thinking coherently and continuously in music. I hold, in a word, that much of *Elektra* is merely frigid intellectual calculation simulating a white heat of emotion. I find that Mr. Shaw once expressed, apropos of Marlowe, the very point I would make here: Marlowe, he says, is 'itching to frighten other people with the superstitious terrors and cruelties in which he does not himself believe, and wallowing in blood, violence, muscularity of expression, and strenuous animal passion, as only literary men do when they become thoroughly depraved by solitary work, sedentary cowardice, and starvation of the sympathetic centres'. Precisely. I would explain the bogus passion and bogus hysterics of a good deal of Strauss's later music in the same way. He drives furiously at us, with all his enormous cerebral energy and his stupendous technique; but at heart he is cold, for all the whipping and spurring. He reminds me, in moments like these, of the beggars who simulate epilepsy in the streets, producing the foaming at the mouth by chewing a piece of soap. I have no objection to the sympathetic and trustful Mr. Shaw believing the fit to be a real one; but really he must not lose his temper because, having learned some of the tricks of the trade, I assure him that I can see the soap.

And now for No. 3. Mr. Shaw heatedly objected to the tone of some of my criticism of Strauss. It was 'neither good manners' (Mr. Shaw is our leading authority on manners) 'nor good sense' for 'writers of modest local standing to talk *de haut en bas* to men of European reputation'; it was an 'intolerable thing, an exploded thing, a parochial, boorish thing', and Heaven only knows what else. Very good; but who is this purist who yells so deafeningly for moderation in criticism? Let us look for a moment at a few passages of Mr. Shaw's own that he appears to have forgotten. He has lately called Schubert a mere confectioner. He once called Marlowe a fool – 'the fellow was a fool'. Unless my memory is greatly at fault, he once called Shakespeare an idiot – though I will accept Mr. Shaw's correction here if I am wrong. But he certainly wrote that *Cymbeline* 'is for the most part stagey trash of the lowest melodramatic order, in parts abominably written, throughout intellectually vulgar, and, judged in point of thought by modern intellectual standards, vulgar, foolish, offensive, indecent, and exasperating beyond all tolerance'. Again, the same poor Shakespeare, 'in his efforts to be a social philosopher', can only 'rise for an instant to the level of a sixth-rate Kingsley'; but Mr. Shaw cannot stand 'his moral platitudes, his jingo claptraps, his tavern pleasantries, his bombast and drivel, his incapacity for following up the scraps of philosophy he stole so aptly', nor 'his usual incapacity for pursuing any idea'. He tells us frankly that his own *Caesar and Cleopatra* is an improvement on Shakespeare. In fact, says Mr. Shaw, 'with the single exception of Homer, there is no eminent writer, not even Sir Walter Scott, whom I can despise so entirely as I despise Shakespeare when I measure my mind against his'. Some unkind people might say that this was a case of a writer of modest standing talking to a man of European reputation *de haut en bas*. Shakespeare's reputation, I fancy, is European; and if I say nothing about the modest local standing, it is solely because I hesitate to incur the responsibility of mentioning modesty and Mr. Bernard Shaw in the same sentence.

I know that he will say to this – that all these dicta of his upon Shakespeare were based upon a study of his drama, and that while blaming Shakespeare for many things he praised him for others. But that is exactly my attitude towards Strauss. If, then, it is right for Mr. Shaw, it cannot be wrong for me; if it is wrong for me, it cannot be right for him. At all events, if he is going to set out to prove the contrary he will need a better equipment than a penful of scurrilous impertinence and a disgracefully bad memory for his own past.

Yours etc.

Ernest Newman

22nd March, 1910.

VI

Sir, – Mr. Shaw, by talking at such length about von Hofmann-sthal's drama, has switched this discussion on to a side track; and 'H.W.M.'s' article* in last week's *Nation*, acute and illuminative as it is on the literary points it touches, shows the necessity of bringing the discussion back to its starting-point. To myself and hundreds of other people there is a good deal that is crude and melodramatic in von Hofmannsthal's play. He is not content, for example, with having Aegistheus slaughtered at one window, but must needs have the poor man chased to another window and the agony prolonged there – for all the world, as one American critic put it, like a bullock in a Chicago stock-yard. But if other people like this and similar melodramatic effects, I am quite content that they should. My concern is not with the drama, but with the music. Surely the real question is not 'What kind of a drama has von Hofmannsthal written?' but 'What kind of music

---

* Meredith wrote on *Elektra* as a play in the *Nation* for 26th March, 1910.

has Strauss written?' It is the music alone that will save the opera
or damn it, as history abundantly proves. Fifty composers have set
Goethe's *Faust* to music; but the greatness of the drama has not suf-
ficed to save forty-five of these works from destruction. And if
Smith writes another *Faust* tomorrow, the literary critics may rhap-
sodize as they please about Goethe's genius; but if Smith's music
is not good his work will not have the ghost of a chance of keeping
the stage. The *Elektra* question, then, is purely a musical one.
My article, indeed, was entitled 'Strauss and his *Elektra*': it was
Strauss the musician that I mostly fell foul of; and it was for daring
to speak in that way of Strauss as a musician that Mr. Shaw got
so absurdly angry with me. Now are we not all more likely to
come to some kind of agreement on the matter if we make sure
that we are all talking about the same thing?

Let me put my own position in a nutshell. No one admires the
bulk of Strauss's work more than I do. But it seems to me indis-
putable that for some years now his musical faculty has been
deteriorating. The first sure signs of this were to be seen in certain
parts of the *Symphonia Domestica*. In *Elektra* I hold it to be most
marked. It takes four main forms. (1) Instead of getting to the very
heart of a situation in his music, as he used to do, he is inclined to
illustrate the mere externals of it; hence the facile and foolish
pictorialism of such things as the 'slippery blood' motive in
Elektra or the orchestral delineations of Klytemnestra's jewels,
the sacrificial procession, and so on. He sometimes does wonders
of virtuosity in this way with the orchestra, but it is all as far from
real music as a pianist's or violinist's display of technique for
technique's sake can be. (2) He is degenerating into a bad and
careless builder. Mr. Shaw may object to the phrase, but I repeat
that it is ridiculously easy to put a score together as Strauss now
does for pages at a time – flinging out a leading motive of three or
four bars' length, and then padding unblushingly for twenty or
thirty bars until another salient motive can be introduced. (2) He
is often downright ugly. There were some shocking examples of
this in the *Symphonia Domestica*. In *Elektra* I do not know who
would not call the opening scene ugly; even Mr. Kalisch, the
most loyal Straussian in England, wrote that a second hearing did

not alter his view that the music was 'needlessly ugly'. (4) His
thematic invention is sometimes positively wretched now. This
may not be so evident to one who hears *Elektra* for the first time,
with all the excitement of the stage action and the orchestration
to distract him, as it will be when he knows the music better. Thus
'H.W.M.' speaks of being carried off his feet as the opera swept
to its end. I venture to say that when he has played through the
final scene a hundred times, as I have done during the past twelve
months, he will be appalled at the banality of the bulk of it; even
the theme of the 'recognition' is spoiled. He will hardly know
whether to laugh or cry – laugh at the barrel-organ jingle of some
of the themes, or cry that a man like Strauss should have sunk so
low. The solo of Chrysothemis is even worse in parts – let anyone,
for example, play or sing pages 45 and 50–51 half a dozen times,
and say if a tune like this is fit for anything but musical comedy
or the music-halls. It is thus not a case, as Mr. Shaw imagines, of
Strauss's art rushing ahead and myself being too slow to follow,
but of his art worsening in quality and my declining to call five
shillings a sovereign. It is not a case of the Wagner of *Lohengrin*
developing into the Wagner of *Tristan*, and so thinking far ahead
of his old admirers, but of the Wagner of *Tristan* being smitten
with a withered hand and degenerating every now and then into
the melodic banalities of *Rienzi*. There is great stuff in *Elektra* –
the recognition scene, for instance, and a score or two of isolated
pages here and there; but there is much that is mere orchestral
bunkum – if I may use that word – and much that is downright
commonplace.

And who are they who are most conscious of these things?
Not the non-Straussians, but those who of old took Strauss for
their leader! He began as a genius, as Bülow said of Mendelssohn,
and is ending as a talent. If Mr. Shaw was dying to strike a blow
for Strauss he should have done it years ago, when Strauss was
worth fighting for; but to sing his praises now, when he has lost
half the power, the originality, the resource, the fund of genuine
feeling that made him so great, reminds me of the people in Mark
Twain's story who valorously broke their night's rest, as they
thought, to see the sunrise on the Rigi, and only discovered when

the other people in the hotel were laughing at them that they had overslept themselves, and it was the sunset they were watching.

Yours etc.

Ernest Newman.

30th March, 1910.

VII

Sir, – Just a last word with Mr. Newman. I make no apology for bullying him: the result has justified me. I leave it to your readers to say whether I have not wakened him up beneficially, as well as put a very different complexion on the case of Strauss and *Elektra*. The anti-Strauss campaign was so scandalous that it was clear somebody had to be bullied; and I picked out Mr. Newman because he was much better able to take care of himself than any of the rest. Most of them I could not have attacked at all: as well strike a child or intimidate an idiot.

I will now repeat my amusing performance of knocking Mr. Newman down flat with a single touch. He asks me, concerning a certain theme in *Elektra* to look at it honestly and tell him whether it is not banality itself. Certainly it is. And now will Mr. Newman turn to the hackneyed little 'half close' out of which Handel made the 'Hallelujah Chorus', and tell me honestly whether it is not – and was not even in Handel's own time – ten times as banal as the Chrysothemis motif? Strange how these men of genius will pick up a commonplace out of the gutter and take away our breath with it; and how, as they grow older and more masterful, any trumpery diatonic run, or such intervals of the common chord as have served the turn of thousands of postboys, dead and alive, will serve their turn, too!

Fancy trying that worn-out banality gambit on an old hand like me!

Now for Mr. Newman's final plea, with its implicit compliment to myself, which I quite appreciate. That plea is that he did to Strauss only as I did to Shakespeare. Proud as I am to be Mr. Newman's exemplar, the cases are not alike. If the day should

ever dawn in England on a Strauss made into an idol; on an
outrageous attribution to him of omniscience and infallibility; on
a universal respect for his reputation accompanied by an ignorance of his works so gross that the most grotesque mutilations
and travesties of his scores will pass without protest as faithful
performances of them; on essays written to show how Klytemnestra was redeemed by her sweet womanly love for Aegistheus,
and Elektra a model of filial piety to all middle-class daughters;
on a generation of young musicians taught that they must copy
all Strauss's progressions and rhythms and instrumentation, and all
the rest of it if they wished to do high-class work; in short, on
all the follies of Bardolatry transferred to Strauss, then I shall give
Mr. Newman leave to say his worst of Strauss, were it only for
Strauss's own sake. But that day has not yet dawned. The current
humbug is all the other way. The geese are in full cackle to prove
that Strauss is one of themselves instead of the greatest living
composer. I made war on the duffers who idolized Shakespeare.
Mr. Newman took the side of the duffers who are trying to
persuade the public that Strauss is an imposter making an offensive
noise with an orchestra of marrow-bones and cleavers. It is not
enough to say that I scoffed, and that therefore I have no right to
complain of other people scoffing. Any fool can scoff. The serious
matter is which side you scoff at. Scoffing at pretentious dufferdom
is a public duty; scoffing at an advancing torchbearer is a deadly
sin. The men who praised Shakespeare in my time were mostly
the men who would have stoned him had they been his contemporaries. To praise him saved them the trouble of thinking;
got them the credit of correct and profound opinions; and enabled
them to pass as men of taste when they explained that Ibsen was
an obscene dullard. To expose these humbugs and to rescue the
real Shakespeare from them, it was necessary to shatter their idol.
It has taken the iconoclasm of three generations of Bible smashers
to restore Hebrew literature to us, after three hundred years of
regarding the volume into which it was bound as a fetish and a
talisman; and it will take as many generations of Shakespeare
smashers before we can read the plays of Shakespeare with as free
minds as we read the *Nation*.

Besides, what I said about Shakespeare, startling as it was to all the ignoramuses, was really the classical criticism of him. That criticism was formulated by Dr. Johnson in what is still the greatest essay on Shakespeare yet written. I did not read it until long after my campaign against Bardolatry in the *Saturday Review*; and I was gratified, though not at all surprised, to find how exactly I had restated Johnson's conclusions.

Yours, etc.

G. Bernard Shaw

(On the broader issue raised here, is not the trouble precisely this: that Mr. Shaw appears to claim for himself the possession of a perfect criterion for distinguishing 'duffers' and 'torchbearers' and for naming other persons qualified to perform the same task of discrimination? Ed., the *Nation*). [2nd April, 1910.]

VIII

Sir, – As Mr. Shaw has said his last word in this pleasant little controversy, may I now say mine? I should not like to lose this opportunity of thanking Mr. Shaw for his lucid explanation of the difference between my criticism of Strauss and his of Shakespeare. The thing is now simplicity itself. Artists, it seems, fall into two categories – the 'duffers' and the 'torchbearers'. You can be as rude as you like to the former, but must be very polite to the latter. But how to know which is which? How to know whether we should bless a given artist for a torchbearer or damn him for a duffer? That also, is simplicity itself: find out on which side Mr. Shaw is, and bless or damn accordingly. 'Any fool', as he wisely says, 'can scoff; the serious matter is which side you scoff at.' The necessity of being on the right side is self-evident; therefore, when in doubt, write or wire to Mr. Shaw. (Telegraphic address: 'Infallibility', London.)

'He knows about it all; HE KNOWS; *HE KNOWS.*'

And now, just a word on what he calls his amusing performance of knocking me down with a single touch. He has looked at the passage in *Elektra* to which I drew his attention, and he agrees with me that it is banality itself. But, he says, 'strange how these men of genius will pick up a commonplace out of the gutter and take away our breath with it' – instancing Handel. I am sure that on reflection Mr. Shaw will see how confused his thinking is here. What he has in his mind is the way in which a great composer will sometimes take an apparently insignificant germ-theme and work it up into wonderful music; as Beethoven does, for example, with the very plain theme of four bars' length that opens the Eighth Symphony, or the mere G and E flat that form the basis of most of the first movement of the Fifth Symphony. No musician here would dream of quarrelling with the theme itself for being 'banal' (which it is not, by the way; it is only modest). It is like the unprepossessing bulb that will some day give us the glory of form and scent and colour of the flower. I blush to have to point out to Mr. Shaw that the melody to which I drew his attention is not a theme of this kind at all. It is not a germ-theme; it is a long melodic passage, meant to speak for itself there and then. It is, in fact, intended for a piece of por-traiture – Elektra, according to the stage directions, dancing about 'like a Maenad'. And the objections to it are two – first, that it is a wretchedly cheap melody, such as no other great musician in history has ever written at the height of his career; and second, that it is hopelessly inappropriate and ineffective as a piece of characterization. This a Maenad! It is only Salvation Sal, or Jump-to-Glory-Jane.

But note that Mr. Shaw, in the act of trying to palliate the banality of the theme, admits that it is banal; these great geniuses, he cries, have a way of turning to gold what they pick out of the gutter. So the theme was picked up in the gutter, was it? And the man who makes this incautious admission is the same man who a few weeks ago cursed me by all his false gods for saying that Strauss must have picked it up on a rubbish heap! Or is there some superiority of the gutter over the rubbish-heap that only Mr. Shaw's subtle brain can distinguish? It is as I hinted in a previous letter. The cheap gilding on the button takes Mr. Shaw in; and so he gets furious with those of us who, having fingered the button a hundred times to his once, are more conscious of the impudent brass of which it is really made. Anyhow the fact remains that on the solitary point on which Mr. Shaw has come down from his sublime generalities and deigned to discuss the actual music of *Elektra* – which I have been vainly trying to get him to do all along – he agrees with me. I have, therefore, every reason to hope that when his knowledge of the score is a little more profound than I suspect it to be at present, he will agree with my indictment of Strauss on the other counts.

Yours, etc.

Ernest Newman.

5th April, 1910.

THE STRANGE CASE OF RICHARD STRAUSS, 1914

being the

THE FURTHER CONTROVERSY BETWEEN ERNEST NEWMAN and BERNARD SHAW
From the *Nation*

I

FOR SOME of us the sitting out of Strauss's new ballet at Drury Lane the other evening was like attending the funeral of a lost leader. For apparently Strauss is now quite dead so far as music is concerned. Hanslick used to say that in England – he might with equal truth have said the whole artistic world over – it is difficult to win a reputation and impossible to lose one. Strauss may congratulate himself on this trait of canine fidelity in the public. The music of *The Legend of Joseph* is bad enough to ruin any man's reputation but his; had one of the younger German composers written it, everyone would have been talking contemptuously of the German vein being exhausted. Whether it is or is not, it is hard to say. Threatened nations, like threatened men, have a way of living long. It is nearly forty years now since Tchaikovsky gave it as his opinion that German music had come to the end of its resources. Well, since then we have seen Brahms – the Brahms whom Tchaikovsky could never understand – taking more and more confidently his place in the great Teutonic line; and we have seen Richard Strauss – the Strauss whom we used to know as a man of genius – enriching music with a new vocabulary, a new idiom, and a new psychology. German music may yet renew its youth, perhaps in the person of some composer sealed of the tribe of Schönberg. But one vein of German music is certainly used up – the post-Lisztian-Wagnerian vein; and in exhausting that, Strauss has evidently exhausted himself also. He is now one of the dullest and at the same time one of the most pretentious composers in Germany.

It is not pleasant to have to say things like this of a man who was once our leader. The obvious *riposte* from the Straussians – of whom there are probably a few still surviving – is that the degeneration may be in the critic rather than in the composer. Mr. Bernard Shaw suggested, when he and I were exchanging compliments over *Elektra* three or four years ago,* that I failed to see the true inwardness of that work because I could not follow Strauss's new harmonic language; whereby Mr. Shaw simply demonstrated his comical ignorance of Strauss, of modern music, and of me. Strauss's harmonic idiom in *Elektra* presented no more difficulties to any ordinarily good musician than a page of average German prose does to a linguist; while in the works that have followed *Elektra* – especially *Ariadne auf Naxos*, the *Festliches Praeludium*, and *Joseph* – the harmony is for the most part relatively as simple as Mozart's. Our complaint against the present Strauss is not that he is a wild pioneer hustling us against our will along an unknown and terrifying road that may lead anywhere, but a tired and disillusioned mediocrity lagging behind his fellows and behind us and beckoning us back to the road that leads nowhere. We can forgive anything in an artist but commonplace. Strauss is now virtually nothing but commonplace. In *Salome, Elektra,* and the *Rosenkavalier* there are quarters-of-an-hour of dazzling genius; in *Ariadne auf Naxos* there are moments of genius not quite so dazzling; in *Joseph* there is not a page of genius,

* February–April 1910 (the previous correspondence).

or even of a talent beyond that of a good hundred composers whom one could name.

What will save *Joseph*, if it can be saved, is the splendour of the *décor*, the beauty of the dancing, and, it may be, the quality of the old story and the suggestiveness of the action. It is true that the authors of the scenario, with a typically Teutonic childishness, have tried to overlay the simple story of Joseph and Potiphar's wife with a bastard sort of symbolism; but on the stage the symbolism does not carry, even to those who have taken the trouble to wade through Count Kessler's super-solemn preface to the score. All that the authors and composer have done is to exploit the naked story for every penny that it is worth, and by transporting it from Egypt to the Venice of the sixteenth century, to give it an almost insolent magnificence of colour. Ten years ago Strauss would probably have treated the subject ironically, as Fielding did in *Joseph Andrews*. Today he talks pseudo-philosophy about it with Count Kessler and Hugo von Hofmannsthal. At one point, and one only, have the German authors added a really effective touch to the story. The greater part of the first scene is a mere quasi-dramatic excuse for dancing; the temptation scene is just what one might have expected it to be; the final scene, with the angel leading Joseph away, is a combination of the last Act of Gounod's *Faust* and the British Christmas card. But the ballet of the women venting their rage and horror on Joseph after the catastrophe – a kind of outward projection of the despair and frenzy of Potiphar's wife after her repulse – not only intensifies the action just at the point where it might have been in danger of thinning out, but has inspired Mr. Fokine to one of his most expressive pieces of mimetic invention.

The Russians, indeed, have done their part of the work magnificently. It is only Strauss who has failed us. It is no question of failing to see his meaning or disagreeing with his bent, as in the case of some of the real leaders of the musical thought of the day. One's objection to *The Legend of Joseph* is very simple: look where one will, the score is a mass of unredeemed banalities. The writing is the merest journalese of music, the self-satisfied, platitudinous orotundity of the leading article and the party

speech. The opening theme, and all the subsequent developments
of it, are simply the eleventh-fold chewing of a ten-times masticated German standing dish. The paradoxical tonalities of the
first dance promise well for a moment, but the interest of the
dance is exhausted in less than a dozen bars. The music for
the boxers is simply the usual late-Straussian bluff; the noises in
the moments of great dramatic intensity are simply the usual late-
Straussian bluster; the affected theme of *Joseph* is simply the third-
rate attempt of a dull mind to invent something 'characteristic';
the finale is imposing only in virtue of its piling-up of orchestral
colour, not of any value in the ideas themselves. Even Strauss's
technique seems to have deserted him; from the mere point of
view of effect the new work is a perpetual disappointment. He has
obviously written himself out, whether for good or only for the
moment remains to be seen. It is pitiable to think that all that is
left of the man who wrote *Don Quixote* is the platitudinarian and
futilitarian who has written *The Legend of Joseph*.

II

THE STRANGE CASE OF ERNEST NEWMAN

To the Editor of the *Nation*

Sir, – Mr. Newman opportunely reminds you that when
Richard Strauss's *Elektra* was produced in London by the enterprise of Sir Joseph Beecham, he encouraged that public-spirited
gentleman by assuring the public, in effect, that *Elektra* was
despicable trash, and that it was just like the impudence of an
inferior person from Germany to attempt to impose on him,
Ernest Newman, with such stuff. Whereupon, I contradicted Mr.
Newman with extreme flatness. And now Mr. Newman assures
us that *Elektra* contains 'quarters-of-an-hour of dazzling genius'.
He adds that *Joseph*, which has now succeeded to *Elektra*, is bad
enough to ruin any man's reputation; that Strauss is now one of
the dullest and, at the same time, one of the most pretentious
composers in Germany; that he is a tired and disillusioned mediocrity; not to mention that he is now quite dead as far as music

is concerned; after which it is hardly worth adding that he is a platitudinarian and futilitarian, that the score of *Joseph* is a mass of unredeemed banalities, the merest journalese of music, the eleventh-fold chewing of a ten-times masticated German standing dish, the third-rate attempt of a dull mind to invent something characteristic, an attempt baffled by the fact that even Strauss's technique seems to have deserted him.

As before, I flatly contradict Mr. Newman. He kept paying out all that ill-mannered nonsense about Wagner after even the *Daily Telegraph* (remonstrated with at last, it is said, by Royalty) had dropped it. I contradicted him flatly; and now he thinks Wagner, on the whole, rather a great composer. He paid it out about *Elektra*. I contradicted him flatly, with the result recorded above. He will say it about Strauss's next masterpiece. I will contradict him flatly (in fact, I do so now in advance), with the same sequel; for Mr. Newman's erroneousness is almost certain enough to be accepted as a law of nature; and his death-bed repentances may be as confidently looked forward to as the revivals of *Peter Pan*.

But from the point of view of journalism, they are open to exception. How many people realize that a whole generation of the English people was deprived of the enjoyment of Wagner's music solely because the critics went on about Wagner exactly as Mr. Newman is now going on about Strauss, and as he formerly went on about Wagner until the grossness of his error was too much even for English editors? The extent to which we are kept out of our inheritance of contemporary culture by mere inconsiderate offensiveness in the mask of criticism is appalling. If Mr. Newman does not like Strauss's music, nobody wants him to pretend that he does. If he is bored by simple diatonic themes such as all the great composers abound in shamelessly, and is so weary of his business that he has no appetite for anything but the very interesting technical experiments of what he calls 'composers sealed of the tribe of Schönberg', let him say so by all means. But do not let him suppose that his weariness justifies him in assailing Strauss or anyone else with libellous insolence seasoned with disgusting metaphors. A gentleman may say that the opening theme of *Joseph* has done service before in "The Minstrel

Boy", in one of the entractes in Bizet's *Carmen*, and probably in
many other compositions besides, just as Handel's 'O thou that
tellest' had done duty in 'God Save the King!' He may poke a little
good-humored fun at Strauss over it if he does that sort of thing
amusingly, and does not forget Strauss's dignity and his own.
But to call the theme the eleventh-fold chewing of a ten-times
masticated German standing dish is not criticism but simple
obscenity. It is not amusing, as obscenities sometimes are. It is
laboriously and intentionally offensive; and the fact that it is
addressed to a foreign visitor of great distinction and of extraordinarily attractive personality, who has impressed Europe as a
genius of the first order, by an English journalist who has some
past errors of judgment to apologize for does not make it any
pleasanter.

Since *The Times* set the example, paragraphs of the news of a
hundred years ago have become familiar in our older newspapers. If the *Nation* could devise some means of printing the
opinions which Mr. Newman will have some years hence,
instead of his first impressions, your readers would be spared the
irritation of being told, at the moment when a masterpiece is
being performed, that it is not worth hearing, and learning after
the performances are over that it contains quarters-of-an-hour of
dazzling genius. – Yours, etc.,

G. Bernard Shaw

1st July, 1914.

(Mr. Newman can (and no doubt will) defend his own taste in
music. But we see nothing obscene in his metaphors. – Ed.,
Nation.)

III

THE SAD CASE OF BERNARD SHAW

To the Editor of the *Nation*

Sir, – It was a voluptuous joy to me to find I had drawn Mr.
Shaw again; but his angry letter about Strauss and myself –
mainly myself – was a disappointment to me. Mr. Shaw is going

off sadly as a controversialist. He has lost his punch along with his temper; and now he is obviously losing his memory, as I shall show. In my article on *The Legend of Joseph* I referred to Mr. Shaw's comical ignorance of Strauss, of modern music, and of me. I must apologize. Comic isn't the word: I should have said tragic.

Mr. Shaw's misunderstanding of Strauss and his position in modern music need not detain us long. He objects to my speaking as I did of 'a foreign visitor of great distinction and of extra-ordinarily attractive personality'. Strauss's personality – about which I know nothing at first hand – has nothing to do with the matter. The fact that Strauss happens to be in this country when his work comes up for criticism has nothing to do with the matter. And that Strauss is now 'of great distinction' I deny. He is not, on the basis of his present work, a distinguished musician at all. He is simply a distinguished financier who deals in music.

Mr. Shaw calls *The Legend of Joseph* a masterpiece. I call it a mass of banalities, a re-hash of the stalest German ideas and most conventional German formulas. To hear Mr. Shaw talk, anyone would think I was the only person in Europe with the temerity to suggest that Strauss is now writing a good deal of poor music. I invite Mr. Shaw to read the press of England and Germany, *passim*, on the subject of *The Legend of Joseph*, and to have a few conversations about it with some leading English and Continental musicians, as I have done. If Mr. Shaw likes commonplace, or if he dabbles so superficially in modern music as to mistake a well-worn platitude for a stroke of originality, that is his affair. It does not concern the rest of us, and all his bellowing will not move us.

I wish Mr. Shaw would make up his mind as to what sort of person I really am in music. During the *Elektra* affair his first view was that I was an old fogey who could not keep pace with the rapid developments of Strauss's harmony. I had to point out to him that my complaint against Strauss was not that he was too advanced – for indeed he is as simple as Mozart in comparison with some other modern composers – but that of late years he has written an appalling amount of music that is mere common-place, bluff, bluster, make-believe, padding, call it what you will.

F

He is not in front of us now, but behind us. Mr. Shaw's latest view of me is as a sort of musical roué whose wearied nerves can respond to nothing but extreme and unnatural titillations. He imagines me to be 'bored by simple diatonic themes such as all the great composers abound in shamelessly', and 'so weary of my business' that I have 'no appetite for anything but the very interesting technical experiments' of 'composers sealed of the tribe of Schönberg'. It may cheer Mr. Shaw up to know that I am not a bit like that. I am perfectly well and happy, and enjoying good music of all sorts and schools, old and new. I have not the slightest objection to diatonic music if it is good any more than I object to a story told in words of one syllable if the words are put together by a man who has something of his own to say. I pass by with a smile Mr. Shaw's reference to Schönberg. He evidently does not understand what my original sentence meant, because he as evidently does not know his Schönberg. If he did, he would know that there is another Schönberg than the one who indulges in 'interesting technical experiments'.

Mr. Shaw imagines that I have recanted over *Elektra*. I must disabuse him of that notion. If he will refresh his memory, he will see that from the beginning I admired certain parts of it. I can assure him that those are still the only parts I admire. My opinion of the work as a whole remains unchanged: quite recently I wrote of it, after hearing yet another performance, that three people seem to have had a hand in the score – a man of genius, a man of talent, and a fool. Mr. Shaw's discovery is only another of his mare's nests.

And now, Mr. Shaw having had his say about me, let me have a word or two with him. He declares that *Joseph* is a masterpiece, and that I will some day recognize it to be such, when I have corrected my 'first impressions'. It will be remembered that Mr. Shaw fell foul of me over *Elektra* before he had heard the opera. There is no need for him to admit that he does not know *The Legend of Joseph*: I can prove it. He was at a rehearsal of the ballet, but for all that he does not know the music, or he would not have made the howler to which I am about to draw attention. 'A gentleman', he says – i.e., some person other than myself – 'may say that the opening theme of *Joseph* has done service before in "The Minstrel Boy". A gentleman might, but a musician would not. I puzzled for a good hour over Mr. Shaw's strange saying. Had he quite lost his reason, and would he be telling us next that the opening phrase of *Tristan* is the same as 'God Save the King'? And then a light dawned on me. There is a theme in *Joseph* that bears, in its first few notes, a superficial resemblance to the tune of 'The Minstrel Boy'; but it is not the opening theme. I have not my score of *Joseph* with me where I am writing this, but the theme occurs, I think, in the middle of the second page. Now this is instructive. No man who had played or read through even the first couple of pages of the score could possibly have said that the 'Minstrel Boy' melody is 'the opening theme'. Mr. Shaw plainly does not know the work; he is, as usual, merely dogmatizing on a matter he imperfectly understands. And the cocksure amateur who thus publicly demonstrates his ignorance of *Joseph* has the assurance to talk of my 'first impressions' of a work which, before writing about it, I had played through at least a dozen times in the course of a month, and of which I had heard two rehearsals and one public performance!

Mr. Shaw on *Joseph* and myself is only a joke and a sore shame. Mr. Shaw on Wagner and myself is a perverter of the truth. According to him, I 'kept paying out all that ill-mannered non-sense about Wagner after even the *Daily Telegraph* (remonstrated with at last, it is said, by Royalty) had dropped it. I contradicted him flatly; and now he thinks Wagner, on the whole, rather a great composer.' This is definite enough: Mr. Shaw charges me with being a one-time ill-mannered disparager of Wagner as a musician. Now when a controversialist possessing the public ear is so lost to literary decency as to attempt to put into circulation so gross a falsehood as this concerning me, I refuse to mince my words with him. I simply give Mr. Shaw the lie direct. Wagner as a composer has always been one of the three supreme gods to me. Mr. Shaw has in mind my *Study of Wagner*, which was published in 1899. At that time I was less near Bach and Beethoven than I am now, and I wrote about Wagner's musical gifts in terms of

almost idolatrous admiration. I could easily fill a couple of
columns of the *Nation* with quotations to prove this, but I will
content myself with referring the reader to pages 42, 47, 48, 249,
250, 257ff., 289, 291ff., 296ff., 305, 312ff., 317ff., 355, 357ff.,
364ff., 379, 384, 392 and 393. So great was my admiration for
Wagner's music, indeed, that a reviewer of my book thought it
his duty to abate it a little. 'Far from disparaging (Wagner's)
musical gift', he wrote, '[Mr. Newman] proclaims that it has
"never been equalled among men", an estimate which quite takes
my breath away, as if someone had said that Watts was a greater
draughtsman than Mantegna.' I had 'fallen under the spell of
Wagner's music', he went on to say, 'and therefore had an
intellectual rather than a musical quarrel with him'. Where and
when did this review appear, Mr. Shaw may ask. In the *Daily
Chronicle* of 9th June, 1899. And the writer of it? None other than
George Bernard Shaw! So that the very man who is now trying
to spread the malicious fiction that I have only arrived at my
present stage of Wagner appreciation through an earlier stage of
'ill-mannered' Wagner depreciation is the same man who,
fifteen years ago, had his breath taken away by what he thought
my excessive admiration for Wagner!

Not content with this primary mendacity, Mr. Shaw adds
that 'a whole generation of the English people was deprived of the
enjoyment of Wagner's music because the critics went on about
Wagner exactly as Mr. Newman is now going on about Strauss,
and as he formerly went on about Wagner, until the grossness of
his error was too much even for English editors'. Again I give Mr.
Shaw the lie direct. If he objects to my handling him thus roughly,
let him give the readers of the *Nation* some proof of his charge
that I ever 'went on about Wagner' in such a way as to turn
English people against him; and let him name the 'English
editors' for whom the grossness of my imaginary error became
in time 'too much'. – Yours, etc.,

                                                    Ernest Newman.

National Liberal Club, London.
7th July, 1914.

THE STRANGE CASE OF ERNEST NEWMAN

To the Editor of the *Nation*

Sir, – I should perhaps apologize to your readers for not having warned them that my first thanks for rescuing them from Mr. Newman's misdirection would be a demonstration by him that I am an abandoned liar. I had better rectify the omission by explaining how it is done.

When a barrister is pleading for the conviction of an educated forger or swindler, or when the judge is summing up (which usually comes to the same thing), they invariably lay great stress on the prisoner's amazing cleverness, on the excellent education he received from his parents, on the hopes that were built on his early promise, on what he might have done but for the fatal perversity which enables the judge to finish with the traditional 'Instead of which you go about stealing ducks'. Mr. Newman never neglects this old and trite method of securing a conviction. But he goes further than any judge has ever gone. When you say to a judge, 'You put X away for ten years, though he was as honest a man as yourself', he does not say, 'You lie; nobody could have spoken more highly of X than I did at the trial.' He stands to his guns. Not so Mr. Newman. If, a year hence, I accuse him (as I very likely shall) of having abused Strauss, he will say: 'You lie in your dastardly throat. If you turn to the *Nation* of 27th June, page 488, column 1, line 1, you will find that I described Strauss as a composer of dazzling genius.' And if (as is not at all probable) I cite Mr. Newman as one of Strauss's admirers, he will exclaim: 'The mendacity of Mr. Shaw is a public scandal. If you turn to the *Nation* of 27th June, 1914, page 487, column 2, last line but five, you will find Strauss denounced as a tired and disillusioned mediocrity in an article signed Ernest Newman (*moi qui vous parle*); and nobody knows it better than Mr. Shaw, as he protested angrily against it at the time.'

Let it rest at that. Strauss, according to Mr. Newman, is a tired

and disillusioned mediocrity of dazzling genius. It is a fine day; but
the weather is extremely rainy and tempestuous.

The fact that in our old controversy in the *Daily Chronicle* I
quoted Mr. Newman's implication that Wagner was a greater
musician than Sebastian Bach (for instance) needs no further
explanation. But Mr. Newman has raked up that controversy to
prove that in those days he was an enthusiastic champion of
Wagner, and I his opponent. If he did not mean this, the raking-
up is an irrelevance. Yet his quotation makes it clear that the
controversy was about his 'quarrel' with Wagner. So he was
quarrelling with Wagner then. Out of my own mouth he has
proved my good faith. On that occasion I was defending Wagner's
greatness against Mr. Newman's disparagements of it exactly as I
am now defending Strauss's greatness against Mr. Newman's
disparagements of it. This is the essential truth of the matter; and
if Mr. Newman is ashamed of having been on the wrong side
then as he is on the wrong side now, the fault is not mine. I did,
and am doing, my best to convert him.

I admit frankly, however, that my opinion of *Joseph* was based
on half an orchestral rehearsal and two performances, all three
conducted by Strauss, the last one (the second public performance) a triumph of conducting and of response to it from the
band. I have since heard another performance; and, though at
some points I missed Strauss's conducting, I was confirmed
beyond redemption in my opinion that *Joseph* is a magnificent
piece of work, and that any lover of music among your readers
who has been prevented from hearing it by Mr. Newman has
been very cruelly deprived of one of the rare opportunities of a
lifetime.

Mr. Newman objects to a judgment based on such experiences.
He declares that his own opinion is based on a dozen performances by himself. As Mr. Newman is not a walking orchestra, I
presume he played *Joseph* on the piano, unless, indeed, his theory
of the excessive simplicity of Strauss's harmony led him to resort
to the accordion. Now, I am bound, in all candour and fair
dealing, to confess at once that if I had played *Joseph* twelve
times on the piano and judged the work thereby, it is only too

probable that my opinion would have been the same as Mr. Newman's. I conclude that Mr. Newman's accomplishments as an executant bear a melancholy resemblance to my own. And I thought, somehow, that he was a fine player. Another illusion gone!

I must apologize for having misled Mr. Newman by calling 'The Minstrel Boy' theme the opening theme. Let me indicate its position more exactly by saying that the work begins with it. It is recognizable as a rhythm before the end of the third bar, though it is repeated several times before it passes, by an irresistible gravitation, into the actual notes of the old tune. When I was a professional critic, we used to describe a theme so situated as the opening theme. I do not know what Mr. Newman calls it; but, at all events, he now knows where it is.

I accept Mr. Newman's explanation that when he alluded to Schönberg he did not mean Schönberg, but another composer of the same name. But I had rather not accept his invitation 'to read the press of England and Germany, *passim*, on the subject of *The Legend of Joseph* and to have a few conversations with some leading English and Continental musicians, as Mr. Newman has done'. If I had done that in the days of the Wagner controversy, I should have arrived at the same conclusions as to Wagner that Mr. Newman has arrived at as to Strauss. I am glad to know now, on his own authority, how he has been led into his errors. My own plan is to listen to a piece of music and say what I think of it. I recommend this method to Mr. Newman as, on the whole simpler, and more satisfactory in its results, than the one he recommends to me.

Mr. Newman's memory betrays him as to *Elektra*. I did not criticize that work before I had heard it. I criticized Mr. Newman years before it was composed; but that is not quite the same thing. Mr. Newman now says he knows nothing at first hand of Strauss personally, and that Strauss's personality has nothing to do with the matter. I confess I did not understand this: I thought that calling a man 'a tired and disillusioned mediocrity' with 'a dull mind' was meant as a personal criticism. I seem to be always misunderstanding Mr. Newman. I am very sorry.

'I wish', says Mr. Newman, 'Mr. Shaw would make up his mind as to what sort of person I really am in music.' I have.

Sans rancune

G. Bernard Shaw.

14th July, 1914.

V

THE QUITE MELANCHOLY CASE OF BERNARD SHAW

To the Editor of the *Nation*

Sir, – In my former letter I deplored the failure of Mr. Shaw's memory. I have now to lament the failure of his eyesight; at least it is to some such failure that I may perhaps attribute his having omitted to read my letter to the end. I accused him, you will remember, of having told two fibs about myself, and I gave him the choice of either justifying them or withdrawing. He has done neither. Has he read what I said to him and about him, or does he think that by keeping silence on these points he will cause the public and myself to forget them? I can assure him that having got him in a corner from which all the dialectical ingenuity in the world will not enable him to escape I am not going to walk away and let him slip out. Not likely! But I will return to this anon. It is no use our continuing to bandy words over *Joseph*. Mr. Shaw says it is 'magnificent', 'a masterpiece'. I say it is platitudinous Teutonic tosh that any decently schooled German musician could have turned out, and that the more thoughtful of them will pray that they may never turn out. Obviously I cannot prove this to Mr. Shaw, any more than he can prove to me that the work is a masterpiece. Let us then leave it for the next five or ten years to show who has blundered. Today I want to have a little fun with Mr. Shaw's desperate attempts to score a point off me here and there.

1. According to him, I have said that 'Strauss is a tired and disillusioned mediocrity of dazzling genius'. 'It is a fine day' – runs Mr. Shaw's comment – 'but the weather is extremely rainy and tempestuous.' It apparently does not occur to Mr. Shaw that though it is rainy today there may have been fine moments last Tuesday. It is surely possible for a man to write a work that has some pages of genius in it, and four years later to write another that shows no genius whatever. I hope this is clear even to Mr. Shaw.

2. Mr. Shaw would fain persuade your readers that I formed my opinion of *Joseph* from 'the press of England and Germany', and from 'conversations with some leading musicians'. I cannot believe he is so stupid as not to have seen the plain meaning of what I said – not that I had derived my opinion from anyone, but that if Mr. Shaw would take the trouble to look into the matter he would find that I was not the only person with a supreme contempt for *Joseph*.

3. Mr. Shaw objected to my speaking as I did of *Joseph*, seeing that the work was by 'a foreign visitor of extraordinarily attractive personality'. I rejoined that the attractiveness or repulsiveness of Strauss's personality had nothing to do with the question of whether his music was good or bad; and now Mr. Shaw plaintively says he thought that 'calling a man a tired and disillusioned mediocrity with a dull mind was meant as a personal criticism'. Cannot Mr. Shaw see that if a critic has never spoken to Strauss in his life, what he says about him can only be an artistic, not a personal criticism? What in the name of reason has 'attractive personality', in the sense in which Mr. Shaw originally used the words, to do with the matter? I believe that Strauss as an artist – as a thinker, let us say – is at present tired, disillusioned, and mediocre; but he may still refrain from beating his wife, or forging a friend's name, or drinking his soup from a sponge.

4. Mr. Shaw would have your readers believe that no idea of *Joseph* can be had from the piano score, even after a dozen readings of it. If that is so, I shall sue Strauss for having got sixteen shillings out of me under false pretences; for if the pianoforte score is not intended to give people an idea of the music,

why is it published? As a matter of fact, such a score tells us a good deal; it makes us familiar, for one thing, with the thematic contours of the work; and we can then listen more intelligently to an orchestral performance. I am told that Mr. Shaw was once a musical critic. It seems incredible, but I am assured it is so by people whom I have found truthful in other matters. In those days did Mr. Shaw ever study the piano score of a new work before he heard it and criticized it? If he did – and it certainly was his duty to do so – he ought to know better than to talk the cheap nonsense he is now retailing. If he did not, then he must have criticized new works on the basis of a single performance – that is, he trusted to those 'first impressions' which he censured me, wrongly as it happens, for trusting to in the case of *Joseph*.

I pass over in charitable silence Mr. Shaw's grotesque attempt to make out that when he spoke of a certain theme as the 'opening theme' he did not mean the theme that opens the work, but a totally different theme that occurs some time later. I leave him to God. 'I do not know what Mr. Newman calls it', he says; 'but at all events he now knows where it is.' This to me, after I had shown him where it is!

Is all this display of damp fireworks intended to make the public and myself forget that I have a crow to pluck with Mr. Shaw over Wagner? I wish to draw him back, gently but firmly, to his first letter. He accused me of 'paying out ill-mannered nonsense' about Wagner years ago, 'after even the *Daily Telegraph* (remonstrated with at last, it is said, by Royalty), had dropped it'. I challenged him to prove this. He makes only a passing reference to the matter – a reference that in its turn is deliberately dishonest, as I shall show in these columns if Mr. Shaw provokes me to pursue the subject. He knows perfectly well that my arguments in *A Study of Wagner* (1899) were directed against Wagner the metaphysician, Wagner the historian, and half-a-dozen other minor Wagners – not against Wagner the musician. But that it was Wagner the composer whom he accused me of disparaging is clear from his own words – 'and now he' (i.e., myself) 'thinks Wagner on the whole, rather a great composer' (the 'on the whole' is merely another gratuitous impertinence). It was

Wagner the composer against whom the *Daily Telegraph* used to fulminate; nor can we imagine 'Royalty' intervening on behalf of Wagner the metaphysician. Mr. Shaw will excuse me, then, if I insist on his either producing his evidence for his charge against me, or apologizing for having fibbed about me.

His other libel was that I ran down Wagner the composer 'until the grossness of (my) error was too much even for English editors'. This charge he must either publicly prove or publicly withdraw. Once more I ask him for the names of those editors. Nay, sorry as I am for Mr. Shaw, I will set him an easier task. According to him, I pursued my career of crime against Wagner for some time before the editors revolted. Presumably, then, the damning articles that caused the revolt are in print somewhere. If Mr. Shaw cannot name the editors who protested, and the articles that were refused, surely he can cite the articles that were printed? But he may save himself the trouble of research. There were no such articles, there were no such editors. Will Mr. Shaw climb down, or must I bring him down?

Ernest Newman.

19th July, 1914.

VI

THE STRANGE CASE OF ERNEST NEWMAN

To the Editor of the *Nation*

Sir, – Allow me one word more. I cannot leave Mr. Newman to be soured and maddened by an imaginary injustice. He believes that your readers may infer from my first letter that he was once dismissed from the staff of a newspaper for abusing Wagner after our editors had discovered that Wagner was a very considerable composer. If anyone has actually drawn such an inference, they have mistaken me. I do not even suggest that Mr. Newman's editors ought to have dismissed him; for though I think that his judgments of his greatest contemporaries are on the whole erroneous, and his critical manners towards them hardly those of one gentleman to another, yet he is too clever and entertaining to be dispensed with; and when great men are in question, the *advocatus diaboli* is useful: indeed I have myself taken that brief in the case of Shakespeare with much benefit to English literary mankind.

Further, I take a sort of paternal interest in Mr. Newman's championship of the delightful toy symphonies of Stravinsky, and the very useful and sometimes exquisite experiments and novelties of Scriabine and of that school generally which was encouraged by the success of Debussy's scale of whole tones, long familiar to organ builders, but strange to the musical public. It is perhaps natural that Mr. Newman should have got into a state of taste in which Strauss's procedure seems so hackneyed that he writes as if you could take the double bass part from the score of *Joseph;* turn it into a figured bass by writing six-four, four-to-three, six-three, etc., under it; and hand it to any bandmaster or church organist to fill up accordingly and reproduce the harmonic effect of the entire work. Mind: I do not say that Mr. Newman has said this in so many words (he will be rude to me again if I do); but if he does not mean this, I respectfully submit that he does not mean anything. The truth that he overlooks in his craving for more Stravinsky is that the greatest artists always belong to the old school; and that the simplicity which is common to Handel's Hailstone Chorus and the exordium of Strauss's *Zarathustra* is the result, not of ignorance or resourcelessness, but of the straightforwardness of the great man who, having something to say, says it in the most familiarly intelligible language, unlike the smaller man who, having little or nothing to say, very properly secures interest by a curious way of saying it. Thus you have Handel, Mozart, Beethoven, Wagner and Strauss denounced as madmen, even by eminent musicians, whilst their personal mannerisms were still strange, and then denounced by the amateurs of strangeness as platitudinous, sententious, and even by such exceptionally hardy and fanatical amateurs of strangeness as Mr. Newman, mediocre.

I now leave the verdict to the good sense, including the sense of humour, of your readers. I should not have begun the controversy (on express provocation from Mr. Newman, who must not complain if he has got more than he bargained for) but for my strong sense of the vast public mischief done by our campaigns of stupid abuse against supreme geniuses like Wagner, Ibsen and Rodin, with the result that whole generations are robbed of their birthright of culture by the misleading and intimidation of the entrepreneurs whose business it is to supply the public demand for the highest art. My sole object was to make it clear to your readers that Mr. Newman's remarks about Strauss need not deter them from attending performances of his music, nor entrepreneurs from venturing their capital upon it, nor public-spirited gentlemen like Sir Joseph Beecham from devoting their fortunes to it.

But, of course, I note Mr. Newman's denial to Wagner of all the qualities that distinguished him from eminent musicians like his contemporaries, Sir Frederick Gore Ouseley and Dr. Stainer (not to mention men still living). To Mr. Newman's mind, this is a handsome acknowledgment of Wagner's position as a composer. To my mind, it represents the extremest length to which anti-Wagnerism can safely go now that no one, without making himself publicly ridiculous, can question Wagner's technical ability. In short, there is a difference between Mr. Newman's mind and mine; and as nothing that we can say or write will alter that difference, we must remain content with having given the readers of the *Nation*, and incidentally one another, a piece of our minds on the subject.

Mr. Newman's last letter proves, especially in his references to pianoforte scores and opening themes, that the more delicate nuances of controversy, however entertaining to the bystanders (for whose sake I hope he will excuse my little attempts) are apt to escape him. I propose, therefore, that we drop it. If he will cease asking me for the name of that imaginary editor who did not dismiss him, I, on my side, will not press him for the names of the hundred composers who could easily have composed *Joseph* and magnanimously refrained, though we should all dearly like to know them. And so I leave the last word with Mr. Newman. – Yours, etc.,

G. Bernard Shaw.

P.S. – I see by a rather jolly article of Mr. Newman's in the *Birmingham Post*, that his hundred men in buckram have now more than doubled their numbers. By the time this appears they will no doubt have run into four figures; but that will not affect my estimate of his critical powers.

VII

THE ARTS AND CRAFTS OF
GEORGE BERNARD SHAW

To the Editor of the *Nation*

Sir, – As Mr. Shaw is kind enough to leave me with the last word – a right that I think would have been mine in any case – I shall repay his courtesy by talking more about him than about myself. I propose today to analyse his technique of controversy.

But first of all let me set Mr. Shaw's mind at rest on one point, and apologize in connection with another. Mr. Shaw rightly opines that I gave him 'expressive provocation' to begin this controversy. I did indeed, and of malice aforethought. For three years I have been trying to decoy Mr. Shaw into another argument. After each article I have written on Strauss I have said to myself: 'This will draw him'; but Mr. Shaw has refused to be drawn. When *Joseph* came along I saw a special opportunity and made a special effort. I knew this was the poorest long work that Strauss has ever written. I know I had only to say so in picturesque language to goad Mr. Shaw into committing himself irrevocably to the opinion that it is a masterpiece; but to make quite sure I baited the trap with an almost too obvious hint to Mr. Shaw that it was his bounden duty to contradict me. The bait took: the unwary Mr. Shaw rushed into the trap: and here we are.

On one point, I admit, he has me; I might have expected, indeed, that his eagle eye would detect the one weak spot in my armour. I was rash enough to say that some two hundred European composers could easily have written a work so commonplace as *Joseph*. But on reflection I see that I was wrong. Not one of them could. I am not like some people I could name: when I recognize that I have done anyone a gross injustice I admit my fault. I apologize to the two hundred.

And now let me display the anatomy of Mr. Shaw's technique. His first great dodge is to turn a blind eye to every awkward question and every dilemma that is presented to him. He reminds me of Montaigne's story of the two Greek wrestlers. One of them was not much good at wrestling, but was a great rhetorician; and each time his antagonist threw him he volubly demonstrated to the spectators that he really had not been thrown at all. I point out to Mr. Shaw that a theme incautiously called by him 'the opening theme' does not, in fact, appear until some time after the opening. Does Mr. Shaw admit that he has blundered? Not a bit of it! Even before he has risen from the mat he assures the spectators that while in one sense the theme is not the 'opening theme' because it does not open the work, in a higher, subtler sense it is the opening theme, inasmuch as the music passes into it by 'an irresistible gravitation'. Mr. Shaw's week, I suppose, begins with Tuesday afternoon; for on an enlightened consideration of the calendar it is clear that the whole of Monday and Tuesday morning are merely 'irresistible gravitations' into Tuesday afternoon. And when I chuckle, as many other musicians have done, over his delicious conundrum of 'When is an opening theme not an opening theme?' Mr. Shaw gravely tells the spectators that 'the more delicate nuances of controversy' are 'apt to escape me'. The rhetorician, in fact, has only been 'downed' by his opponent's ignorance of the more delicate nuances of wrestling.

Mr. Shaw's other most familiar trick is to paint a gross caricature of his adversary's opinions, and then argue, not against the man, but against the caricature. I tell Mr. Shaw, for example, that plenty of musicians besides myself despise *Joseph*. Whereupon Mr. Shaw appeals to the crowd: 'You see, ladies and gentlemen, this abandoned person actually confesses that he derived his opinion of *Joseph* from other people.' The only exercise I have had throughout this controversy has been chasing round after Mr. Shaw, putting my foot through one after another of his imaginary portraits of me, and substituting a genuine photograph for it. I would not go so far as to say that this inveterate practice of his is primarily conscious and purposive; it seems to derive ultimately from a congenital inability to see what is plain before him without first running round the corner and standing on his head. But this copious natural faculty for seeing truth from an angle that hopelessly distorts it has been developed by the dire necessity of extricating himself, at any cost, from the difficulties into which his many controversies land him – controversies often begun by his incurable mania for lecturing professional people on subjects in which he is only an amateur. (The amateur is writ large over Mr. Shaw's latest remarks on Scriabine and Debussy.) In the end it is hard to say where the natural unconscious impulse ceases and the conscious exploitation of it begins. Always there is the unblushing attempt to be the interpreter not only of his own views but of his opponent's; always the opponent's views are grotesquely manipulated to suit Mr. Shaw's purposes; always from this welter of absurdity is drawn the inference that Mr. Shaw wants. 'Joseph contains a lot of diatonic music', runs one of his preposterous syllogisms. 'Mr. Newman dislikes *Joseph*; therefore Mr. Newman dislikes diatonic music'. Which is like saying that I never, never, never eat fruit, because Mr. Shaw has seen me decline to have a rotten apple forced down my throat. '*Elektra* seems to me music of an advanced harmonic idiom', was a former syllogism of Mr. Shaw's: 'Mr. Newman does not like some parts of *Elektra*; therefore Mr. Newman, plodding old fogey that he is, does not like advanced harmonic idioms.' Then the tune changes. When Strauss writes another work, so obvious in idea that the brain of a musical rabbit could grasp the bulk of it, Mr. Shaw elaborates an antithetical syllogism: '*Joseph* is simple and rather old-fashioned music; Mr. Newman does not think much of *Joseph*; therefore Mr. Newman is a furious foe of simple and old-fashioned music.' The next misrepresentation follows as a matter of course. 'If Mr. Newman detests simple music of the "old school", he must necessarily lust after the "strange" music of the "new school." Now Stravinsky, in my opinion, writes strange music; therefore Mr. Newman's god is Stravinsky.' This is the latest caricature through which I have to put an avenging foot. In all my life I have not written ten sentences about Stravinsky. What Mr. Shaw has in his mind is clearly a recent article of mine on Strauss in the *Birmingham Post*, which he admits having read. After expressing my regret that our one-time leader Strauss should have lost our confidence by degenerating into a platitudinarian, I said that 'in works like *Joseph* he has no message that can interest us; and so we turn to younger men like Stravinsky, who, though we cannot always see eye to eye with them, yet give us the impression that they are personalities, that they have something of their own to say that is worth saying, that they thoroughly well know how to say it, and that something big may some day come of one of them.' Observe the extreme caution of the phrasing. I have not given my artistic conscience into Stravinsky's keeping; he is simply a young composer who, though he sometimes puzzles me, always interests me – a composer who, in my opinion, is worth keeping one's eye on. How does Mr. Shaw translate this guarded declaration for your readers? 'You have Handel, Mozart, Beethoven, Wagner, and Strauss denounced as madmen, even by eminent musicians, whilst their personal mannerisms were still strange, and then denounced by the amateurs of strangeness as platitudinous, sententious, and even by such exceptionally hardy and fanatical amateurs of strangeness as Mr. Newman, mediocre.' I will not ask Mr. Shaw where I have 'denounced' the eminent old musicians he mentions; he is not good at giving this authority for his charges. I merely ask the reader to glance once more at my own remark about Stravinsky, and to try to discover, if he can, what ground there is in it for Mr. Shaw's description of me as a 'hardy and fanatical amateur of strangeness'. Mr. Shaw is really incorrigible. I beg anyone who may do me the honour to be interested in my opinions on music to get them direct from me, not from Mr. Shaw, who is simply not to be trusted in these matters.

For the last time I would remind your readers that Mr. Shaw, in spite of many appeals from me, has neither substantiated nor withdrawn the statement he made concerning me in connection with Wagner. With touching solicitude, he hopes I will not complain if I have 'got more than I bargained for'. My only complaint, my only regret, at the end of this controversy is that it leaves me with a grievously diminished opinion of Mr. Shaw's sense of honour. – Yours, etc.,

Ernest Newman.

3rd August, 1914.

VI

CONTRIBUTIONS TO THE
NATION
1912-1913

THE CASE OF ARNOLD SCHÖNBERG, 1912

IT IS not often that an English audience hisses the music it does
not like; but a good third of the people at Queen's Hall last
Tuesday permitted themselves that luxury after the performance
of the five orchestral pieces of Schönberg. Another third of the
audience was only not hissing because it was laughing, and the
remaining third seemed too puzzled either to laugh or to hiss; so
that on the whole it does not look as if Schönberg has so far
made many friends in London. It will be remembered that a few
months ago an audience was in a similar state of bewilderment
after Mr. Buhlig had played the three pianoforte pieces that form
Schönberg's opus 11. In Vienna, it is said, the performance of the
five orchestral pieces caused a riot. London, at any rate, stopped
short of that on Tuesday, outraged as its susceptibilities evidently
were.

Nevertheless I take leave to suggest that Schönberg is not the
mere fool or madman that he is generally supposed to be. The
fact that he has a following in Germany goes for little, for there
is always a certain number of people there on the look-out for a
new banner to fight under. But he is believed in by musicians,
such as Busoni, whose competence no one will dispute. The book
on Schönberg that has just been issued in Munich – written by a
number of his pupils – is, if a little too uncritical in its admiration,

at all events the work of men of undoubted musical attainments. What, then, is the truth of the matter?

On Tuesday night I tried the experiment, for the first time in my life, of listening to a complex modern work without any previous knowledge of the score; and from the muddle of my own impressions I can readily understand how the music must have struck the average man in the audience. But I know some others of Schönberg's works thoroughly – for example, the String Quartet in F sharp minor (op. 10), and the six songs of op. 8, as well as his brilliant, thoughtful, and extremely suggestive book on harmony; and I remember that while my first impressions of some of this music were very much the same as those of Tuesday, I saw a good deal more in it at the twentieth reading of it than at the first. Schönberg can write very expressively at times. But he is curiously unequal. I have come to admire and like, almost throughout, songs such as the 'Sehnsucht' and 'Voll jener Süsse', by which I was repelled at first; but I do not think I shall ever come to like the 'Drei Klavierstücke' of op. 11, or the ending of the third movement of the F sharp minor quartet, or certain things in the five orchestral pieces. The truth is that Schönberg has visions of possibilities in music for which neither he nor anyone else has as yet been able to find the right idiom. It is unquestionable that modern harmony can expand almost indefinitely. The problem is how to keep it still coherent and logical as it grows more subtle and complex. It must, like prose or poetry, talk sense, and, like painting, it must be recognizably veracious. The trouble is that you cannot test the truth of music, as you can test the truth of poetry, or painting, or sculpture, by comparing it with any external original. Who, then, is to say what is right or wrong, false or true? If a composer like Schönberg tells us that his music is the honest transcript of emotions really felt, who has the right to sneer at it simply because it conveys no emotion at all to him? The very fact that the material of musical expression is not eternally fixed, as words and colours are, but alters from one generation to another, is enough to make us cautious in our condemnation of any new idiom. May it not be that the new composer sees a logic in certain tonal relations that to the rest of

us seem chaos at present, but the coherence of which may be
clear enough to us all some day?

All we can do is to go by the safest steps we have, reasoning
from the known to the unknown. Schönberg's harmony owes its
complexity, in the main, to three causes. He builds up chords with
notes that seem to be hopelessly dissonant. He passes abruptly
from one chord to another that is apparently unrelated to it. And
he writes a seemingly reckless sort of counterpoint, regardless of
the dissonances made by the clashing of the parts at certain points.
Now my own experience is that a good deal of his harmony that
sounds repulsive or incoherent at first becomes lucid and enjoyable
with further experience of it. This merely means that he is here
thinking a little in advance of most of us. But in other cases I am
afraid he is merely experimenting. In his *Erwartung*, for example,
he has chords composed of eleven and twelve notes. I give one of
these as a curiosity, going from the bass upwards, the notes are A
natural, B natural (an octave higher), D sharp, F sharp, C natural,
F natural, A sharp, C sharp, E natural, G natural, C natural, and
E flat. If the composer himself were to tell me that this chord was
the one inevitable expression of something in his soul at the
moment, thrown out instantaneously in the white heat of his
vision, I should politely decline to believe him. The thing is a
piece of pure manufacture; and if we were to add or subtract a
couple of notes I am confident that Schönberg himself would not
notice the change. So with some of his counterpoint. As Richter
said once when he was asked to admire the polyphony of the
Works of Peace section in *Ein Heldenleben* – 'anyone can make any
number of themes go together, so long as he doesn't care what it
sounds like'. The many-voiced modern orchestra admits of a
most elaborate contrapuntal texture; and so accommodating and
tolerant is the modern ear that it will accept almost anything that
does not sound utterly horrible. But I, for one, decline to believe
that much of Schönberg's counterpoint is anything more than a
deliberate piecing together of themes that have no vital imaginative connection with each other. You cannot add to or take away
from a single part in the tissue of, say, Mozart's *Eine kleine
Nachtmusik* or Wagner's *Tristan*. I have seen extracts from the

score of Schönberg's orchestral poem, *Pelleas and Melisande*; and I will undertake to add half-a-dozen new counterpoints to his without the hearer being a penny the worse off. On the other hand, the harmonic crudity that the ear resents at first in some of his work disappears when we know the music and think of it not as a succession of chords but as the combination of various counterpoints; we can then even take pleasure in the dissonances.

My own experience of Schönberg, then, leads me to the conclusion that he is a man of undoubted gifts who, in his later work, is aiming at the transcription of new shades of emotion into a musical language that he has not yet succeeded in making logical and lucid. Perhaps this is to write him down as a failure. For genuine imagination, projecting outwardly a vision veritably seen, always makes its own language; and it may be that Schönberg's many fumblings prove him simply to be lacking in imagination and vision of the right fire and intensity. But whether he succeeds or not in doing what he is now trying to do, it will have to be done some day by some one. The next vital development of music will be along the lines of the best of Schönberg.

MAHLER'S SEVENTH SYMPHONY, 1913

MAHLER IS still very little known in England, and judging from some of the criticisms of his Seventh Symphony, which was excellently given by Sir Henry Wood at the Queen's Hall on Saturday last, he is still less understood. That he has a great following in Germany is not in itself a very impressive recommendation, for there are so many circles in Germany each burning to call the true Messiah its own and no one else's, that whatever a musician may do there he is certain of a following of some sort. Mahler, however, numbers among his adherents a great many not only of the merely 'advanced' but of the steadier heads of modern Germany. It is at least arguable that his nine Symphonies repre-

sent on the whole the most significant body of work done in the
symphonic form since Brahms; while even people who are not yet
on the intellectual or musical level of the Symphonies are as a
rule sensitive to the beauty and the power of his songs.

It will not do, as several critics tried last Monday, to dismiss
him as a merely clever manipulator of enormous orchestral
masses. Richard Strauss has really a great deal to answer for!
We have so often seen him – as in the *Symphonia Domestica* – using
an orchestra the size of which was out of all proportion to the
value of the ideas he was expressing, that it has become almost
a fixed principle with many people to assume that every work
demanding an orchestra of 110 must necessarily be another case
of more cry than wool. The truth is that under certain circumstances an orchestra of 110 is quite a reasonable combination; it
certainly did not seem to me to be excessive in the Symphony of
Mahler, for the simple reason that I never felt that splashes of
colour were being laid on to hide a deficiency of ideas. What
struck me was rather the exquisite balance between the means and
the end, the perfect certainty both of Mahler's thinking and of his
style. One can hardly imagine a composer more sure of himself
in latitudes not accessible to ordinary feet; and this combined
sense of bigness and certainty is one of the rarest impressions in
the concert room, and the surest sign of our being in the presence
of a master. The smaller men give it us occasionally; among the
men whose normal association is with the greater and graver
things, perhaps only Bach and Wagner can be counted upon for
it at all times. One needs to hear only a chance phrase of Wagner's
in the concert room, quite dissociated from its context, to realize
how the ardour of his thinking fills every vein of every phrase.
We had an illustration of this at the commencement of last
Saturday's concert. Plunged as we were without a moment's
preparation into the *Waldweben* from *Siegfried*, no one, surely,
could fail to be conscious that he was in the presence of a master
whose merest word constrained us to listen, such pregnancy, such
concentration, such power to call up associations far wider than
itself, were there in the smallest theme. I, for one, always felt this
largeness of brain and of hand in Mahler's symphony; I do not

see, indeed, how anyone could read a single time through the score without being conscious of it. With all his ambition and his fervour, and what is erroneously called his megalomania, there is never a trace in him of the fumbling that does so much to spoil our enjoyment of the real greatness of Bruckner's ideas – never a sign of struggle with problems either of thought or of technique. Or just one sign, perhaps. I am not sure whether it is the composer's imagination or our own that relaxes a little during the final movement; no doubt both find the strain an abnormal one. The Seventh Symphony, it may be frankly confessed, is too long: probably no composer of purely instrumental music can hope to sustain the interest at the same high level for an hour and twenty minutes. But apart from this natural slackening of the tension during the *finale*, I cannot, for my part, see any sign in the work of a mind aiming at an expression beyond its natural powers. The Symphony seems to me extraordinarily rich in ideas and firm in texture, and the work all through of a great man.

Mahler must be a hard nut to crack for the amiable gentlemen who are obsessed by the theory of a 'national' consciousness that must somehow create for itself a 'national' school of music; and he is correspondingly comforting to those who hold that art is not a matter of nationality but of personal temperament and experience, and that, other things being equal, the finest art is likely to come from a crossing of races and of cultures. Mahler was apparently half Jewish and half Bohemian; the blend of Slav and Semite in him, in itself a rich one, was further enriched by a world-wide culture, not only in music but in art and philosophy – for his brain was as eager as his blood. The soul of him burned the body out, indeed, at the age of fifty-one. Yet with all this crossing of inner forces and outer influences in him, there could not be a style less obviously or consciously composite than Mahler's; at no point in it do you feel that any of the elements of it have been merely 'lifted' without being assimilated. Even the most intrepid of hunters-out of 'national' characteristics in music would blanch at the task of deciding which feature of Mahler's music was Jewish, for example, which Slavonic, and which German. What has evidently happened is that each of the currents in him has raised the others to a new power. The one traceable affinity to other music in the Seventh Symphony is to be found in some of the waltz-like melodies of the third movement, that are unmistakably children of that 'Viennese spirit' to which Schubert gave such delightful expression. But they *are* living children, not mere imitative waxwork figures. They are, in a sense, Vienna and Schubert, but they are also unmistakably Mahler. But the Symphony is throughout, I should say, the product of a mind of unusual distinction.

The charge of megalomania seems to me quite unjustifiable. I can nowhere see any of the signs – so sadly plentiful in some other music of more ambition than achievement – of the frog swelling himself to the size of the ox, and bursting in the process. The themes are of peculiar pregnancy; they have personality of their own, independently of the uses to which they are put in the course of their development; they are not merely figures but characters, which is more than can be said of many symphonic themes. The colouring is amazingly sure both in the mass and in detail; Mahler is one of the few men who can make us feel that a melody has not merely been invented in the abstract and then scored for this instrument or that, but that melodic line and colour were conceived simultaneously and are inextricably interblended. None of us can say how much of the elevating effect of the fine theme with which the symphony opens is due to the contour of it and how much to the veiled yet eloquent tone of the tenor horn; one can no more think of the two factors in separation than one can imagine the melody of the prelude to the third act of *Tristan* in any other colour than that of the cor anglais. The surety of Mahler's colour sense, and at the same time the perfect fusion of the colour with the idea, is shown again by the way he uses the guitars and the mandolines in the fourth movement. So far from their giving us the impression of being dragged in for mere effect by a composer who was at the end of his resources on normal lines, these instruments seem here the most natural thing in the world, so perfectly do they fuse with the rest of the orchestra, and so essential are they to the ideas at this point. But behind all this certainty of style and of technique is an imagination of a very unusual kind, vivid, ardent, and vast, and with the power of turning everything that passes through it into natural music. He gives us none of the clues to his vision that the writers of avowed programme music do; but he is clear enough for all that, and to minds that can enter into his with imaginative sympathy he is one of the subtlest forces in modern music.

SCRIABINE'S *PROMETHEUS*, 1913

WITH THE curious ignorance of everything that goes on outside London that is so characteristic of the Londoner, the device of giving Scriabine's *Prometheus* twice at the same concert last Saturday was announced as an innovation so far as England is concerned. It is not unknown to Manchester, however, and I remember that on the occasion of the first performance of Debussy's *L'Après-midi d'un Faune* in Liverpool some years ago, the work was repeated in the second half of the concert. It is a pity, indeed, that the practice of playing big new works twice at the same concert is not more prevalent. Last week at Queen's Hall we had an interesting sidelight on the relations between the critics and the public. Concert-givers and theatrical managers pretend that the disparaging articles of the critics upon new works do more than anything to kill their chances. The critic knows that his words influence the public very slightly, if at all; if the man in the street has so much faith in the critic's judgment, he ought obviously not only to stay away from things of which the critic disapproves, but fly post haste to the things the critic admires. No amount of ridicule of musical comedy for its brain-lessness and unoriginality manages to keep the public away from it; and no amount of enthusiasm over a great work of a new type suffices to inspire the public with any faith in it. On Saturday the public gave itself away; probably not more than half of the people who heard the first performance of *Prometheus* remained for the second. They went out with their noses in the air and a look of outraged virtue – and this before a single critic had delivered himself of a judgment on the work!

One could foresee that *Prometheus* would be a poser to the plain music lover, whose education has stopped short at Wagner and Strauss. But in truth it is often a difficult problem even for those of us who believe that music can no more cease its evolution with Wagner and Strauss than with Bach and Beethoven, and who keep our ears always astrain for any authentic new note that may be borne to us on the wind. It is absurd for any of us to dogmatize about a work that aims at carrying the idiom and the vision of music to a point as far beyond Strauss as Strauss is beyond Tchaikovsky; the more confidently any critic tries to sweep it off the board as the mere effusion of a musical lunatic, the more certainly he writes himself down as a superficial duffer, intrepidly denying the existence of things simply because he cannot see them. I do not contend that everything in *Prometheus* is clear even at a second hearing, or that there may not be a good deal in it to which no number of hearings would reconcile us. But I do urge that to a listener with an imagination it mostly talks in a perfectly lucid language of things that have never been expressed in music before.

The linking of Scriabine's name with that of Schönberg is a gratuitous error. Schönberg is really a better composer than his music would sometimes lead us to imagine; but his style is to some extent obviously a calculated one. It is the idiom of a man who was consciously determined from the first that however he might write, he would not write like other composers. Scriabine has developed as naturally as Beethoven or Wagner or Strauss, beginning, as they did, with his roots in the past, and gradually evolving a highly individual style of his own as his whole personality developed. Whatever may be thought of his later style, there is no affectation in it on the musical side, and there is no fumbling. What struck some of us in the *Prometheus* was the almost infallible certainty of the adaptation of the means to the end throughout; only a composer who is at once master of his ideas and of his technique can work so surely as this. Whether, however, the brain as a whole is evolving harmoniously, whether it may not be developing a strain of excessive idealism, losing itself somewhat in the void of the thought that lies in the far beyond of the other side of music, and failing to see its vision not merely with theosophical but with musical clearness, failing to find the firm enclosing line that alone can make the vision as real to us as it is to him – on these points one cannot be wholly sure.

The truth probably is that certain parts of *Prometheus* – as of still later works of Scriabine such as the recently published pianoforte sonata – will never be quite clear to us because they were never quite clear to the composer, either because he has not thought his way exactly enough through the subtleties he is envisaging, or because music's means of expression are not yet equal to the task he imposes on them. I cheerfully present these parts of *Prometheus* to the ordinary objector to the work, for him to make what capital he likes out of them. But to the rest – and that much the greater part – I firmly pin my faith. *Prometheus* is the one work I have ever heard that seems to me to approach the new territory that music will some day make its own. It is in essence the most immaterial of the arts; but circumstances have forced it to develop so far upon more or less material lines. It first of all had to win for itself, by means of rather rigid rhythms and formal designs, the faculty of coherent thinking upon a large scale. Then the purely human impulse surged up within it, and – mainly under Wagner – substituted for the set design the modelling of the tissue of music upon the forms and vicissitudes of the emotions themselves. But music of this kind needed an obvious and detailed 'poetic purpose' – the plot of the opera or the story of the symphonic poem – just as much as the older music needed the material scaffolding of sonata or fugue. Clearly music will be able to dispense with even this 'poetic' support in the future, and yet speak to us quite plainly of mysteries as far surpassing the operatic or symphonic-poem subject in subtlety and remoteness as music in general surpasses words in general; it is all a matter of how lucidly and logically a composer can think in this tenuous atmosphere, what body he can give to his visions, and how far we can think and see along with him. A rough analogy to this progress of music to immaterialities ever more and more refined may be had in the theories men have held upon matter. To the first philosophers, matter was solid substance; to the later ones, a bundle of atoms; to those still later, a play of electrons. Always the immaterial mystery encroaches upon the material fact, or upon the mystery a shade more material.

It is surely evident that the true home of music is among these ultimate immaterialities of thought, because it is the only one of the arts that can ever hope to express them. That home it will one day win. To my mind we have nowhere come so near to it as in the best of this music of Scriabine's. I care nothing for the theosophy that is tacked on to it by the composer and the annotators, and think that this is as likely as not to confuse or prejudice the hearer. But listening to it solely as music, only a congenitally unimaginative dullard, I fancy, or a musician sodden with the futile teaching of the text-books and the Conservatoires, could help feeling that here is music that comes as near as is at present possible to being the pure voice of Nature and the soul themselves. One needs no programme note to have the picture flashed upon one's brain of the soul of man slowly yearning into conscious being out of a primal undifferentiated world, torn by the conflict of emotions, violently purging itself of its grossnesses, and ultimately winning its way to the light.

And all this is done, not on the familiar 'poetic' lines of the symphonic poem, but a stage further behind the veil, as it were; the wind that blows through the music is not the current stage and concert room formula, but the veritable wind of the cosmos itself; the cries of desire and passion and ecstasy are a sort of quintessential sublimation of all the yearning, not merely of humanity, but of all nature, animate and inanimate. No amount of criticism of the work in details can diminish the wonder of such an achievement as this. Its thematic texture may not always be distinguished, and the piano part may, as I believe, be mostly an error; but the fact remains that here is an imagination of extraordinary subtlety and scope, and a most remarkable faculty of musical expression. The only fear is lest the theosophist in Scriabine should overpower the artist in him.

ARIADNE AUF NAXOS, 1913

ARIADNE AUF NAXOS has been a failure in Germany. So far as the music of it is concerned, there is little doubt that it will be a failure in England also. For the play preliminary to the opera there is more hope – at any rate when done in the style we were treated to at His Majesty's Theatre last Thursday – because of its naked and unashamed exploitation of the current English comedy humour. The whole thing was so bad that Sir Herbert Tree would almost certainly make a fortune by taking it on a long provincial tour. Sir Herbert is a patriot *pur sang*. He scorns the foreign joke: if he is to keep company with Molière, the flimsy Frenchman must get rid of his alien graces and tune himself to the key of the English musical comedy comedian. *Le Bourgeois Gentilhomme* in its latest English dress and with its latest English acting might well be taken, by any casual and unlettered visitor who strolled into the theatre while the performance was on, for the latest transplantation from the Gaiety. It is true that Molière's wit and humour would out even through such a translation and such acting – all the coarsening in the world cannot quite kill it: but a Frenchman would be hard put to it to recognize some of these clumsy caricatures for the finespun characters that Molière drew, while an Englishman will recognize them all as types made familiar to him by the comic English stage of the last fifteen years. After the first bad joke or two that has been foisted upon the original and upon Hofmannsthal we could anticipate most of the others. We might have foreseen that Jourdain would threaten Nicole with a slap over the jaw, that when Jourdain was told the title of the new opera he would ask "Arry?' and be told in reply 'Adne', that as his song had something to do with a lamb there would be references to ham and damn, and so on. One of the characters is asked by Jourdain what he is getting at: another is informed that M. Jourdain can't stand slow music at any price.

And as the translation – or rather adaptation – so the acting. Apart from the Dorante of Mr. Philip Merivale and the little bit of work Miss Neilson-Terry and Mr. Creighton had to do as Dorimène and the Composer respectively, there was not a single style – hardly even a single voice – that had the least suggestion in it of the breeding and the elegance of the old French comedy. Jourdain, it is true, has neither breeding nor elegance in the usual senses of the words: but he is not the clumsy clown Sir Herbert Tree made of him. He is the most lovable noodle in all dramatic literature: his little vanities are never objectionable, whereas the vanities that Sir Herbert Tree puts upon him hurt one as horribly as the clothes he dressed him in – they were a quite needless riot of colour-cacophony. The rest of the play had to live up to the awful standard of over-emphasis set by those appalling clothes – or was it that Sir Herbert Tree wore them so ill? In the true musical comedy vein, an elaborate finger-post was set up in front of each joke, the adapter and the actor presumably having always in their minds the least intelligent member of the audience, and being determined that he shall miss nothing for want of having it pointed out to him. Even the farewell sentences that Hofmannsthal puts into Jourdain's mouth when, at the end of the opera, he finds that his titled guests have slipped away in the darkness, could not be left to carry their own point, as they certainly ought to anyone who is mentally qualified for admission to a theatre. 'I wish', says Jourdain, 'I had been born a Count or a Marquis, and had been endowed with that certain something with which they know how to give the Great Air to everything they do.' As if this were not enough, Sir Herbert Tree, or Mr. Somerset Maugham, or both of them, must needs add 'even when they are rude'; and curiously enough it was just these words, and the excessive emphasis and the knowing look with which they were uttered, that established the most confidential relations between the actor and the audience.

But however skilfully the wine of Molière's wit may be doctored to suit a theatrical palate brought up on vinegar or beer, nothing can save such a work as *Ariadne auf Naxos*. The libretto and the music are surely the poorest things ever put forth by two men of world-wide reputation. The unfortunate thing about the combination of Hofmannsthal and Strauss is that it too often brings out the worst qualities of both of them. Like so many other German writers, Hofmannsthal is apt to mistake brutality for strength, and horseplay for humour; and in Strauss he has a musician who, with all his genius, has in him a certain strain both of rawness and of stupidity. The Ægistheus episode in *Elektra* as Hofmannsthal has written it, would have been rejected by most composers as too crude a piece of melodramatic effect: Strauss applies the whole force of his orchestra to making a still rawer head and still bloodier bones of it. And no one but a composer whose humour, as in *Ein Heldenleben*, had a touch of the cackle of the village idiot or the bladder-banging of the village green in it, would have set himself with such gusto to underlining in his music all the puerilities of the inn scene in *Der Rosenkavalier*. The humour of *Ariadne auf Naxos* is inane beyond words. There is some sprightliness in the music of the quartet of buffoons, but it is nothing to become enthusiastic over: while the coloratura aria of Zerbinetta is mostly tedium itself.

The whole of the comedy, indeed, could be cut out of the opera without our missing it: perhaps some day a concert version of the work will be arranged, consisting solely of Ariadne's opening lament and the music that follows the arrival of Bacchus. There would be little of the greater Strauss in this, but it would be interesting enough for a while. The music of the opera as a whole makes it even more certain than in certain parts of *Der Rosenkavalier* that the bloom has gone off Strauss's imagination and the vitality out of it. Occasionally there is a great note of human feeling – especially in Ariadne's opening scene – that no other living composer could sound; but for the rest it bears the same relation to Strauss's really fine music as ordinarily competent journalism bears to great literature. The small orchestra of thirty-six players that he uses makes it hard for him to dazzle us, as of old, with purely technical cleverness; and the essential poverty of some of his ideas is unmistakable now that they are seen without their gorgeous trappings. But he is still clever enough to keep on talking volubly and persuading us to listen even when he has nothing very urgent to say: a good deal of the Bacchus music, for example, is simply the machine-made rhetoric of the skilled old oratorical hand.

One of the most distressing features of the score is the added proof it affords us that Strauss has exhausted his old idiom without having been able to discover a new one. His melodic sense – which is as much as to say his power of creating in music – has come to a standstill. He is apparently conscious of it himself, and tries to atone for the failure of it in two ways – by harmonic eccentricities that cannot blind us to the poverty of the ideas underlying them, and that are becoming as manneristic as certain formulae of Debussy; and by an affectation of Mozartian simplicity and limpidity of melody. His attempts at the imitation of Mozart invariably end, both here and in *Der Rosenkavalier*, in a banality of cadence that destroys whatever illusion they may have begun by creating. In any case there is no path to be opened out into the future by imitating Mozart; if a new idiom is to come, with Strauss or with another, it will have to be as the natural efflorescence of all his best ways of thought and of ours. At present Strauss is drifting like a rudderless boat in a stormy sea. He has no impulse strong enough and sincere enough to carry him through a work at the one white heat: he wastes himself in experiment, in imitation, and in bluff. The full measure of his weakness may be seen in the incidental music of Molière's play. The one good thing in it is the brilliant piece of characterization that accompanies the fencing scene. The arietta and the duet could have been written by dozens of other men. The rest of the incidental music is either ordinary or stupid. He is a sore disappointment now to those of us who once felt that the future of music lay with him more than with any other composer of our day. When one thinks of the splendid work he has done, and then sees him clowning clumsily in company with Hofmannsthal, or writing music as dull as it is meretricious to accompany the serving of a dinner or the putting on of a pair of trousers, one feels somewhat as the more decent-minded of Noah's sons felt on a famous occasion.

G

VII

CONTRIBUTIONS TO THE
NEW WITNESS
1915-1918

STRAUSS'S NEW SYMPHONY, 1915

IT IS rather disturbing to those of us who have been led by certain writers to believe that Germany is economically almost at her last gasp to find that her musical life seems to be going on very much as usual. In France, music has virtually stopped; the Paris opera houses, I believe, do nothing more than just 'carry on' till better times shall come. The production of an important new work in Paris at present is unthinkable. Berlin, however, has just had the first preformance of Strauss's new work, the *Alpine Symphony*, and has taken the production, even in war time, as a matter of course; nor did it shrink from the expense of bringing the Dresden orchestra to Berlin to perform the work. It has been suggested to me that all the musical activity of Germany during the past twelve months – the numerous concerts and operatic performances, the many productions of new works – has been simply so much 'window-dressing' on the part of the authorities, who are anxious to give both resident neutrals and their own people the impression that Germany is unmoved by all the assaults of the Allied armies upon her. It may be so, but none of us over here has information sufficient to warrant an opinion either way.

The only long account I have yet seen of the *Alpine Symphony* is that written by Dr. Edgar Istel – an able German critic and

179

historian – in the *Berliner Morgenpost* of 29th October, the morrow of the production. For the first time in many years, a new Strauss work has been performed without attracting the critics of the leading papers of the civilized world. It is true that Dr. Istel speaks of the presence in the audience of 'many famous foreign conductors and musical critics' – by which he probably means that Turkey and Bulgaria had sent the flower of their musical culture to Berlin. It is, of course, impossible for any of us to procure a score of the new work, owing to that curious kink in our legislators that makes them keep German music out of this country while letting German incendiary bombs in. I do not profess to follow their reasoning, but we have to bow to their decision. Such information as I have about the *Alpine Symphony* at present is derived almost entirely from Dr. Istel's long article, which, on the face of it, seems trustworthy enough. The work is in one movement, lasting a full three-quarters of an hour. It is, of course, scored for a very large orchestra, the composer demanding 'at least' a hundred and twenty-one players, among whom are to be twenty horns. We all know from experience what force attaches to Strauss's 'at least'; like *Salome* and *Elektra*, the new work, if it is to get any performances at all, will have to be content with much fewer instruments than a hundred and twenty-one. Strauss has not only employed once more our old friend the wind-machine of *Don Quixote* – how, indeed, could one describe the Alps without a wind-machine! The only wonder is that Strauss has not used an ice-cream freezer as well! – but has introduced a thunder-machine. Were the mad King of Bavaria still alive, he would no doubt complete the realism by taking the roof off and letting the snow in on the audience, as he is said to have let some tons of rain fall on the actors during the storm in the *Valkyrie*.

Dr. Istel sums up at the commencement of his article that the new symphony is 'one of the best of Strauss's works, though the conclusion is not on the same height as the rest, and some curtailment would do the work no harm'. Later on, however, it peeps out that the critic is not too favourably impressed by it. He praises its general painting of the Alpine *Stimmung*, and especially what seems to be a remarkable representation of a waterfall in music. But he shies at Strauss's excessive devotion to a detailed programme. Everyone knows Beethoven's *mot* as to his *Pastoral Symphony* being 'more an expression of emotion than painting'. Strauss's *Alpine Symphony* is apparently more painting than emotion. There is a remark in Beethoven's sketch book to the effect that any one who knew country life would understand the *Pastoral* without any finger-posts in the score. The score of the *Alpine Symphony* seems to be so full of finger-posts that I suspect before the tourist has had time to read the name on one of them he will be bumping into another. Here are the stages of the itinerary: 'Night: Sunrise: The ascent: Entry into the wood: Wandering by the brook: By the waterfall: A vision (or scenery; we cannot be certain, without knowledge of the score, of the precise meaning of *Erscheinung* in this connection): In the flowery meadows: Losing one's way in bramble and thicket: On the glacier: Dangerous prospects (views): On the summit: A vision: Mists creep up: The sun sets gradually: An elegy: Calm before the storm: Thunder and tempest: The descent: Sunset: All sound dies away: Night.' It would have only been a step further into the arms of the American symphonist who described in music a day in the country – the first movement representing the journey to the scene of the picnic, and the finale, which depicted the homeward journey, being simply the first movement played backwards.

However, the symphony may be no more dependent on sign-posts of the objectionable kind than other works of which the composers have not been as frank as Strauss in exposing their programmatic basis. The only thing in the work that can really matter is not the programme but the music. If this is bad, the programme will not save it; if it is good, it will take the programme up into itself and reanimate it. It is interesting to see, by the way, how the passion for musical illustration has grown upon Strauss in recent years. There is no rational objection to illustration *per se* in music; it would be folly to condemn a practice that has been followed, in one form or another, by perhaps four-fifths of the world's composers. It is no more absurd of Strauss to try to suggest the cracking of whips in *Elektra* than it was for Mozart to suggest the criss-cross of duelling swords in *Don Giovanni*, or for Elgar to suggest the tinkling of the thirty pieces of silver in *The Apostles*, or for Mendelssohn to suggest the hee-haw of the donkey in the *Midsummer Night's Dream* overture. The only question, in each case, is whether the realism is visibly foisted upon the music and remains an unassimilated excrescence upon it, or is taken up into and dissolved in the pure being of the music. The less 'external' the realism is, of course, the better; we may object to the wind-machine – except in humorous music like that of *Don Quixote* – but we cannot reasonably object to those suggestions of blinding or shimmering light in which Ravel and Stravinsky excel. A list of the natural phenomena that have been more or less successfully translated into tone would surprise, by its very length, the old-fashioned aesthetician who regards the sphere of music as touching at no point the spheres of the other arts. The truth seems to be that everything that music can do in the way of painting, even by a mere *tour de force* of orchestration, is legitimate if only it be embodied in an art-form of which the very essence is a simultaneous appeal to eye and ear. It is for this reason that a hundred things are right in opera that would be wrong in a symphony, and a thousand things right in a ballet that would be dubious in an opera. Strauss's flirtation with the quasi-ballet form in *The Legend of Joseph* may have been prompted by a feeling that the field for descriptive music is wide enough, but that it is irrational to expect full freedom for a composer of this bent in the purely instrumental, non-representative forms, in which the imagination has to do the work of the eye. But it seems to me strange that composers should still be so slow to recognize the possibilities of a form that would differ as greatly from ballet as ballet does from opera – the union of music and the cinematograph. The brain of a Fokine exercised upon the possibilities of the cinematograph would certainly open out a whole new field of beautiful suggestion. One ventures even to say, in advance of all knowledge of the score, that little harm could be done to such a work as the *Alpine Symphony* by playing it to the accompaniment of panoramic scenes, while the appeal of many portions of it might actually be deepened. But in the last resort, the one question still is the quality of the music. Dr. Istel apparently holds no very high opinion of it, apart from the brilliance and suggestiveness of the orchestration. The themes seem to be shorter than the generality of Strauss's melodies – a necessity, indeed, if a closely woven symphonic texture is aimed at. But Strauss has never been particularly successful in the management of fragmentary thematic matter of this kind, as was shown rather painfully in the *Symphonia Domestica*. It will presumably be a long time before the *Alpine Symphony* is given in England; but one hopes the time is not far distant when it will be possible to procure a score of it without 'trading with the enemy'.

BORIS GODOUNOV, 1916

I

MANCHESTER SHOULD be grateful to Sir Thomas Beecham for its month of opera in general, and for its introduction to *Boris Godounov* in particular. One's admiration for that work increases each time one sees it or plays through it: there are times when one is inclined to say that the discovery of it is the most important event in the musical history of Western Europe during the last decade. Sir Thomas Beecham is giving the opera in French. He may have no alternative at present, for the English tranlsation does not always fit the music very well, we have no English Boris, and in M. Bouilliez, who apparently does not sing in English, we have a Boris who, though lacking Chaliapin's extraordinary plasticity of face, is not only a fine singer but a capable actor. Still, I am afraid *Boris Godounov* will never disclose its full secret to the British public until it is sung in English. It was clear to me last Friday, for example, that only those who already knew the opera felt the full pathos of the Idiot's song. To the spectator who stands outside the opera and listens to it sung in an incomprehensible tongue, Moussorgsky's Idiot is simply the

English village idiot, with the tin kettle on his head and the straw in his mouth – a figure half silly, half comic. To anyone who knows or can hear the words, the character is what Moussorgsky meant it to be – a symbol of some of the saddest elements in Russian life and history. And I for my part – I cannot say whether other people saw it in the same way – felt all the evening that the Russian music and the French speech were here incompatible, and that precisely because the music is so *very* Russian. That is to say, the music and the characters so distinctly suggest the map of Russia that I cannot help wondering all the time why they are talking French. It may be objected that it would be equally anomalous were they to talk English; but that is not so. English being our ordinary medium of expression, it sets up in us no foreign connotations whatever music is sung to it; whereas any other language does. And as the connotations set up by *Boris Godounov* are, for the most part, so purely Russian, I have an uncomfortable feeling of disharmony the whole evening. Many people would have the same feeling if they were to hear *Pelléas et Mélisande* sung in German.

For some years I have been arguing against the fallacies that lurk in the cry of 'national music'. It may be thought, then, that in declaring *Boris Godounov* to be, for the most part, purely Russian, I am surrendering some of my own contentions. That is nor so, however. The case of *Boris Godounov* is really an argument in my favour. The main objection to making music an expression of 'the national spirit' is that it simply cannot be done, there being no such thing nowadays as a 'national spirit' in art or literature. A nation is made up of many intellectual and moral types, no one of which has the right to regard itself as 'the' nation. When some of us express this view we are asked the naïve question, 'But could such a work as *Die Meistersinger* have been written by anyone but a German?' The answer – an answer, I think, not lacking in comprehensiveness – is 'Yes' and 'No'. The *Meistersinger* might easily have been written by a non-German of genius who happened to have absorbed, and been absorbed into, the great German tradition, as the Fleming Beethoven was, or the Hungarian Liszt, or the Croatian Haydn, or the Jewish Mahler and Mendelssohn, or the Hungarian-Jewish Joachim, or the Styrian Wolf. But the *Meistersinger* could not have been written except by someone who had become German in this sense, whatever he may have been originally in the ethnic sense. Tradition, sympathy, environment count for more than mere race in art. 'National music' will become harder and harder to write as time goes on, and will eventually disappear, for the simple reason that travel and the easy access to scores and performances of the music of every nation will make of each composer not a mere German or Frenchman or Englishman, but a citizen of the world. The village pump may be a more immediate cultural influence than *Tristan* or *Pelléas* or *Boris*, but it will not be so intense or so durable an influence. In the seventeenth century a very little thing said in music by the man next door counted for more with an inhabitant, say, of Worcester than a stupendous thing said in music by someone in Paris or Leipzig; but that kind of world is gone, never to return.

In future the language of music will become more and more cosmopolitan for the very reasons that once made it 'national'. 'Nationalism' in music is like dialect in speech: the only means we have of detecting it, indeed, is by some peculiarity of melody or rhythm. Where these do not lie on the surface of the music it is difficult to 'place' any music with certainty. And national peculiarities in music originated, I imagine, much as dialects have done – a community shut off from other communities has developed certain oddities that could hardly be expected to persist except under the same conditions of isolation. How these oddities began it is difficult to determine. In language some of them may have been due to a peculiar racial formation of the organs of speech; but I imagine that the main reason for a whole district adopting a certain accent or burr is, in the main, merely unconscious imitation of a variety that has somehow come into existence. Thus even grown-up English people who have lived some years in America or Scotland unconsciously drop into an American or Scotch way of speaking. No one, surely, will contend that a 'national' trait in music, such as the little flick at the end of the tail of a Hungarian melody, came into being for the sole reason that there was something in the nature of the race that made it imperative that it should write melodies just in that way or die. I take it that what has happened is that at some time or other someone has hit upon this melodic turn, it has commended itself to other musicians, and has gradually become stereotyped like the inflections of the spoken language, or like the dress of the district. Or the melodic turn may have been motived in the first place by some peculiarity of rhythm or cadence in the popular poetry of the district; or, again, it may have been determined by the steps of some local dance. The oddities of a particular scale are clearly due, in many cases, to the limited resources of primitive instruments. Let us assume, for example, that the flute used in a given district has only four holes. From such a flute only a limited scale could be produced by the ordinary person. The constant hearing of such a scale would accustom the inhabitants of the district to thinking in terms of it; and so their melodies would come to exhibit the peculiarities of omission that we notice in a good deal of primitive music. I do not contend that *all* primitive scales are the result of such a process as this, but it is, at any rate, a conceivable process for some of them. The essential thing to note is that the oddities of 'national music' must all be capable of some such explanation. There must have been *real* causes for them: to attribute them to the spontaneous ebullition of a 'national character' is simply to use words that have no relation to reality. Once the oddity had become established it would exercise as rigid a sway over the inhabitants of that district as the syntax of their language; and as long as the community kept very much to itself, as primitive communities necessarily did, nothing could break the tyranny of the mode but a revolution from the inside. But a revolution from the inside, in view of the conservatism of all islanded communities, would be difficult. Children would be so accustomed to the 'national' trait from their birth that it would remain a part of their thinking for the whole of their lives, something no more to be questioned than the genders of nouns or the inflections of verbs. So strong would be the unconscious 'pull' of the peculiarity that people would impose it even upon melodies that were originally conceived without it. A communal mannerism is thus as tyrannical as an individual mannerism. How strong the influence of tradition can be in these matters is well shown by an anecdote that is told of Remenyi, the Hungarian violinist with whom Brahms toured in his adolescent days. Everyone knows the typical turn at the end of a Hungarian melody – the note above the tonic, the tonic, a double appoggiatura, the tonic again, the note below the tonic, and finally the tonic. This turn had bitten so deeply into Remenyi's musical being that he used to terminate the theme of the slow movement of the Kreutzer Sonata with it, thus converting it at once into a Hungarian tune. It is peculiarities of musical dialect of this kind that people generally have in mind when they speak of national music. It is by means of such local turns that they are enabled to recognize this melody as Hungarian, that as Russian, a third as Norwegian, a fourth as Irish; and so definite are the associations thus set up that by the use of these oddities of dialect clever musicians of other nations can write 'Hungarian' or 'Norwegian' tunes that no one can distinguish from genuine products of the country.

II

'Nationalism' in music is in the last resort dialect in music. As I have said, we can only be quite sure of it when historical and other circumstances have combined to fasten upon the melody or the rhythm of a country or a district a certain formula which, every time that we hear it, shall remind us of the map of the place. Yet, paradoxically, this clue is not a certain one. Precisely because the 'nationalism' is embedded in a formula, any clever person of another nation can use that formula just as he can don a foreign costume. It would not be difficult to cite examples of music of all sorts that had one national stamp and quite another national origin. The adherents of the nationalist theory, indeed, cannot come to the most elementary agreement among themselves as to what nationalism in music is. Let us look for a moment at the instructive case of Mr. Edwin Evans. It is only a few months ago that Mr. Evans' patriotic soul writhed within him at the thought that Englishmen were writing German music instead of English music. We should never achieve, he said, the Emancipation of Music in

England so long as people over here persisted in writing in an 'obsolescent [German] vocabulary that was never at any time a national medium of expression for English ideas. I once wrote', he continued, 'that an Englishman writing German music was as inexpressive as a Japanese in a bowler hat, and I am of the same opinion still.' That was the Mr. Evans of October, 1915. Now for the Mr. Evans of May, 1916. From a letter of Mr. Evans to the *New Statesman*, that has reached me through my press-cutting people, I gather that he has been in controversy with Mr. Turner, whose charge of anti-nationalism he repudiates. Mr. Evans, it seems, has written two 'Proses Lyriques' in French – because 'they just happened to suggest themselves to me in French'. These have been set to music by Mr. Goossens. I do not know the works, but apparently they are in a French idiom, and apparently Mr. Turner has pounced on that fact. Mr. Evans' reply to him is instructive. 'The texts being French, I venture to suggest that Mr. Goossens was indubitably right in giving them a French setting.' He protests against another critic having also objected to 'the Frenchness of the music', which Mr. Evans holds is the right thing under the circumstances.

I will not say much about the adaptable quality in Mr. Evans' patriotism that allows him to regard it as a crime in one Englishman to write German music, and a virtue in another to write French music. I will only remark on the instructive admission that an Englishman, if he is clever enough, *can* write 'French music' at will. After this delightful little exhibition the less, surely, that is said about nationalism in music the better. If Mr. Goossens' music to the 'Proses Lyriques' is really 'French', then on the nationalist principle it must be unnatural music – a Chinaman, say, in kilts. If it is good music, as Mr. Evans would no doubt contend, then nationalism obviously has not counted. What Mr. Goossens has done, apparently, is to make use of an idiom or an atmosphere that has become fashionable on the other side of the Channel during the last few years. He has flavoured his song according to the recipe, and no one, from the mere taste of it, could tell whether it had been made in Paris or in Peckham. Wherever it was made, it is French songs just as Worcester sauce would be Worcester sauce if it were made, from the same in-gredients in Wigan. Music of this kind is, in the larger acceptation of the term, dialect music. The composer talks with an assumed accent; he puts on a costume; and if he looks the part, and talks the part, I for one will have nothing to say against him in the name of nationalism. Better far that Mr. Goossens, or anyone else, should write good music in the French, the Russian or the Kamschatkan style than that he should write commonplace music in the English style.

The sole question is, not whether a musician shall derive his style from the parish pump or from an imported vintage, but whether, having derived it from one or the other, or from both, it is a style worth listening to, a style in which he can express himself easily and fully. And this, of course, implies the further and the vital question – has he a self that is worth expressing? The strong point in Moussorgsky's admittedly Russian style is not that it is Russian, but that it is Moussorgsky's. He talks an idealized dialect for a great part of his time; but this kind of dialect happens to be *the* medium for his particular kind of thought. With Moussorgsky it is not a costume that he has put on for the moment, but his very skin. That is why he never wearies us, as other practitioners of nationalism do: with him we are never conscious of theory, of artifice. We feel that he, at any rate, was God-guided when he made his idiom – or a large part of it – out of the folk songs of his district. For this idiom suited admirably most of the emotions he had to express, most of the scenes he had to depict. That it did not suit them all is evident from portions of *Boris Godounov*, as even partisans of the nationalist theory are compelled to admit. It stands to reason that precisely in so far as an idiom is penetrated with 'nationalism', it is unsuited to a *milieu* that lies outside the national. The folk-song theory, even with regard to Moussorgsky, breaks down as soon as we leave a special *milieu*. We are told that certain sections of *Boris Godounov* – the music of Boris' death scene, the love scene between Dmitri and Marina, Boris' aria in the second act, the hustling of the two Jesuit priests, as well as the people's welcome to the pretender in the first scene of the fourth act, and some of the Doume scene –

were originally composed for an opera based on Flaubert's
Salammbô, and afterwards adapted to the present work. Now,
some of these scenes are precisely those in which the Russian
element in the music is most pronounced, and rightly so; it is as
right that a Russian crowd should sing like Russians as that the
scene painter should give them a Russian landscape to sing in.
But just because this music suits the Russian characters and the
Russian setting so well, I cannot for the life of me see how it
could have suited the characters and the setting of *Salammbô*. I
cannot imagine Salammbô and Hamilcar and Matho in Russian
furs and talking with a Russian accent. Even in *Boris Godounov* as
we now have it, there are scenes in which the nationalist theory
comes to grief. The very qualities in Moussorgsky's idiom that
make it so congruous with Russia make it incongruous with lands
that are non-Russian – which is why the music of the Polish girl,
Marina, is relatively unsatisfactory. Here again, of two things one.
If only a Russian can write Russian music, then by parity of
reasoning only a Pole can write Polish music, and therefore
Moussorgsky is bound to fail when he tries to put Polish music in
the mouth of Marina. Or else, if this Polish music is a success, and
a Russian has made it so, then surely a Pole or a Bohemian or a
Breton could equally well write successful Russian music, and the
whole theory of the inevitableness of nationalism falls to the
ground. As a matter of fact, most people agree that Marina's music
is anything but a success, and that she is anything but a living
character. Here the national idiom that Moussorgsky tries to
exploit is merely costume, and a costume that sits ill on him. As
Mrs. Newmarch says, 'He (Moussorgsky) who penetrates so deeply
into the psychology of his own people, finds no better characterization of the Polish temperament than the use of the polacca or
mazurka rhythms. . . . The method becomes monotonous.
Marina's solo takes this form, and again in the duet by the
fountain we are pursued by the eternal mazurka rhythm.' But
Moussorgsky had no choice. If you write in an idiom that is free
from dialect, you can make all your characters talk what is
essentially the same speech, and yet differentiate them – as Othello
talks the same tongue as Iago and yet is different, or the Cornish

Tristan talks the same tongue as the Irish Isolde and yet is different. But once you begin to use dialect as a differentiating feature, you are compelled to use it to the end; and if you tell us to recognize a Russian character by his singing Russian music, you are obviously bound to make a Polish character recognizable by giving her Polish music to sing – which, in the very terms of the case, you, if you claim as a Russian to be alone qualified to speak for Russia, must admit that only a Pole can do.

The very strength of the folk song element in Moussorgsky, then, is also a weakness on occasion. There are other sections of the opera in which the dialect that is so effective in the case of the chorus is, by Moussorgsky's own practice, admitted to be inappropriate. The more complex the character, the less 'Russian' does it become, the less dialect does it speak. The method serves admirably for the crowd, the child, the nurse, the drunken monk; it does not serve for Boris, who talks a language as removed from that of the chorus as the language of Tristan is from that of a German folk-song. Is not the truth of it all simply this – that in Moussorgsky we have the chance association in a man of genius of a dialect idiom with an unequalled faculty for describing popular life – just the life with which dialect is most congruous?

No musician ever observed a crowd so keenly as Moussorgsky (it may be, of course, that a Russian crowd has more individuality, more colour, than a Western crowd), and for the expression of this crowd in music he found within himself an idiom that, in its curious reiteration of certain formulae, had in itself something of the psychology of the crowd – the same limited range of ideas, the same tendency to the repetitive. Wherever this reiteration of formulae within a narrow psychological range is justified – as in his mob music, his death music, his child music – Moussorgsky's dialect is a wholly adequate instrument of expression. But a sure instinct withheld him in the greater solo parts of *Boris* from using this dialect idiom in circumstances in which it would have been psychologically false.

GRANADOS AND HIS *GOYESCAS*, 1916

THE DEATH of Granados in the *Sussex*★ was the greatest loss the artistic world of Europe has sustained by reason of the War – and in saying this I have not forgotten the name of Rupert Brooke. The news of his death, and the excitement caused by it, were probably the first intimations most people had that Spain had an important school of music of its own. A few professional musicians knew something of the work of Albeniz, who figured in the ordinary music-lover's eye as musical Spain; but hardly anyone in England, except a star pianist or two and the people who came into contact with them, knew even the name of Granados. I myself am ashamed to confess to a very limited acquaintance with his music – an acquaintance, however, that shall be speedily extended. It was about three years ago that I met with the first set of his pianoforte *Goyescas* – a year or so, I should think, after their publication. Rarely has any new experience of mine in music been at once so immediately and so durably pleasurable. Many of us had begun to feel, with regret, that the days of great writing for the piano were over. At that time we knew nothing of Medtner, who has specialized upon the piano as truly as Chopin did, and who has developed a virile idiom and a system of pianoforte sonorities that are quite his own. Scriabine was becoming too insubstantial to satisfy us. Debussy had already shown that he had written himself out; we were tired of his pompous affectations of originality in his piano works, and equally so of the glittering futilities of Ravel. For these two – the Old Pretender and the Young Pretender – we had no further use; Granados came to us like a godsend. Here was a mind unmistakably original, that talked to us most fascinatingly of people and places we had never seen before; yet it was an originality that never lost itself in experiment, was always master of an orderly and logical speech, always realized infallibly in tone its own vision. Granados instantaneously exercises the subtle power over us that never fails to be exercised

★ Granados lost his life when the *Sussex* was torpedoed on returning from the U.S.A. on 24th March, 1916.

by the rare minds that even in their own day are at once romantic and classic – not only glimpsing new territories of thought and feeling but subduing them, giving passion new wings yet not launching it so far that it loses itself in the void, putting forth the maximum of energy of gesture and of eloquent facial play without for a moment ceasing to be graceful and beautiful. In none of the music of Granados that I know is there even the suspicion of a grimace, a shout, or a convulsion. All is smooth and strong and supple, the play of the big muscles just showing grandly through the velvet skin.

The most original mind must, of course, have had a progenitor. Granados derives ultimately from Chopin – that source as fecund for certain forms of life in modern music as the classical stream itself. Granados has expanded all the typical Chopin elements – the richly savorous harmonies, the melodic line that is at once tense and flexible – now making straight for its point like some irresistible projectile, now diverting itself with all sorts of caressing arabesques – the proud, nervous rhythms, the sense of ancestry and breeding, of an old and very refined civilization flowering to its very best in a last great scion. The texture of Granados' music, like that of Chopin's, is of the kind that makes you want to run your fingers over it, as over some exquisite velvet; the flavour of it is something for the tongue almost, as well as the ear. An exceedingly adventurous harmonist, he never writes a chord or a sequence that does not both sound well and talk continuous sense; to play through some of his pages is like a joyous wading knee-deep through beds of gorgeous flowers – always with a sure way through, and the clearest of light and air around us. I do not think there is any modern piano music that, for pure beauty and fullness of sound, can compare with his. Both Debussy and Ravel have exploited with extraordinary success some of the cooler or more metallic resonances of the piano; Scriabine has shown of what elusiveness it is capable; Medtner has blended both the thickness and the fluidity of its resonance – some of his music reminds us of a sturdy crag covered with glowing rock plants; but Granados' texture has almost every quality. His main bias, however, is towards an organ-like richness. I know no other piano music that so constantly has the resonance of four-hand writing. Yet it is all playable, though much of it is, of course, very difficult. A first-rate pianist himself, Granados solves with ease the most terrifying of the problems set to pianistic mankind by Providence's regrettable oversight in endowing it with only two hands. His writing is almost invariably that of the practical artist; it is only now and then that he is a little thoughtless, not so much as regards piano technique as in the matter of notation – he could have simplified the reading of page 22 of the first set of the *Goyescas*, for example, by writing it with the key-signature of E flat or G flat instead of in the open key with a perfect hail-storm of accidentals. He obtains superb effects of organ sonority by writing massed chords high up in the right hand, with rich harmonies sweeping up in arpeggios from the deep bass of the piano right to the treble. But he has every device at his fingers'-ends. At times the harmony will be skeletonized down to its bare essentials; but it is always just the essentials, for he has an infallible instinct for getting the richest possible effect with the fewest possible notes, simply by the feeling for the different sonorities of the same chord in different spacings. An excellent illustration of this faculty of his is to be seen in the passage commencing at bar 29 of the second of the first set of *Goyescas*. At the end of the first of the second set, again – 'El Amor y la Muerte' – he symbolizes the death of the majo with a couple of funeral-bell effects that are as cunningly calculated for the piano as the bell effects in *Boris Godounov* are for the orchestra. But the fascinations of the Granados piano technique are endless: one would like to talk about it by the column.

As everyone now knows, the *Goyescas* are based on certain etchings of Goya. Never before has an artist so profoundly entered into and coloured the soul of a musician. Other composers have played at taking pictures as the starting-point for their ideas; but in the case of Granados there has been not merely a stimulus of the musician by the painter but a complete penetration. Granados has made Goya's majo and maja part of his own flesh and blood; and he seems to have re-created not only a type but a period and a milieu. How completely these figures had taken possession of him is shown by the fact that they almost wholly engrossed his musical thinking during the last few years of his life. This obsession gave rise to two curious phenomena that are surely unique in the history of music. The first set of *Goyescas* (1912) consisted of four pieces, each of them descriptive of some episode in the life of the majo and the maja – the 'compliments' of the majo, the conversation of the pair through the grill, the fandango in the lantern-lighted barn, and the maja's outpouring of her soul to the nightingale in the garden. A strange and beautiful world of feeling surges across these pages – gaiety, pride, the sensuous joy of the dance, a noble and refined melancholy. It all seems to be born out of the South, as the music of Sibelius is born out of the mysterious lakes and forests of Finland. The *Goyescas* are not in any sense programme music. In their genesis and their development they are obedient only to the laws of music, not those of the picture; but all the same they create a singularly definite impression of certain beings in a certain environment. They were so real to Granados himself that he had to return to them, as one returns to a living household, in the second set of the *Goyescas*. The first of these – 'El Amor y la Muerte' – is a masterly fresh working of some of the old themes: they are taken now as accepted symbols, and made to play new parts, live out a new drama, like the leading-motives in the third act of a Wagner opera. Again there is no programme, yet the logic, one feels, is both that of music and that of poetry. Then came a further strange evolution of these ideas. Granados had a series of dramatic episodes written upon the etchings, the whole forming an opera that embodies the main scenes of these. To this opera he transferred bodily the greater part of the music of the pianoforte *Goyescas*. This was the work produced in New York a few months ago; Granados was on his way home again when the German assassin slew him, at the age of forty-eight. I have not seen the work on the stage, but I understand it was not a success, and I am not surprised. It is perhaps unfair to judge it in the English version, which is maddeningly inept, the verbal accents persistently falling on the wrong notes and giving the composer's syncopations especially a preposterous rag-time air. But even from my own limited knowledge of Spanish I should say that the fitting of words to the music has been a failure, and was bound to be so. These superb instrumental melodies and rhythms are only coarsened and lose most of their resiliency by being passed through the thicker medium of speech. The style, again, seems to me too purely pianistic to make good orchestral music; and I feel that the very unity of rhythm and colour that is so admirable in the piano works – silhouetting the types and painting the milieu as it does – must inevitably make for monotony in a stage setting. But the operatic work is still splendid stuff to play through at home; and here and there not only do the words give a new precision to the piano phrases, enabling us henceforth to play these with greater understanding, but we get the impression that in the pianoforte *Goyescas* Granados must have worked upon an unformulated but fairly definite scenario, and at one or two points – in the nightingale scene, the final love-duet, and the death of the majo – probably even conceived the music to actual words of his own.

WAGNER, DEBUSSY, AND MUSICAL FORM, 1918

I

SO FAR as I have observed, none of the English articles called forth by the death of Debussy – not even the ablest of them, such as that of Mrs. Newmarch in the *Contemporary Review* and that of Mr Edwin Evans in the *Fortnightly Review* – have addressed themselves seriously enough to what will surely be one of the vital questions for the musical historian of the future, the question of Debussy's form. By 'form', of course, I do not mean mere pattern, still less the ready-made suits, the musical reach-me-downs, that are sold in the conservatoires and given away with the text-books as 'form'. I mean simply the art of saying what you want to say, and indeed all there is to be said on the given subject, fluently, lucidly, and, above all, coherently and continuously. The difficulties of doing this will obviously increase with the scale of the work. A brilliant American critic, enthusiastic for Grieg and Franz and other exquisite miniaturists, will have it that mere size has nothing to do with the value of the work of art. But surely, though the cameo may be as perfect in its way as the cathedral, its way is a smaller way. The problems of symmetry, of the balance between the detail and the embracing whole, become much more difficult as the work of art spreads itself out further in space or in time; and humanity tacitly agrees to think the *Götterdämmerung* or Goethe's *Faust*, with all their imperfections, greater than a flawless nocturne or lyric.

In the reaction of composers and critics during the last decade or two against the grandiloquences of German music, there has been a tendency to lose sight of the fact that form, in the higher sense, is as vital a concern of the modern musician as it was of the classic. Form is to art what logic is to thinking: we simply cannot get far without it. For one reason and another, the greater German musicians of the last two or three centuries have given special attention to the problem of filling extended works through and through with this logic. They have not always succeeded, for coherency on a large scale is far more difficult to achieve in music than in any other art. It is relatively easy when the problem is simply the filling of a mould or the endless repetition of a decorative pattern, as in much of the work of Bach. It becomes harder when this pattern-working has to be combined with dramatic or pseudo-dramatic psychology, as in Beethoven, Wagner, and the modern symphonists, for here two very self-willed horses have to be run in harness. The result is that perfectly designed musical works on a large scale are exceedingly rare – there are only a symphony or two of Beethoven and an opera or two of Wagner, together with an odd movement or an operatic act here and there. I venture to think that the supreme master of form in music is not Beethoven or Wagner but Hugo Wolf. Nowhere but in Wolf do I find, in work after work, the perfect adaptation of means to end, not a note too few, not a note too many, the idiom and the mode of treatment always varying with the emotional subject, the music always working itself out from

the first bar to the last as if under the control of a logical faculty
that was never in the least doubt as to its aim and never swerved
from the straight pursuit of it. To some people this praise may
seem excessive; I can only say that this is my own conviction after
some fifteen years' study of Wolf. But Wolf's marvellous achievements were all on the small scale of the song: a composer who
could realize the same formal perfection in the symphony or the
opera would be the greatest master of musical form that the
world has ever seen.

It is perhaps because of an instinctive feeling that musical logic
on the grand scale is so exceedingly difficult that mankind
extends to imperfect musical works a tolerance it would never
dream of giving to, say, a piece of architecture of the same size
and the same incoherence. *Boris Godounov*, for example, is not
even a badly constructed building. It cannot even be called a
building at all: it is merely a collection of fragments that the
architect has dumped down near each other on the same plot of
earth, lacking even the ability to give them a factitious air of
coherence by joining the outer walls of one to those of another,
and running a corridor through here and there. Nothing was
more symptomatic of the lack of balance and basis in English
musical criticism than the assumption by so many of our critics,
in 1913 and 1914, that this and other Russian operas had made an
end of Wagner and his theories and ideals – that here was a new
musical value that annulled, as Nietzsche would say, all previous
values. The truth is that, so far as form is concerned, Wagner
began where Moussorgsky and the others left off. They would
no doubt have despised his later form; but they would have
despised it because they were incapable of grasping it. He was
speaking a language the subtleties of which they could not understand: he was away among the subjunctives of the irregular verbs
while they were pluming themselves, like children, on being able
to join a noun and the present indicative of a verb in exercise one.
So little had they of the root of musical logic in them that they
could not even distinguish between genuine logic and chop-
logic. For them, as for a good many composers and critics of our
own day, 'working-out' was merely a 'German' device, mostly

employed by Germans to give an appearance of 'development'
to their ideas, and in any case unsuitable for any but 'German'
music. There would have been the less to say in reply to this,
narrow of view as it is, had the Russian composers of the mid-
century succeeded in making a formal instrument for their own
music even approximately as good for 'development' as that of
the Germans. But they never managed to do so. The 'Invincible
Five' mostly showed an invincible feeble-mindedness wherever
form was concerned. Their operas, their symphonies, their
symphonic poems, their chamber music, are little more than
beautiful pearls badly strung. In comparison with Beethoven and
Wagner these men are no more than gifted children, visited with
beautiful and charming intuitions, but incapable of the subtler
co-ordinations, and quickly tiring at their play.

I think it would be much better to recognize frankly that the
constructive sense of Debussy also, so far as the larger forms are
concerned, was no more than that of a child, than to hint vaguely,
as Mrs. Newmarch and Mr. Evans and some smaller writers have
done, that a work like *Pelleas and Melisande*, if it does not actually
supersede the Wagnerian structure, at all events presents a structure comparable to it in its own way in value. For my own part,
much as I admire the imaginative qualities of the best parts of
Pelleas, I have never been able to see it, so far as regards its form,
as anything but a confession of artistic bankruptcy. Perhaps I am
harder to please than Mr. Evans; but with the best will in the
world I cannot see in the opera the invariably infallible touch that
he apparently sees in it. Debussy, he says, achieves his end (of
'letting his music reflect the moods of the characters in all the
fluctuations indicated by the text') 'with *unfailing subtlety* by the
simplest means, sometimes by no more than a couple of chords
whose only intrinsic merit lies in the sureness with which they
were selected. On every page there are instances of this.' Well, I
open the vocal score at random at pages 244-7; and so far from
either the method being subtle or the touch infallible, I cannot see
anything in either of them but what any musician of intelligence
could achieve with one hand tied behind his back. If the touch
were infallible, not a note could be altered without ruining the

tissue; but we could easily alter the vocal recitative in many ways, and substitute other chords in the orchestra for those of Debussy, without even a Debussyite who did not know the score by heart being able to detect the substitutions. It is curious, and quite amusing, that the school of criticism that is never tired of girding at Brahms for his padding should not have a word of condemnation for padding so egregious and so easy as this. Debussy has signally failed to achieve a consistent style for *Pelleas and Melisande*. The work is not musically *one* in the sense that *Tristan* is; it is no more than a collection of beautiful musical fragments held together by Maeterlinck's poem. Debussy has not solved the problem of operatic form; he has merely evaded it, bluffing his way through when the eternal difficulties became too great for him. He reminds us of the Scottish preacher who used to say: 'Now we come, my brethren, to a deeficult passage; and having looked it boldly in the face, we will pass on.'

II

Not being a believer in rooted and inalterable race-characteristics, I am not going to say that there is something in 'the French genius' that hinders it from erecting large and solidly built structures in music. It is the fact, however, that the French musicians have never shown much capacity for architecture on the great scale, especially in purely instrumental music. Couperin and Rameau may match Bach himself in some of their clavier miniatures; but they have nothing to set beside the vast imaginings of Bach in his organ works. French music has nothing to compare with the mighty formal structures of Beethoven, Wagner, or even Strauss. Berlioz had grandiose visions, but was rarely able to realize them. (César Franck I regard as a Belgian who worked in France.) In our own day we have seen the French composers insisting, to excess, as I cannot help thinking, on ideals that they regard as characteristically French. They pride themselves on their super-modernity. A devil's advocate might make out a case against them as being excessively old-fashioned in some respects. They cry 'Back to Rameau', forgetful that Rameau was Rameau because *he* 'went back' to nobody, but expressed himself in terms of his age. For two hundred years at least, music has been labouring anxiously to master the art of weaving great continuous tissues. It has longed to express all the fullness of life and thought: and it has known instinctively that such expression is only possible in the larger forms, where the thought can gather itself up page by page until at last it becomes a mighty river of life. By turning their backs on this development the French are deliberately restricting their capacity for expression. It is with their music as with their prose. How we all love that admirable French prose, the clarity of it, the certainty of it, the absence of sprawling effort in it; and yet how we tire at times of its calm poise, its short-breathedness; how we long for a more majestic surge in it, a broader sweep, a wider arc, a more ringing chest note, something of the music of the madder elements of the volleying winds in the great spaces of the earth! It is tradition – a tradition, certainly, of good taste, but none the less harmful – that keeps French prose so limited in rhythm. It is tradition in its most harmful form that has latterly kept French music so thin-chested in its emotional expression and so miniature in the matter of form. The composers have been trying to live up to a 'French' ideal. In other words, they have been slaves where they thought themselves particularly free. They saw only the German menace: they did not see that an artist is equally a bondsman whether his chains are forged abroad or at home.

French criticism, and the English criticism that has taken its cue from France, has been much to blame for accepting the theories of a little *cénacle* of French musicians without proper critical examination. Criticism has its academics as composition has: and a critic who prides himself on repeating none but the very latest aesthetic formulae may be essentially as petrified an academic as any teacher of the art of composition according to Brahms or Parry. The English public is just beginning to realize the truly academic nature of much of the criticism that has taken upon itself, during the last few years, to popularize the older Russian 'nationalist' composers. Instead of seeing the men of 1860 through the eyes of 1910, it lazily preferred to see them through the eyes of 1860; the propaganda on behalf of Moussorgsky and the rest of them has been, in large part, merely a *rechauffé* of that of Stassov and Cui – much as if Wagner were now becoming known here for the first time, and the propagandists were serving up to us selected opinions of Liszt and Bülow. But the English public has not yet realized that much of the critical theory that is now being used to buttress up the weaknesses of the modern French music is almost equally old-fashioned. I have read a great many French and Franco-English attacks on 'German form'. I have hardly seen one among them that indicated that the writer had brought his knowledge of German form up-to-date. The general stock-in-trade had been a few easy gibes at Brahms – as if Brahms were fully representative of German form! Even so acute a critic as Mr. Edwin Evans has not always been free of the *cliché*. In his excellent little speech at the French concert in Steinway Hall a fortnight ago, he said something, if my memory serves me well, to the effect that while the French mind was searching for something new, something personal in music, it had always been the failing of German music that it was too content with established forms – accepted moulds into which the thought could be poured with the minimum of trouble. (I am not, of course, attempting to reproduce anything like Mr. Evans' actual words. I am only phrasing his argument, a fortnight after, as I understood it.) But it has been precisely in Germany that the most serious efforts have been made, during the last hundred years, to break up the established moulds and create new ones. The revolution wrought by Beethoven in the symphony in his middle period was itself a very great one; and in his last quarters we see him making a titanic effort to achieve yet another form. It is singularly unfortunate that the theorists, in discussing modern symphonic form, should mostly get no further than Brahms, who merely extracted a few formulae from the Beethoven tissue of the middle period, and completely ignored the pregnant prophecies of Beethoven's later works.

Later there came the complete smashing of all German moulds by Wagner – a revolution in form to which there is no parallel whatever in the music of France. And with Wagner, as with

Beethoven, criticism is still half a century behind the times. The average Wagner biography is extremely copious for the earlier years and ill-informed as to the later. No biographer except Glasenapp seems to be aware that in his last years Wagner thought seriously of writing a symphony – but not a symphony in the older style. Here, as in the opera, he wanted to create a new form. His symphony would have been in one movement; and in place of the conventional system of theme-contrast he would haved aimed at a continuous melodic web. That is undoubtedly the model for the symphony of the future. Wagner had in him by instinct what Debussy never had – the desire for flawless logic in music. How clear-eyed he was in this matter we may see from a passage in one of his letters to Frau Wesendonck on the subject of *Tristan*. His 'most delicate and profound art' (of which he has been made conscious by his work on that opera) is 'that of transition'. He knows that a long musical discourse should proceed, like any other discourse, step by step, that each bar should grow organically out of the one that precedes it, and into the one that follows it; and he points with justifiable pride to the second act of *Tristan* as his 'highest achievement in the art of the most delicate and gradual transition'. 'The beginning of this scene portrays the most intense emotions of abounding life: the end, the holiest and deepest longing for death. There are the pillars; now see, my child, how I have woven a bond that leads from one pillar to the other. This, then, is the secret of my musical form – a form which, I boldly assert, embraces every detail with such harmony and clearness of development as hitherto has never been conceived.'

In face of facts like these, it really will not do to try to make out that the French, *qua* French, are all agog for contemporaneousness in music while the Germans, *qua* Germans, are content to lumber along, ass-like, with the century-old burdens upon their backs. Neither Beethoven nor Wagner succeeded in realizing the new form of which he dreamt; but at least they both had a sense that new forms were necessary. Debussy and his fellows have laboured under the delusion that form could be replaced by style, that the one thing to be sought after was *justesse* of expression.

Debussy in particular came, in his latter years, to a condition in which expansion of wing was rendered impossible by his incessant anxiety as to the sheen of his feathers. That the capacity for more extended tissue-weaving was not quite atrophied in him seems to me evident from the ballet *Jeux* – the finest work, I think, of his last period. Why he did not oftener trust himself for a long flight of this kind I cannot say; one wearies, in most of his other works of this period, of the tiny fluttering of the wings in the restricted little home-built cage, the perpetual preoccupation with the effect of the moment, the inability of the thought or the emotion to get into a decently long stride. It remains as true today as it ever was that the supreme art of composition is the art of transition. It need not be in the future the same kind of transition as in the past. The older technique of coherence, the product in part of musical lyricism, in part of the instinct for decorative pattern-weaving, will not serve for a music that, like Debussy's *La Mer*, leans more towards impressionist painting. But this kind of music will never be the equal of the older music until it achieves an equivalent technique of transition: we cannot endure for ever an art that resembles a series of lovely miniatures roughly pasted together to look like a big picture. And French music will not achieve such a technique as this until it realizes that 'style' is no more a French than a German or an Italian or an English monopoly, and that style without substance is hardly more than the grin without the cat.

VIII

CONTRIBUTIONS TO THE
NEW YORK POST
1924-1925

THE SPEED OF MUSIC, 1924

ONE OF the younger English musical critics, who has a comprehensive distaste for most composers except Mozart, astonished me a little while ago by writing this: 'All modern musicians play Mozart, in my opinion, much too fast. The habit produced by modern music of listening to blocks of sound makes one unconsciously liable to dash through Mozart and pass over all the exquisite detail. In order to fasten and sharpen our attention, it is necessary to play Mozart more slowly than it was customary even to play him in his own day.'

With this I find myself unable to agree, just as I was unable to agree with the two ladies on a London bus whose conversation I happened to hear the other day. We were going down Regent Street, and one of the ladies remarked how interesting the shop windows were. 'Yes', said the other, 'but they don't give you time to see them properly. They ought to run the buses slowly down Regent Street', regardless, I suppose, of the mere men who have no great interest in the shop windows, but are possessed only with a base utilitarian desire to get from one spot to another as quickly as possible.

The ladies were strangers to me. But I should not be at all surprised to learn that they were the maiden aunts of my young friend the musical critic. They, like him, evidently thought that when you had a good thing you could not linger too long over it. But I confess I cannot see how we should gain by playing Mozart, or any other composer, on the principle of the slow motion pictures. We might, it is true, be made, in this way, a little more conscious of the detail; but is detail, in itself, of such great account? It has to be there, and always is there in the finest work; but to insist overmuch on it is to destroy the picture as a whole. We merely substitute a lower intellectual interest for a higher one. It is interesting to have the manoeuvres of a couple of boxers slowed down by the cinema to such an extent that every detail of every movement, of every blow, is made clear; but is there the thrill in this that there is in the real thing?

We have, I think, to be particularly careful in this matter of the tempo of the older music, because speed is merely a relative, not an absolute conception. All agreed-on measurements, whether of time or space, imply a fixed standard. If there is no fixed standard, the same term will have different meanings for different people or different epochs. Now nothing can be more certain than that the twentieth century idea of speed is very different from that of the eighteenth century. As everything in the modern world goes faster than it used to do in the old, what our ancestors would probably have regarded as scorching seems to us little more than a crawl. The railway train, the motor car and the aeroplane have made what a hundred years ago would have been regarded as a dizzy speed, to us, quite a sober one. It appears to us of today positively incredible that people should ever have been run over by a horse-drawn cab.

Only a paralytic could achieve that feat nowadays; but we have only to look back a few years to realize that the most agile of us had then to put on the same speed to get out of the way of the horse-cab as we now have to escape the rush of the auto-mobile. Or rather it *seemed* the same speed. In truth it was very different. We skip out of the way of the automobile at twice the speed, at least, that we used to work up to avoid the horse-cab; but it seems no faster, because everything else in the street is correspondingly faster.

Apply these considerations to music, and you see at once that all our notions of the tempo of the older works have to be revised. What may have seemed a breakneck pace to a musician of the eighteenth century is probably only a canter to us. I am not urging that all old music should be taken prestissimo, but only that it should be translated, as it were, into the modern speed-language.

Mozart's or Haydn's normal pace, could we now discover it, would, I conjecture, be found too humdrum for us today; it would seem like jogging along in a 'growler' while the rest of the town was whizzing past us in Rolls Royces. And for old music of which the very essence is speed, music that was intended by the composer to convey in its own day a sense of gay adventure, with the pulse accelerated beyond the normal, we should surely adopt a tempo that is to the average speed-sense of today what the original tempo was to the average speed-sense of *that* day – that is to say, a tempo rather faster than our forefathers would have thought proper.

This need involve no sensation of hurrying, so long as the technique of the performers is clean enough to define everything as sharply at the quicker tempo as at the slower; and the technique of a first-class modern orchestra is certainly equal to this. The singers are in a different case. Partly from lack of technique, partly from ordinary human disabilities, they cannot move with the speed this new conception of the older music demands of them. Our singers may be better than those of a century or two ago in some respects; their musical sense is bound to have been deepened and enriched by the remarkable emotional developments of music since Beethoven. But the average of *agility* among them is certainly lower than it was a century ago. There are many old Italian operas that would probably be successful today in a thoroughly competent production – works like Rossini's *Il Signor Bruschino*, for instance.

But it would be difficult to get a cast together that could sing this kind of music at the pace and with the elasticity it demands. Even with the best technique, the average human larynx cannot hope to achieve the agility of the average violin. We were made very conscious of this in England a few years ago, when Sir

Thomas Beecham, who is an exceptionally brilliant Mozart conductor, used to try to play the more animated numbers of the Mozart operas at a speed corresponding to our modern notions of vivacity. From the orchestra he could get whatever he wanted, and the effect there was exhilarating beyond description. But the poor singers, struggling as they had to do with the knotty consonants of the English language, could not keep pace with him and the orchestra; they were like a cart-horse harnessed to a racer. Sir Thomas Beecham used to do the same thing with the quintet in the second act of *Carmen*; he gave us a pace so sprightly that I have never been able to tolerate the quintet under any other conductor. But again the singers, hustled as they were, acted as a sort of brake on the wheel.

I sometimes suspect that music *en masse* is becoming slower than it was in the eighteenth century and the early nineteenth. One of the things that puzzle us most in reading the criticisms of that period – Stendhal's may be taken as typical – is the Italian view that Mozart was 'too learned'. Music, it seems to us, could hardly go more nimbly on its feet than Mozart's operatic did. But we have only to compare it with Cimarosa's to see what the people of that day had in their minds. The Germans were too harmonic for a purely melodic race, as the Italians were then. Now music that is largely harmonic is always bound to be, in the main, less agile than music that is predominantly melodic. Mozart's wider range of harmony had the effect of slowing his music down relatively to that of the Italians, who were satisfied with fewer chords, that gave the melody more freedom.

A movement like the ensemble in Cimarosa's delicious little opera-ballet, *Le Astuzie Femminili* – one of the fastest things, surely, in all music – was beyond the powers of any German musician of the day, even Mozart. It is, indeed, to the Italian opera of the generation from Cimarosa to Rossini that we have to go if we want an idea of what sheer pace in music means. And the joy in and by and for itself, which can be as exhilarating in music as in motoring, will never come back into music until someone simplifies it harmonically. We poor mortals cannot have everything at once. If we want the intoxicating spin of the blood that comes with fifty miles an hour, we must give up the thought of enjoying the scenery. If we want the exhilaration of a pace like Cimarosa's or Rossini's, or Mozart's in some of his ravishing symphonic finales, we must surrender the delights of harmonic introspection.

Perhaps one of these days another Rossini will come, a healthy, joyous animal who will bother as little about modern problems of harmonic expression as Rossini bothered about the problems of Beethoven. If he does come, he will sweep the modern world as his predecessor swept the old; for to the man of today even more than to his grandfather, speed *qua* speed, is irresistible in its attraction. Meanwhile, let us see to it that Mozart and Rossini and the other light-footed ones of the past go at a pace appropriate to our altered modern conceptions of speed.

LETTER FROM A LADY, 1924

IN COMMON, I suppose, with the rest of my colleagues I have received the following letter from Mme. Lucrezia Bori:

'Dear Sir, – Pardon me for my seeming but innocent effrontery. We Spanish women are not in the habit of writing to newspapers, especially to take exception to criticism of our professional work. No one more than I respects the musical critics in their duties to the public. When I sing badly or act badly, certainly it is within their province to tell both me and the public so, provided they explain in simple language where and why I sang or acted badly and just how I should correct my faults.

'However, when my kind musical critics take me to task regarding my costumes, I reserve the right (even though I am not a Joan of Arc) to cross swords with them. Some of these critics took serious exception to my costumes as Giulietta, the Venetian courtesan, in the second act of *The Tales of Hoffmann*. I don't think I am mistaken in assuming that they all belong to the more serious or sterner sex. Such being the case, as a woman

H

I may be permitted to question their authority as arbiters of the feminine toilette.

'Consequently, to show that I bear no malice, I am prepared to give a nice little tea party in honour of the musical critic (male, of course), who will submit to me the best original sketch of a smart eighteenth-century Venetian courtesan's evening frock suitable to the scene in question.

'Of course, he must be honour bound to create this design without the aid, direct or indirect, sympathetic or unsympathetic – may I even say without the knowledge? – of his wife or sweetheart.

'Naturally, the musical critics of fashion journals are not eligible in the contest,

                    LUCREZIA BORI'

Nothing, I am sure, could have been further from Mme. Bori's thoughts than obtaining publicity. I must apologize, therefore, for inflicting upon her something so repugnant to her as a singer, and can only justify myself on the ground that her letter raises a question of some interest to opera-goers.

Let me, by the way, say that if critics there who were so abandoned as to 'take serious exception' to Mme. Bori's costume as Giulietta, I was not one of them. I am glad to say I did not notice it, which is a tribute to her singing, for it is my experience that a musical critic's preoccupation with a singer's costume varies inversely with his interest in her vocal art. I remember a French Tosca who, in the second act, wore a frock so tight and so diaphanous that when I came to write my notice on the performance I found, to my astonishment, that I had not the faintest recollection of how she had sung, or, indeed, if she had sung at all.

I confess my total inability to design a dress for a Venetian courtesan, not to mention that I do not know whether we critics ought to regard Mme. Bori's assumption of aquaintance on our part with such subjects as a reflection on our morals or a tribute to our charm. But there have been occasions when even I, a mere specimen of what Mme. Bori flatteringly calls 'the more serious or sterner sex', have ventured to have an opinion of my own as to the appropriateness of some detail or other in an opera singer's appearance. I have never been able to understand how rough and starving Russian peasant women always manage to look as if they had stepped straight out of a beauty parlour – judging from the evidence of the forest scene in *Boris Godounov* – or how Manon, in Puccini's opera, managed to tramp the rough prairie for all those weary miles in satin shoes without either hurting her feet or damaging the shoes; or how Wotan and Fricka, in the second scene of the *Rhinegold*, sometimes manage to have gold ornaments about them before the existence of gold is known to the gods – a point, by the way, upon which Wagner once expressed himself strongly in a letter to Hans Richter.

And while we are reforming opera from the sartorial standpoint, why should we not take oratorio in hand? Could anything be more absurd than Elijah in evening dress, or the Daughter of Zion in a transformation? Would not oratorio singers put more realism into their work if they were properly garbed? For my part, if I had the power I would insist on all oratorios being sung in the costume of the period – with a possible exception in the case of the *Creation*.

A NOTE ON PUCCINI, 1924

THE NEWS of Puccini's death would be received with especially melancholy interest in New York, where, no doubt, his new opera, *Turandot*, would have been produced as soon as possible. There seems, however, to be a little uncertainty as to whether the opera is quite finished. It would be a great pity if it were not; for it would have been interesting to see whether the new promise of his latest published work – the three one-act operas – was being fulfilled.

Puccini was evidently changing in the triptych; he was shedding a lot of his sentimental grossness and acquiring a fresh lightness and quickness of touch. One is inclined to believe that he deliberately experimented in the one-act form to cure himself of his tendency to prolixity and overemphasis. In the old days he would certainly have made full-length operas of both *Il Tabarro* and *Suor Angelica*, with the big scene of each – in the one case the revenge, in the other the revelation of the death of the nun's child – drawn out with the same deliberateness, the same slow, calculated piling of effect on effect, horror on horror, as in the second and third acts of *Tosca*. The one-act form not only forced concision on him but gave a new intensity to his expression: and of course he had developed greatly as a musician in the last few years.

His method of harrowing us in the crucial scene of *Suor Angelica* is precisely the same as in the final scene of *Tosca* – the maddening reiteration of the one slow, heavy phrase. But in the later work the obsession motive, as we may call it, is at once simpler, more direct and more poignant, it had to be, indeed, to permit of our enduring its being repeated so very many more times than the corresponding phrase in *Tosca* is.

There were always two strains contending for mastery in him. There was the Puccini who dipped his thumb into the paint and drew with the thick of it, and the Puccini who was a masterly miniaturist. The two Puccinis are to be found side by side in all his works, but most of them show a decided predominance of the one or the other. *Tosca* is almost throughout gross, thick-fingered, thick-lipped, while *Madam Butterfly*, apart from the rank sentimentality of the love music, is the Puccini of the lighter touch. There are beauties and poignancies so exquisite in *Madam Butterfly* that we can hardly savour them properly in the theatre; they belong rather to chamber music. We have always to distinguish between Puccini the dramatist and Puccini the musician. His knowledge of stage effect has become a commonplace of criticism. But his musical art is generally at its grossest when he is planning these theatrical knock-down blows. The musician that musicians prefer to think of is the Puccini of the more delicate moments of *La Bohème* and *Madam Butterfly*, and, above all, of *Gianni Schicchi*.

It was this last work, more than anything else, that made us feel that a new Puccini was beginning to realize himself. His Bohemians are all charmingly handled; but, to say nothing of the pathos of their darker moments, there is about them even in their gayer moments a wistfulness that is hardly consistent with comedy. But in *Gianni Schicchi* we get the genuine comic spirit both in the play and in the music. It has been said that Puccini derives from Massenet in his lighter moods and from the early Verdi in his moods of sentimentality and brutality. But he himself put this distinction out of court when he gave us *Gianni Schicchi*. That delightful work comes from a truly Italian, not a French, tradition.

The finest flower of this tradition is Verdi's incomparable *Falstaff*; but *Gianni Schicchi* comes a good second to it. Here, as in *Falstaff*, we get the authentic musical language of comedy, easy on the lips, polished of accent, and always suave to the ear. And that Puccini himself was conscious of a new orientation in him is shown by his treatment of the familiar idiom of Italian opera lyricism in the song about Florence and in the appeal of Gianni Schicchi's daughter to him. Puccini here plays all the accustomed Italian tricks on us, but without any desire to take us in; he is all the while smiling at them and us and himself. He had outgrown these little personal and racial nonsensicalities, but he still turns a kindly and tolerant eye on them, and caresses them even while he is ridiculing them. At sixty, seemingly, Puccini was not only changing but developing, as Verdi did at about the same age, winning his way into a clearer air. We must wait for *Turandot* to see what further changes went on in him as a musician between sixty and sixty-five.

TWO OPEN LETTERS UPON THE SEASON AT THE METROPOLITAN OPERA HOUSE —PERFORMANCES FROM THE POINT OF VIEW OF THE VISITING CRITIC AND THE MANAGEMENT, 1924

Dear Newman, – By this time you must be pretty well fed up on literary communications from persons more or less associated with musical activities in our little old New York. You must at least be impressed with the itch for writing that seems to be epidemic in our musical circles. I think, therefore, that you can understand my hesitancy in adding to the accumulating contents of your waste-basket.

Well, my dear boy, as we were both born under the Union Jack, though I am quite an old, while you are a new, importation into this land of liberty and free speech, perhaps you will indulge me as a former (may I say?) neighbour, as we started life with the Irish Sea between us.

You, perhaps, know that I am associated with an institution known as the Metropolitan Opera Company in a certain non-descript capacity. I don't know exactly what I am in the institution – publicity secretary seems the most dignified title – in vulgar parlance, press agent.

My status thus being established, you may take me in a Pickwickian sense or otherwise, when I tell you frankly – but understand me not officially – that you have certainly spanked us good and hard since you arrived in America to record your impressions of operatic and other musical events in New York. I would be the last one to say that, from time to time, your 'observations' on some of our performances have been unreasonable. But, my dear old man, there have been times when – let me say it frankly – I think you have been hardly fair to the opera management in its serious and honest endeavours to provide our very exigent public with the best that physical conditions and available human elements can in these days furnish.

It is a long time since I have seen any operatic performances in England, and I am not in a position, personally, to compare operatic productions in the British capital with those of the Metropolitan. I cannot, personally, pass upon the dramatic judgment effectiveness of the Italian operas given in Covent Garden in recent years. I do not know whether the caperings of the Bohemians when Puccini's opera is given there are more veristic than the play-acting of our artists; or whether your Andrea Cheniers sing to the audience instead of addressing the Revolutionary Tribunal. I do know, however, that the spaces of the Metropolitan Opera House certainly are larger than those of Covent Garden, and that in these Italian operas and others, if the singers do not to some extent diverge from the strict requirements of artistic stage management, the people in the gallery and in the back of the house would hear very little of the voices for which they paid their good money to hear.

However, old man, all this is merely *en passant*, and I am sure you will take it in the spirit in which is it written. Even though you do not spank us and find fault with things that I am sure you would easily pass over if you knew all the difficulties latter days have brought (even in America) to the production of opera, to meet the present demand in New York – to the organizing of a season of twenty-four weeks in which we are compelled to give seven, eight and nine performances a week – never repeating an opera on subscription nights (for unlike European opera houses, where subscribers are willing to hear the same opera half a dozen times, here our subscribers would raise a howl if they were compelled to hear any opera a second time) I am quite sure you would be less caustic in some of your comments on our evening entertainments if you could spare the time to drop into my office and see 'how the wheels go round'. I am certain that the last thing you would find would be 'Anarchy'. I have had the honour to be on Mr. Gatti-Casazza's staff for fourteen years. If he is an 'Anarch' then 'Anarchy is Heaven's first Law'!

Finally, in order to square myself, let me add that while I think you have occasionally given the Metropolitan Opera a bit of a tough deal, I am quite with you on the transitory quality of the jazz craze and the illusion as to the value of so-called 'national' opera and music. After all there are only two kinds of music – good music and bad music. The one survives and the other doesn't. And there you are!

Fraternally yours,

William J. Guard.

*   *   *

My Dear Guard, – I suppose that, however clearly one may try to express oneself, somebody or other is sure to misunderstand one. Perhaps, therefore, I ought not to be surprised at your reading into my recent innocent remarks on the subject of opera in New

York an invidious comparison between the Metropolitan Opera House and Covent Garden. A glance at my articles, however, will show you that no such comparison was made or intended. It would be impossible, for you cannot compare the existent with the non-existent. International opera – that is to say, opera of the kind that we now get at the Metropolitan and used to get at Covent Garden – is virtually extinct, for economic reasons, in the latter place. The last great season in London was in the months that preceded the war in 1914.

In that year we had a short season that was an attempt, under very difficult circumstances, to revive an old institution in a greatly changed world. The season, in spite of one or two striking performances, was not a success. We had no more international opera in London till the summer of this year, when a season was hastily patched up to meet a contingency that had suddenly arisen. We had a few pretty good performances of the *Ring* and *Salome* and *Ariadne in Naxos*, some first-rate performances of the *Rosenkavalier*, and a few mixed performances of the staler Italian operas. The 'grand season' in London seems to be a dead institution. The London public in the past did not mind paying high prices to hear the stars; but it refuses now to pay star prices and not get the stars – who, indeed, do not appear to exist now.

You will see, then, that my criticism of the Metropolitan way of giving opera was not prompted in the least by any vainglorious feeling that we have a better way in London. As a matter of fact, public opinion in England is slowly but steadily moving away from foreign opera towards opera in English. The desire is becoming intense to have a genuinely national opera, on the lines of the big Continental cities – opera sung not by birds of passage, in all sorts of languages that the people do not understand, and at prices that a heavily taxed people cannot pay, but by English or English-speaking singers. The British company that Sir Thomas Beecham ran during the war showed us in England what could be done in this way. Few of the singers had voices that would permit them to rank as stars in the big international theatres; but by dint of their constantly playing together under a man of genius who was competent to supervise every factor of opera, we got an ensemble not merely of singing but of action, of psychology, of scenery, of production, that made the performances extraordinarily interesting and enjoyable. Opera became something that a man of intelligence could listen to with his whole intelligence, not merely with his ears. But unfortunately Sir Thomas Beecham could not continue his good work. His company was wrecked; and we are now trying to rebuild the ship and re-man the crew.

I go into all this because I should not like either you or my New York readers in general to think I had been guilty of the crude impertinence of coming here as a guest and arrogantly telling New York it is inferior to London. Quite the contrary. We have nothing in London just now as good as the Metropolitan. My argument was that, with its human material and its financial resources, the Metropolitan could easily be very much better than it is. If I say that I have been somewhat disappointed in the singing as a whole, purely *qua* singing, that is hardly a disparagement of the Metropolitan. Of those I had not already heard I had perhaps been led to expect too much from report. The plain truth is that as regards great opera singers the whole world is rather in a backwater at present; but that is not the fault of the Metropolitan–though everyone who knows anything of the singers of today could mention one or two who would be an improvement on some of those we are hearing this season in New York.

My criticism of the Metropolitan performances was, in the main, this – that they seem to indicate a lack either of the power or of the will, on the part of those in authority, to impose that authority upon the singers, to rid some of these people of the quaint notion that nothing matters in the opera of the evening but themselves and their voices, and to make them realize that they are only parts of a dramatic whole. I went into this question in some detail in my previous articles, and I will not inflict it upon my readers again. I would only say that not only do you not refute me, but you actually agree with me. You do not attempt to deny the truth of my criticisms; you only say, in effect, that things are as they are because of the difficulty of making them any different. May I remind you that *qui s'excuse, s'accuse*?

You do not deny, for example, that some of your singers commit that first and greatest sin against operatic art – stepping out of their dramatic characters to face the house (in some cases even to approach the footlights) and addressing the audience directly. Your excuse is that the Metropolitan is so large that only thus can they make themselves heard. You are surely not serious. If there were anything in what you say, we should find the whole company, in every opera, lining up to the footlights to sing. But many of the singers manage to make themselves heard perfectly without coming out of the dramatic picture; and if these can do so, why cannot the others? The plain truth is that they could, but will not. They care little for dramatic truth; they are vain of their voices and want applause; to get it they will stop at no inartistic trick; and instead of having their errors pointed out to them and being bidden to correct them by those in presumed authority over them, they are, if we may take your letter at its face value, actually encouraged in them. I have sat and wondered how some of the things I saw and heard were made possible. Now I know.

The only other feature of your letter that calls for a reply on my part is your appeal *ad misericordiam*. You ask us to take into account your internal difficulties and troubles. With all possible sympathy, we cannot. Neither the press nor the public has anything to do with the private difficulties of an artist or an artistic institution. The press and the public are concerned solely with results. You yourself would be the first to refuse to take a workman's difficulties into consideration when purchasing the product of his work; if, for example, you were asked to buy a pair of shoes the soles of which were badly fitted to the uppers, you would reject them even though you were assured that the trouble came from the shoemaker having injured his hands at baseball. If you were viewing an exhibition of pictures, you would not regard it as any excuse for a piece of bad colouring that the artist's wife had left him. If, at a recital, a pianist pedalled badly, you would not, on being told that he suffered from an ingrowing toe-nail, declare that his pedalling was ideal.

Ernest Newman

IVOR STRAVINSKY AND HIS WORKS, 1925

IT WOULD be interesting to be born again about the middle of the next century, to see what the historians of music make of the case of Stravinsky. Never, surely, has any composer attracted such universal attention on the strength of so little vital achievement. At the age of forty-two and a half he has to his credit – what? Some youthful works of no great importance. Two small works of genius, *L'Oiseau de Feu* (1910) and *Petrouchka* (1911). An uneven but often remarkable opera, *The Nightingale* (1914), that forms the basis of the orchestral piece of the same name. A work still more remarkable at its best, but also still more uneven, *Le Sacre du Printemps* (1912). Since 1914, mostly a succession of failures and half-successes: *Mavra*, *L'Histoire du Soldat*, and a number of small instrumental pieces and songs with an occasional charming little thing like *Renard* and an interesting work like *Les Noces*, that, however, is too purely Russian to capture the musical world as a whole.

Since *Le Sacre du Printemps* and *The Nightingale*, in fact, he has done next to nothing that, had it appeared under any signature but his, would have drawn the general attention to him. And all this at an age when Mozart and Schubert and Chopin and Mendelssohn and Purcell and Weber were dead, when Schumann's work was finished, when Hugo Wolf's work was finished, when Strauss had to his credit such permanent contributions to the world's repertory as *Don Juan*, *Tod und Verklaerung*, *Till Eulen-spiegel*, *Zarathustra*, *Don Quixote*, *Ein Heldenieben*, *Salome*, and a number of songs and smaller works; an age when Beethoven had written seven of his symphonies, *Fidelio*, the *Leonora No 3*, *Coriolan* and *Egmont* overtures, all five of his piano concertos, his violin concerto, all his quartets but the last five, all his trios, and all his piano sonatas except the last five or six; an age when Bach had written a large number of works that are still very much alive, including the first set of the '48', the 'St. John Passion' (he was forty-four when the 'St. Matthew' was written), and the Brandenburg Concertos.

I am not making any comparison between Stravinsky and these

other composers. I am only pointing out with what a meagre quantity of notable work (for a man of his age) he has managed to focus the attention of the whole musical world upon himself for so long.

What is the secret of it? *Le Sacre du Printemps*, surely; and not so much that work itself as the controversy that has raged over it. It started out with an extraordinary piece of good luck. It was first produced in Paris, and there was almost a riot in the theatre. Those of us who know Paris know that this really meant nothing. In no town in the world do people make so much fuss about so little where art is concerned. In London or New York or Dresden, if a work that is out of the common is given for the first time, people either like it or dislike it, but they do not break out into physical violence over it either way. But in Paris, the most conventional city in the world, there is a venerable tradition that tradition must be made war upon.

There is nothing so conventional as youth; it says and does the same things at the same age in every epoch. In Paris the young artists who are the unconscious victims of this hoary convention are always looking for some new convention to protest against. In the early years of this century almost the whole world was beginning to weary a little of the music of the great classical period of about 1700 to 1900 (not one person in a million knows anything of the magnificent music of the sixteenth and early seventeenth centuries), and longing for something new, something less romantic, less emotional. A few people in Paris decided that Stravinsky was the new man, and *Le Sacre du Printemps* the beginning of the new era. It was to them what Victor Hugo's *Cromwell* was to the generation of 1830. The people who were shocked at the *Sacre* thought it necessary, in face of the shouts that were being raised for it, to shout even more loudly against it. So there was a charming scene that night in the Théâtre des Champs Elysées; heads – or at any rate hats – were broken; and the *Sacre* was launched with a réclame that falls to the lot of few works.

Then the inevitable happened. There is always a certain number of people who make a point of being in what they regard as the van. The *Sacre* became their slogan. European critics who would have laboured in vain to get much of a hearing for themselves by writing about music in general made quite a reputation for themselves for a time by taking Stravinsky under their protection. They assured the world, without any false modesty, that they were the pioneers, the men with the future-piercing vision, and anyone who did not say what they said was a reactionary. That made it easier still. Few people can stand being called reactionaries; it hurts their self-esteem. They never think of inquiring into the meaning of the word, or its applicability to the case in point: they see the cat jumping, and the herd instinct prompts them to jump with it. So quite a pretty legend grew up around the *Sacre* in every country that had not heard it, or, having heard it once or twice in 1913 or 1914, had forgotten it during the long years of the war. The legend was that this was the most remarkable work our generation had heard, or was likely to hear unless Stravinsky himself happened to surpass it: there had at last been what Nietzsche would call a transvaluation of values.

Such a legend could exist only so long as the *Sacre* was neither published nor performed. As soon as it became generally accessible and audible it began to be recognized that it was a work of very mixed quality. It was absurd to talk of only the future being able to grasp it; there was nothing in it to puzzle any musician. It was simply the Stravinsky of *Petrouchka* developing a step further, with all the former Stravinsky's excellencies and limitations. His musical gift is really a rather small one. Left to himself he can invent comparatively little that is vital, as we can see in the new piano concerto. For his best thematic material he has always been largely dependent upon Russian folk-song or popular song, as in *L'Oiseau de Feu* and *Petrouchka*, where the best tunes are not his own. His limitations are many. His qualities are few but remarkable. He has brought a new psychology into music – the psychology of the primitive soul. He has created a texture entirely his own; and we can never weary of admiring the superb certainty of his orchestration.

How then does the *Sacre* stand today? The novelty of it has worn off. A good deal of its first effect was purely physical: it was impossible to sit unmoved under that torrent of sound; the mere noise in certain parts set up a profound disturbance in us. But this effect could not last: the time was bound to come when we were no longer to be shaken by the sound purely as sound, but sat through it calmly and examined the value of what was being said. Perhaps one-third of the work, we now see, is first-rate: the voice of the primitive world itself, harsh, powerful, menacing, speaks through this music. But a great deal of the music has all the familiar faults of the Russian nationalist school – the short-breathed phrase, the limited mental outlook, the endless, tiresome repetition of the same little figures. The section entitled 'Augures Printaniers: Danses des Adolescents', begins magnificently – what power there is in the mere rhythm! – but it soon lapses into the usual Russian triviality. That incessant repetition of the same figure is the mark of the savage or the child in music. The whole evolution of music in Europe has meant getting away from this kind of thing, and learning how to talk connectedly and organically in tones; and the clock will certainly not be put back by Stravinsky and his primitive methods.

Several of my friends were disappointed with the performance we had of *Le Sacre du Printemps* the other evening. I ventured to suggest to them that it was not that the performance was not as good as some previous one they had heard, but that the work itself impressed them less – that they were, in fact, unconsciously discovering its frequent commonplace. This is an experience I myself have more than once gone through in connection with other music; it takes us a little time to realize that we have hitherto overestimated a work, and so we naturally assume, when the first disillusionment comes, when the accustomed thrill fails to arrive, that it is the performance that is at fault. I never had much opinion myself of the section entitled 'Rhondes Printanières' (after, that is to say, the first few bars of the *sostenuto e pesante*, the rhythmic effect of which is superb). But though the later handling of the theme made no appeal to me, as music, in the score, I used to be, if not impressed, at any rate thoroughly shaken, by the effect of it in the concert room.

The other evening, however, I was not even shaken; the effect had been from the first a purely physical one, and my nerves

decline to respond to it any longer. I fancy that as time goes on a
good deal of the *Sacre* will cease to move us for the same reason;
but if that means the passing from the repertory of the work as a
whole we shall all be sorry, for there is some splendid stuff in it.
But what has become of the Stravinsky who wrote the *Sacre* in
1912? To pass from the best parts of this to the new piano concerto is to feel that in declining from the ranks of genius he has not
even, like Mendelssohn or Strauss in similar circumstances,
remained a talent, but has overshot the mark and become a
mediocrity.

IX

THE SPIRIT OF THE AGE

(From the *Fortnightly Review*, 1930)

I

TO DESCRIBE, as I am expected to do, 'the general characteristics and tendency' of the music of the day in a single
short article is a difficult, if not impossible task, for the international field is wide, the tendencies are manifold, and the general
situation changes every few years. Moreover, it is anything but
easy to make some of the technical points clear without the liberal
use of the musical quotations. This article, however, is intended
not for the expert but for the general reader, to whom I will
explain as best I can the change that has come over the face of
music during the last two decades or so, and the reasons for the
change. But I feel that I am writing this article a mere matter of
three hundred years too soon. An eminent German musician,
Alfred Lorenz, who has devoted himself particularly to investi-
gating the laws that control both the course of musical history
and the operations of the individual musical mind, has given us
the soundest reasons for believing that a radical change in the
orientation of music comes about at the end of every three
centuries. Every student knows that a face-about of this kind
happened at the turn of the sixteenth and seventeeth centuries,
when the polyphonic style that had been the goal of musical
endeavour for some three hundred years was rejected in favour of
a homophonic style, that found its first outlet in the Florentine
opera. On Lorenz's theory, another revolution was due about
1900; and it is from approximately the beginning of the new

225

century that the change dates of which the whole musical world
is now feeling the effects. It is quite an error to attribute this change
to the war. The main forces had been at work long before the
war; they were rooted in the very nature of the art, were basic
elements in the great secular cycle; and the contribution of the war
and the subsequent peace to the disturbance was really so slight
that the historian of a hundred years hence, surveying the field
and trying to trace the laws that underlay the course of events,
will probably dismiss these influences in half-a-dozen lines.

No man can foresee the future of music even for a generation.
But we can learn something by a study of the past, for, on the
principle that Nature never does a thing merely once, we may
anticipate that, *mutatis mutandis*, history will repeat itself, and that
both the theories of the present time and the works written in
conformity with them will have little enduring value, but will
mostly be the mere historical curiosities that the music and the
speculations of the Florentine Camerata of 1600 are now. I shall
return to this point at the end of my article.

II

An art, like a civilization or a community, develops its maximum of efficiency by the suppression of certain internal forces
for the benefit of others, and collapses when the suppressed forces
can no longer be held under. Artists who are working under the
same general influences and are inspired by the same general
ideals come to a tacit agreement to concentrate on certain elements
and to pass over others. It is the law of the line of least resistance;
the problems to be solved by any given artistic *genre* are so many
and so complex that the human mind instinctively simplifies its
problem by ignoring everything but the essentials of it. It took
Europe at least two centuries of concentrated effort to develop the
art of polyphony to the perfection it had attained by the end of
the sixteenth century. But polyphony had not annihilated the
other main elements of music; it had only driven them under-
ground, and the time was bound to come when they would force
their way upward and disrupt the musical polity that had kept

them in subjection. This point needs to be grasped at the outset if we are to understand the meaning and the reason of the musical revolution of today. Vocal polyphony attained its marvellous solidity and complexity of texture at the expense of certain other elements of music. The life of music, like life in general, is a constant struggle between opposing principles; and musical history in future will probably be written from this standpoint. Music is perpetually distracted by the fight of two basic elements for mastery. We may call them, roughly, the song element and the formal element. The former tries to realize itself by means of a point-to-point expression of human emotions that have their correlatives in words. The latter aims at the organization of the musical mass into designs that exist in virtue of their own inner life. Each element, if it is not checked, will tyrannize over the other. On the one hand we will get 'poetic' music that is so intent on following emotional suggestion that the inner structure of the work becomes weak: the symphonic poems of Liszt may serve as illustrations. On the other hand we get music that is a model of formal organization but expresses next to nothing – as in the case of an academic symphony or fugue.

I cannot pursue this principle here in all its ramifications. My present purpose is merely to show how the principle operated in musical history three hundred years ago. The vocal polyphonists achieved their marvels of weaving and structure by ignoring, in the main, the 'poetic' side of the musical impulse. The Florentine reformers revolted against polyphony because, as they said, the sense of the words was lost in it. Why sing words at all, they asked, unless you mean the sense of them to be caught; and how can you catch their sense, or even their essential accent and rhythm, when four or five voices are singing different words at the same time? The words, and the inner life of the words, had necessarily been sacrificed in order to obtain a musical mass that existed in virtue of laws of its own – the skilled weaving of part with part, the entrancing play of contrary rhythms co-operating to the one architectural end. The Florentines threw all this overboard to concentrate on the rights of the words and what was meant by the words; their ideal was a melodic line that 'expressed' the words supported on simple harmonies that gave an added emotional intensity to both the words and the melodic curves and accents and dynamics generally. Their immediate success showed that their reform was not peculiar to them, but was in the air of the time; a long-suppressed element in music was determined to come into its own again.

III

The revolution of 1900 was also the revolt of certain suppressed elements against others that had had power too long in their own hands. The revolters attacked both the ideals and the language of the current art. The two, indeed, were part and parcel of each other; neither could be undermined without the other collapsing. Instinctively obeying that law of the line of least resistance to which I have called attention, composers for many generations had put aside many of the theoretic possibilities of the musical language in order to make a thoroughly serviceable instrument of the remainder. There are twelve notes in the scale – the seven diatonic ones that make up the octave (the final note of the octave not being counted separately), and five chromatic notes. The basis of the composers' thinking was diatonic; there are a few fundamental chords that form the plasm out of which the whole of music, as we knew it until yesterday, was evolved; even chromaticism in its subtlest form (Wagner's *Tristan* is the great historical landmark in this respect) is only a subtilization of the diatonic, the chromatic harmonies being derived from the diatonic by greater and greater sophistication of the fundamental relations between the original seven notes and their five dependents. On this foundation was built, in the course of generations, a language and an art that seemed to be equal to the expression of any musical idea that the mind of man could conceive.

But its very perfection bore within it the seeds of its decay. About the end of the nineteenth century it was visibly crumbling, both internally and externally. The language had become so complete and so perfect that it was too easily manipulated; and the great men of the romantic movement had sunk so many wells into the depths of emotion that any number of small men could now, with the minimum of individual effort, pump up something that, if not examined too critically, was a very fair imitation of the real thing. Emotional expression in music had become too easy; the more adventurous minds turned with contempt from it, seeking for an expression that would give them the thrill that comes only from conflict with a substance that has to be subdued before it can be worked in with any pleasure. Simultaneously the old tissue of the language of the art was breaking up. There was really no reason, in the nature of things, why the twelve notes of the scale should for ever live together under the constitution, so to speak, that had been imposed on them. Was not another constitution possible? The great classical and romantic composers must have had intuitions of some of these other possibilities, but they refrained from exploring them; for their instinct told them that an artist will not get very far if he ventures on the experiment of making a new language as he goes along. If the mind is to work easily, it must take a great number of things for granted. But some of the smaller minds, which are always more inclined to the speculative than the great instinctive minds, were long ago questioning the finality of the accepted relationships between the notes of the scale; and it was only a matter of time before some man of genius would show the possibility of other relationships. Glinka hit upon the whole-tone scale about 1840; Liszt sketches it as a curiosity in a letter of 1860. In the process of time, Debussy took it up and worked it systematically; and with the coming of the whole-tone scale a new chemical factor was introduced into the musical language that was to lead to the gradual disintegration of it as musicians had hitherto conceived it.

Let me here explain, for the benefit of the lay reader, that the two crucial divisions of the scale in the older system – known as tonality – are at the fifth and the fourth. These divisions determine tonic, dominant, and subdominant harmony, and therefore, of course, all the chromatic subtilizations of these. Abolish this traditional division of the language of music into three main tonal relations – those of tonic, dominant, and sub-dominant – and the fabric already begins to crumble. The whole-tone scale does abolish this distinction, for now the octave is not made up of five full-tone intervals plus two half-tones (E to F, and B to C), but simply of six full tones, the scale now being C, D, E, F sharp, G sharp, A sharp, C. The old harmonic society, that was based on the clearly-defined relations of a king-chord, two prime-minister chords, and some dependent people-chords, has thus been undermined. The next step was inevitable. Kingship and aristocracy went by the board; the scale was completely democratized; each note was declared to be as good as any other note, to be as capable of performing the same functions; the old tonality had given place to atonality.

IV

Thus it came about that the new musical world kicked out the old with both feet, as it were; it would have nothing to do with the too-easy expressional methods of its predecessor, and it aimed at abolishing the old musical language and setting a new one on its throne. In theory the revolution was a complete success, for every thoughtful musician was becoming doubtful of the too facile emotionalism into which the art was in danger of degenerating, and sighed for an expansion of the musical language that might be expected to bring with it an expansion of musical thought and a sorely needed aeration of some portions of it. In practice, however, things were not so easy as the enthusiasts had imagined they would be.

I have sketched the development in the broad, as it will probably appear to the historian of the future. Looked at in detail, however, it is complicated by all kinds of cross-currents. There is really no such thing as 'modernism' in the sense of a common policy, a common aim, a common language among the new composers. The revolt against the past has taken various forms in different men and in different environments; nor has the same man, with one or two exceptions, pursued the one consistent course throughout. What we see is many varieties of attempts, some of them instinctive and convulsive, some of them almost wholly speculative, to revive a decaying art by the infusion of new blood into its veins, or by giving its flaccid muscles a new tone and its stiff joints a new articulation. A good deal of what is done is purely and deliberately negative; the composers have no very clear idea of what it is they want to say, but are bent merely on doing something directly opposite to what the nineteenth century did.

As I have tried to indicate, the older art was all of a piece; to this fact it owed both its excellencies and its defects. All the elements of the art ran in easy harness with each other. The type of melody was conditioned by the basic nature of the harmony; the tonal harmony in turn could not develop beyond the limits allowed it by that type of melody; the rhythm was not only correlative to these types of harmony and melody but was planned to assist a certain type of structural design, and was in turn limited by the possibilities of range of the standard types of design. With a musical language the principles, the vocabulary, and the grammar of which were universally accepted, composers could build without the necessity of having to be always making new bricks; with the result that building became too easy. The new spirit attacked the old fabric mercilessly at every point. War was declared on the facile emotionalism into which the art of the nineteenth century was rapidly drifting; a more cynical, more sceptical generation laughed at the soul-searchings of its fathers, and, priding itself on its superior hardness, took a wild delight in substituting the roughest dissonances for the melting chromaticism of later nineteenth century harmony. In its passion for exploring the soul, the older art had concentrated over-much on the literary side of music. The new art, accordingly, partly out of sheer bravado, partly out of a fundamental misunderstanding of the complex nature of music – for there is no sound musical aesthetic as yet – swore it would throw 'literature' on the rubbish heap and devote itself purely and simply to 'music', i.e., the spinning and weaving of notes by and for themselves alone. There was a general tendency, in theory at any rate, to regard words not as concepts to be re-expressed in musical ideas, but merely as vocables to eke out a 'purely musical' line of melody; while some brights spirits showed their contempt for the delusions under which such *crétins* as Schubert and Schumann and Brahms and Hugo Wolf had laboured by choosing for their vocal music texts with a ridiculous meaning or no meaning at all; in one case a number of cuttings from the newspapers of the day were chosen.

The older music having expressed too well the over-refinements of a dying civilization, resort was had by some of the revolters to the plainer or wilder or more brutal spirit of their own 'folk', or to the crudities of primitive races. The great thing was to prevent music from 'thinking' too much; for the dubious new aesthetic held that 'music *per se*' had nothing to do with anything 'outside itself', and particularly with those problems of the soul with which the older composers had tortured themselves and their listeners, and which were now held to be the province of literature alone. (Stravinsky's objection to Beethoven, for example, is that he is 'too philosophical'.) And while these and other attacks were being delivered on the inner spiritual substance of the old music, attacks equally ruthless and systematic were launched against its methods. Since it was all of an organic piece, it could be reformed only by a drastic dissolution of its principles of unity, a liberation of each of its elements and a development of them separately along new lines. Exigencies of structure had formerly led to 'themes' being cut more or less to pattern. This was to be abolished; no longer would the composer's idea hobble along in the chains imposed on it by the four or eight-bar phrase that had come from the dance or the song. Melody was to be 'free', not clamped down to a conventional harmonic base; hence the new vogue of un-accompanied suites for single instruments, in which the arabesque fancy of the composer could have unfettered play. Tonality was to give way to atonality or to polytonality – which latter may be roughly defined as writing in two or more keys at once. An end was to be made of the standardized devices of the past for getting design and structure – the repetitions, the sequences, the 'develop-ments', and so on. The new music was to have not only a vocabu-lary but an articulation of its own.

v

These principles were worked out with the most rigour in Central Europe, among the pupils and adherents of the Schönberg School. The theory is perfect in its thoroughness and exquisite in its symmetry; perhaps the best expression of it is to be found in an essay by Erwin Stein on 'Neue Formprinzipien' that will be as valuable to future historians as the manifesti of the Florentines are to us. The only trouble is that music cannot live by theory alone. It is easy enough to draw up, on paper, a scheme for composing in a new manner; the difficulty is to get men of genius to conform to it, and it is the men of genius who from time to time transform the face of music. These pestilential fellows go a way of their own, and have a way of making the rank and file follow; and I cannot see any man of genius of the future going to school to Schönberg or Erwin Stein or any other theorist. The master's path and methods will be determined for him by the substance and the chemistry of his own spiritual constitution. And indeed the evolution of the new art is already following, in the broad, the course that could have been predicted for it from a study of similar revolutions in the past. The pioneers will certainly not enter the Promised Land; they will be to the music-ians of a century or so hence the fascinating historical curiosities that Peri and Caccini and Gagliano are to us. Already, indeed, a score of names that proudly decorated the banner of 'progress' no more than ten years ago are so discredited that to come across them now in a treatise of that period brings a smile to the face. The lesson of history is plain. In the first place, no great composer ever uses the whole of the *theoretic* possibilities of the day; and composers who insist on trying to do so are doomed to quick exhaustion and ultimate sterility. A compromise will have to be found between the exaggerated claims of the new language and the established rights of the old, so much of the former being added to the latter as it can comfortably assimilate. There are abundant signs of this process already; all over Europe the wild men of ten or fifteen years ago are cutting their claws and trim-ming their hair.

In the second place, the next big and relatively stable develop-ment of the art will take a form that no theorist can accurately forecast. The men of 1600 were confident that they had swept polyphony from the earth; they would have been very astonished could they have revisited the glimpses of the moon a century later and found polyphony in vogue once more. They thought they were founding music drama on the lines of the ancient Greek tragedy; what really flowered from their noble efforts was Italian opera – a very different thing. They could not foresee that vocal music as they conceived it would have to mark time for a long period while instrumental music worked out a new language and methods of its own; and that it would not be until the greatest master of instrumental music, two centuries later, had endowed that branch of the art with a new life, that the greatest master of the music drama, half a century later still, could gather into the one focus all the forces that had been unconsciously pressing towards a common goal through all these generations. There are similar surprises in store for any of us who survive another century or so; we can be sure of nothing except that whatever form evolution may ultimately take, it will be one that nobody can at present foresee. The theoreticians imagine that they are shaping the music of the future. They flatter themselves; the next great man will take a course determined for him by his own constitution, and will act as if the theoreticians had never lived. The theory of opera had been worked out fully and symmetrically on paper, by all sorts of writers in the eighteenth and early nineteenth centuries; in the very year of Wagner's birth, one Mosel published a treatise in which the theoretic ground was surveyed in the most thorough and painstaking way. But if Wagner had died in boyhood, we should still, in all probability, be very much where the world was in 1813 in the matter of music drama. The vital and wholly personal contribution of Wagner was the infusion of the Beethoven system of thematic development into the veins of vocal music; and no theorist could have foreseen the possibility of the final results of that. The thing had to be created before it could be conceived.

VI

I will permit myself only one prophecy – that instrumental music in the immediate future will become far less speculative, and opera much more so. Wagner, who knew as much about the inner life of music as most men, used to point out that pure instrumental music could not possibly allow itself such licences as dramatic music; a harmonic combination or transition, the audacity and seeming unreason of which would be explained and justified by the words and the action of an opera, would, he said, merely puzzle the listener in a symphony. That is as true now as it was half a century ago. Already we see signs of the unconscious application of it to the new music. Opera, particularly in Germany, is experimenting in the boldest fashion, and with great success; while few purely instrumental 'modernist' works are being produced that strike the nail on the head. A harmonic texture of the kind we get in Alban Berg's *Wozzeck* would be to a great extent meaningless in a symphony; but meaning is given it by the stage action and the words. Opera can experiment with 'life' in a way and to an extent that absolute music cannot; and the audacity with which the new German opera is getting to grips with life will in time endow the musical side of opera with new resources. Meanwhile absolute music will have to go more slowly, for the reason that Wagner stated so clearly, until opera has at last provided it with a new kind of nourishment that it can assimilate without injury to itself. A new development of instrumental music, in turn, will permit of a new blood transfusion into the veins of opera, as in the case of Beethoven and Wagner; and so *ad infinitum*.

But though a study of the laws that have operated in the past gives us some warrant for forecasting the very broadest lines of the next development, none of us can see even the next ten years in anything like detail. We must rid ourselves of the flattering notion that our theorizing is going to determine matters one way or the other. Ours is the much more modest task of the spectator, interested in the marvellous new game that is being played for our benefit on the vast field of history, and eagerly awaiting the coming of the next really significant figure, who will give the game a turn which not all the speculation in the world will help us to forecast.

WOLF'S INSTRUMENTAL
WORKS
1940

(From the *Listener*)

WHATEVER MAY be true of other nations, it seems to be a law of German music that the best songs are possible only to composers who are capable of fine work on a larger scale than the song. It may be objected that Robert Franz managed to write a number of good songs without having the smallest claim to be considered a composer on the larger scale. I still think, however, that the proposition holds good in the main. Franz, excellent as some of his songs are in their way, was not a giant even in his own sphere. For the rest, we have only to recall the names of Schubert, Schumann, Brahms, Strauss, Mahler and Reger to see that a genius for turning out the best songs implies a genius for working also in other and larger forms.

How then does this rule work in the case of Hugo Wolf, whose commanding genius as a *Lieder* composer is beyond dispute? Ought he not to have a name for himself also as a composer of instrumental works, or of operas, or of both? Why did he produce so little in these two genres, and do such specimens as he did produce warrant the belief that had a longer life been granted him he would have helped to make history as an opera composer or a symphonist? To answer these questions is not easy; we have to take into consideration not only the nature of the genius of the man as revealed in his songs but the peculiar circumstances of his life.

Severe Self-Criticism

Wolf's published instrumental works are only three in number: a string quartet in D minor, written between 1877 and 1880, a symphonic poem for orchestra, *Penthesilea* (1883), and the *Italian Serenade*, which we possess in two forms, as a work for small orchestra (1893-4), and in Wolf's later arrangement of it for string quartet. The reader will not resent being reminded that Wolf was born in 1860 and died in 1903. In the summer of 1897, his mind having given way, he had to be placed in an institution. He was discharged, supposedly cured, in January 1898. He remained at liberty until October of that year, when he was taken to the Lower Austrian Asylum in Vienna, where he died four-and-a-quarter years later. His working life thus ended when he was no more than thirty-seven.

As a boy he tried his hand at not only songs but instrumental works in various genres – piano pieces, music for strings, a concerto for piano and violin, and even a symphony. It is noticeable that practically all these works were left unfinished; in the case of the symphony, which dates from 1876, he worked for a while at the first movement, the scherzo and the finale in turns, but in the end completed none of them; and the reason for this I take to be that faculty for self-criticism, that capacity for being perfectly honest with himself, that was one of the basic features of his artistic constitution. It is at once strange and pathetic that this rare faculty did not desert him even when his mental life in general was already in process of decay. During the early part of his first internment he sketched some new matter for his *Penthesilea*. While at liberty in 1898 he played the symphonic poem one day to a friend; when he came to the added section he stopped, appalled at the commonplace of it, and would have burned the manuscript then and there had not his friend dissuaded him.

I take it that not only did this habit of self-criticism cause him to leave so many instrumental works projected in his early days unfinished, but it made him excessively, needlessly, doubtful about the two or three works he actually completed. We of today find it difficult to share those doubts. The *Penthesilea* is a more than creditable work for a young man of twenty-three making his first experiment with the orchestra. Though there is necessarily inexpertness – largely the result of over-eagerness – in the technical handling of the orchestra, the thinking throughout is undeniably orchestral; the music has not been conceived in terms of the piano and then 'scored'. On the face of it, here was a work of the richest promise for Wolf's future as an orchestral composer. The string quartet of three or four years earlier is an even more remarkable achievement; it shows a ripeness of mind and a sureness of craftsmanship which it is hard to associate with a boy of nineteen. Why then did not Wolf continue along these paths? Why did he let the instrumental side of his genius lie completely fallow in the ten years' interval between the composition of *Penthesilea* and that of the *Italian Serenade*?

Once more it seems to me that the explanation is to be sought in his exceptional honesty with himself. Remarkable as the symphonic poem and the quartet are in many ways, they do not break absolutely fresh ground in the way or to the extent that Wolf's songs do. We can truly say of the more striking of the two works, the quartet, that it short-circuits most of the German chamber music of the half-century before its birth, going back both in spirit and in texture to the later chamber music of Beethoven, and that it has no reason to feel embarrassed even in that august company. But Wolf himself, I imagine, must have said to himself in later years that it was not sufficient to work in the shadow even of such giants as Beethoven and Goethe. In the *Lied*, Wolf had opened out not only a new world of thought and feeling but created a new musical language for the expression of it. He was probably clear-eyed enough to see that as yet he had not managed to give as purely personal a substance and colour to his instrumental thinking; and so, I conjecture, he decided to wait until what he desired came to him of its own accord, as it had done in the case of the song. For some four years from about the end of 1887 he kept pouring out one amazing lyric after another. Then came a longish spell of relative quiescence in which his mind ran mostly on opera, and then, between 1896 and 1897, a brief return to the song. But all through these years of mastery he seems to have made no further attempt to find himself in purely instrumental music. Perhaps he felt that when the time was ripe, instrumental music would find him as the song had done; and for that time he was content to wait.

It is perhaps significant that even the *Italian Serenade* is an uncompleted work. Wolf had originally intended it to be in three movements; but he never got any further than a sketch of some twenty-eight bars for the slow movement and one of about forty bars for the finale, which was to be a tarantella. He must have known that in the Serenade he had created a miniature masterpiece in an idiom of his own; and no doubt he abandoned the work because his faculty for self-criticism told him that the other movement did not promise to be so completely individual.

The Serenade, in its orchestral form, is scored for strings (with a solo viola), two flutes, two oboes, two clarinets, two bassoons and two horns. It yields its full charm only in this form; but if we did not already know it with its orchestral colour and fragrance we should be perfectly content with it as a string quartet. In either version it is a peculiarly tricky piece to perform, because of the difficulty of finding exactly the right tempi. I myself have heard it many times, but never once as I know it to be in itself. It is generally either over-weighted by too slow or trivialized by too fast a tempo.

BEETHOVEN: THE LAST PHASE

(The *Atlantic Monthly*, 1950)

I

THE OBJECT of the series of which this article forms a part is the study of some great thinker or man of action in a period of crisis that made an obvious dividing line in his life. To achieve anything of this kind in the case of a composer, however, is peculiarly difficult, by reason, to put it paradoxically, of the immaterial nature of the material in which the musical creator works. Music is simply air in motion; and though the sound-symbols written down by the composer at a particular time may have taken the form and colour they did because of some volcanic experience of his in the outer world, or of some psychological change within himself at that or some earlier time, it is always dangerous to try to read into the notes an expression of the experience. In the case of the poet or the prose writer there is as a rule no such difficulty; what we know him to have experienced is plainly visible in, or inferable from, something he has said, even if it be only in his letters. But in the case of the composer we have to be very cautious in arguing from his life to his work, or vice versa: that way psychological dilettantism lies, the superficial blending of romantic biography with sentimental aesthetic of which musical criticism presents us with too many dubious examples.

We may have the best of reasons for believing that a certain experience of eye and ear on the road to Damascus led to a Saul being transmuted into a Paul; but only the sentimentalist ignorant of the profounder psychological processes of a composer can persuade himself that Mathilde Wesendonk 'inspired' Wagner to write *Tristan and Isolde*. A view of the matter more consistent with modern psychics would be not that Wagner wrote *Tristan* because he was in love with the lady, but that he was in love with the lady simply and solely because he was afire just then with *Tristan*; something of the glory that transfigured the universe for him while he was under that influence happened to catch the golden head of Frau Wesendonk and surround it with an aureole; but when the artistic fire within him had died down he soon saw that pretty head for the quite commonplace thing it really was, and the aureole faded in the light of common day.

In the same way, knowing as much as we now do about the subconscious functioning of the musical master minds, we must beware of attributing, as the romantic biographers have been prone to do, too direct an influence upon Beethoven's music of his deafness, his frustrations in love, the cares brought upon him by his nephew, and so on. Some impress upon him, of course, these things must have made; but may it not be arguable that the peculiar quality of the music of Beethoven's final phase – which is the special subject for inquiry in the present article – would have been very much the same had the circumstances of his worldly life been quite different? May not the change in him that finds such marvellous expression in the music of his last few years be traceable to something in his very being as an artist that had been silently developing in him according to its own laws for many years, independently of, even if to some extent parallel with, the circumstances of his outer life?

The reader will be familiar with the traditional division of Beethoven's lifework into three 'styles'. It would indeed be astonishing if some such division were not observable. The work of every artist of great brain power who has had a fairly long life shows as a matter of course a first period of struggle between his dawning individuality and a transmitted routine, a second period in which he achieves a happy compromise between the two, a complete solution of all his problems of expression and form, and a third period in which an expansion of his imagination and subtilization of his craftsmanship draw him on into regions hardly explored until then, in which new and more difficult problems call for new solutions.

A process of this sort is obvious in Beethoven's case. It is true

I

that the works of his final period are still, to a large extent, an
enigma that has baffled the most ardent of his students: true also
that when the critics come down to actualities they differ from
each other as to which works mark the passage from the first
style to the second and which from the second to the third. On
one point, however, everyone is agreed – that in the works unmistakably of his third period, of which the last two piano
sonatas and the last five quartets (with the Great Fugue) constitute
a definite unity, a territory with a spiritual climate and a flora
and fauna entirely its own, we are confronted with what seems
to be virtually a new Beethoven: such music had never been
heard in the world before, and we may doubt whether its like
will ever be heard again. All who have fallen under its spell agree
that here music explores the profoundest depths of the spirit and
soars to the loftiest mystical heights. But I would join issue with
the doctrine that this 'third' style can be marked off at all sharply,
either in chronology or in substance, from the two that preceded
it. On the contrary – and this is the thesis I shall try to establish –
the third period seems to be merely the full realization of impulses
and the sublimation of technical procedures that had been subconscious controlling forces in Beethoven's musical nature from
the beginning. Undoubtedly the works of the last period point
to a 'crisis' in his mental life; but that crisis, I would urge, came
about neither through any pressure on him from the outer
world nor from a conscious quest on his part for new expressions
and new forms.

II

For a thesis of this kind to have any real validity it must be
demonstrated in terms of the man's music alone, without any
resort for support to romantic biography – with its arbitrary
tracing of musical effects to nonmusical causes – or to the equally
arbitrary reading of poetic 'programmes' into purely instrumental works. It must be shown – or at all events some evidence
must be tabled – that certain procedures of melody, of rhythm, of
phrase structure, of form, and so on, which are regarded as peculiar

to the works of Beethoven's last phase are to be found also in
abundance in earlier works of his, thus suggesting the lifelong
persistence in him of essentially the same moods, the same idioms,
a partiality for the same psychological adventures.

This necessitates my saying a preparatory word or two on the
subject of what I have elsewhere called a composer's fingerprints –
basic formulae of expression, personal to him, that recur constantly
in a man's music, though sometimes in shapes so subtilized by the
circumstances of the moment that they may escape our detection
for a long time. The scepticism in some quarters as to the existence
of these fingerprints in composition, or of their value to criticism,
would be less confident if the sceptics were aware how searchingly
and with what illuminative results, the same phenomenon has
been studied in poetry and prose for something like a century.

The dominant style-elements of many writers from Cicero
onwards have been brought to light by style-analysis. Émile
Hennequin demonstrated long ago Flaubert's unconscious
tendency to follow a certain pattern of construction, from word
to phrase, from phrase to sentence, from sentence to paragraph,
from paragraph to chapter, from chapter to book; while in a
brilliant essay he laid bare the verbal elements that constitute the
style, and therefore give us clues to the thinking, of Victor Hugo.
More recently Alphonse Le Dû has shown in minute detail
Hugo's unconscious proneness to certain rhythmical patterns in
both his poetry and his prose. W. F. Jackson Knight has subjected
Virgil's accentual symmetries to a similar analysis; and more than
one writer has demonstrated the curious ways in which a verbal
image in Shakespeare will not only beget a cognate image but call
up from the depths of his subconscious, by some strange un-
foreseen compulsion of its own, a side-line of thought which had
certainly not been part of the poet's conscious purpose when he
began.

Undoubtedly there exist in the composer also definite irresistible biases towards certain basic formulae personal to him. In
some cases the finger-print exists as a mere tic or mannerism of
speech, occurring on every page he writes but not bound up in his
subconscious with any particular psychological state. It is the

easiest matter in the world to show the existence of a harmless tic
of this sort in Puccini. Weber has a marked bias towards a certain
formula of melodic structure, and in his case it often stands in the
way of truth of dramatic expression, for the composer's unconscious use of it on all sorts of occasions is apt to give much the
same musical physiognomy to dramatic characters differing very
much from each other in themselves and in their milieu.

As a rule these basic individual formulae of speech persist
throughout a composer's lifetime; but occasionally one makes a
fleeting appearance fairly late in his career – that is to say, the time
of its taking possession of him, and the duration of its spell over
him, can be more or less definitely fixed. Frank Walker has
recently drawn our attention to a case in point in connection with
Hugo Wolf, a certain melodic-rhythmical formula being so
specifically associated with his work during a particular brief
period that, as Mr. Walker says, 'if an unknown song of his were
discovered in which this "fingerprint" occurred, we should be
able at once to surmise the year, and almost the month, of its composition.' Our Greek scholars, we may remind ourselves, long
ago employed this method of 'stylometry', as it has come to be
called in literary circles – in which, as Professor Grube has put it,
'special attention is paid to the frequency of certain expressions
and particles which any writer uses all but unconsciously' – to
determine the chronological order of the composition of Plato's
Dialogues; for 'some turns of phrase that occur in the early works
gradually disappear, and *vice versa*'.

III

Of all the composers whose work I have studied from the
stylometric point of view, I have found Beethoven the easiest to
systematize, the one in whom the unconscious inclination towards typical melodic-rhythmical formulae is most marked – a
fact which of itself, considering the towering greatness of the man,
should dispose of the innocent notion in some quarters that to
demonstrate these biases in a composer is to lower him in some
way in our estimation. There is probably some subtle organic

reason for the formation and fixation of these unconscious biases in an artist; possibly they represent a subsurface effort at economy on the part of the artistic faculty, the establishment of broad, smooth, chartered highways, as it were, in his thinking that enable him the better to concentrate on the intellectual adventures he will seek to find on the road.

Be that as it may, there can be no doubt that Beethoven shows an irresistible tendency to express essentially the same moods and conflicts of moods, in much the same way from the beginning of his career to the end. This statement can be proved only by plentiful citations, which are impossible in the present article. I can only ask the reader to accept the statement provisionally as part of the working hypothesis upon which the present article proceeds. He will no doubt know that Pirro and Schweitzer have proved conclusively that Bach has a sort of musical 'language' of his own, in virtue of which he more or less unconsciously employs, in one work after another, the same musical symbol to express the same mood or define the same external image.

To prove a similar psychical process in the case of the purely instrumental music of a composer is necessarily more difficult, but I believe it can be done in Beethoven's case. He has a certain rhythmic type-formula, for example, for impressive statements in four-four time, and another for similar statements in three-four time: the type is modified in this work or that, but basically the *ad hoc* formula remains the same. The critics have all seen in certain movements of the final quartets and piano sonatas an expression of something that we may call joy, or contentment, or ecstasy. But I think the essential point has remained unperceived – that in his musical 'language' various *types* of joy or happiness are inseparably associated by him with definite type-constructions of notes. His use of the trill for certain expressions of mystical ecstasy could alone be made the subject of a whole long essay.

The point towards which I am working – with some difficulty because of my inability to make use here of musical citations – is that there is fundamentally nothing new, for Beethoven, in the incomparable works of his last phase, which are only the *approfondissement* of psychological elements and the subtilization of technical procedures that had constituted the substance of his music from the beginning. These last great works of his are the product not of a crisis in his actual life but rather of his emergence from an *internal* crisis that had been piling up steadily within the artist in him for many years. What then was the nature of that crisis?

In his latter years, when he was completely deaf, friends used to write out what they had to say to him, while he, of course, replied viva voce. The 'Conversation Books' that have survived therefore record only his interlocutor's remarks, leaving us to guess as best as we can at Beethoven's. It is rather like overhearing only one side of a telephone conversation, and necessarily the full tenor of the talk often evades us. But there is a page in a Conversation Book of the winter of 1823 that seems to have a bearing on the subject that is now engaging us. Schindler has said to him, 'Do you remember how I had to play you a few years ago the sonata Op. 14? Now it is all clear.' His next remark, in answer to something Beethoven had said, is of no importance to our inquiry. But after that we find him writing 'Two principles also in the middle movement of the Pathétique'; and after having, one surmises, gained the composer's assent to this, Schindler continues, 'Thousands don't grasp that.'

Schindler seems to have been drawing the Master's attention to a recurrent feature that had struck him in his music – that of a system of thought and construction based primarily upon 'two principles' posed in apposition; and Beethoven agreed with him, for Schindler tells us elsewhere, apropos of the piano sonata Op. 14, No. 2, that 'in the second sonata this dialogue and its import are more pregnantly expressed, and the apposition of the two main voices (i.e., the two 'principles') is more palpable than in the first. Beethoven called these two principles "the pleading and the resisting. . . . ." '

Though Schindler did not realize it, he was on the way towards a perception that is vital now for the full understanding of Beethoven's mind and work. A certain principle of polarity can be seen to underlie all this thinking, a tendency to conceive and manipulate things in antitheses. We can trace this tendency from its cell form to its full organic growth. It reveals itself first of all in a bias towards an antithesis within the narrow limits of a phrase, then in an antithesis within the sentence, then in the dramatic antithesis of leading themes indicative of a conflict of psychological 'principles' – and so on to the total work as a purposeful antithesis of movements.

And my thesis here is that in the wonderful music of his final phase he merely transplants to another psychical plane his lifelong impulse to achieve a balanced unity in terms of this polarity. And the crisis, the great dividing line, came not through the stresses of his outer life but from the natural evolution of his innermost being as an artist. The whole of his more significant work had been one attempt after another, in the most protean forms, to balance forces in the world of ideas and emotions which he felt to be locked in an inveterate struggle; and all he does now, in the last phase, is to transfer the polar conflict from the outer to the inner world; the drama is henceforth wholly internal.

IV

At this point it becomes necessary to say a word about Bettina von Arnim, the remarkable girl who made Beethoven's acquaintance in Vienna in 1810. For the authenticity of two of the composer's letters to her few would now go bail; but I see no reason to doubt the essential veracity of the account she gave Goethe of Beethoven's conversation with her. She makes him speak of his sense of loneliness in the world of men: 'I have not a single friend; I must live alone in myself. But well I know that God is nearer to me than to the others of my craft; I consort with him without fear; I have always recognized and understood him, and I have no fear for my music – it can meet no evil fate. To grasp it is to be freed from all the misery that others drag about with them.' (This, be it observed, in 1810, more than a decade before the composition of the great works to which this description by Beethoven himself of the inmost nature of his music is peculiarly applicable.) 'When I open my eyes I must sigh,' Bettina makes him say, '. . . for I must despise the world which has no inkling of the fact that music is a higher revelation than all wisdom and philosophy; it is the wine which inspires one to new engenderings, and I am the Bacchus who presses out this glorious wine for mankind and makes them spiritually drunken. When they have become sober again they have fished up all manner of things which they can bring with them to dry land.'

To realize the full truth of this self-analysis we have to go to the works of his last phase, not to those he had produced by 1810, when he was only forty – for by that time he had got no further than the sixth symphony, the fifth piano concerto, the E flat major quartet, Op. 74, and the F minor quartet, Op. 95. Several of the mightiest works of all, among them the Ninth Symphony, the Missa Solemnis, the Hammerklavier sonata, Op. 106, the last two piano sonatas, and the last five quartets, were still in the womb of time. As regards Bettina, then, we must decide either that Beethoven really did talk to her, half reminiscently, half prophetically, very much as she represents him as having done, or, if she were romancing, that this young woman of twenty-five had an insight into the essential but as yet imperfectly revealed Beethoven that placed her head and shoulders above not only all critics of her day and his but most of those of the next half-century.

For it was undoubtedly as an outpouring of bacchic exultation that Beethoven regarded some of the music of his middle phase, with the more reflective moments of a work figuring as a reaction against this mood, an antithesis or counterpoise to it. In 1818, at the time when he was engaged on the mighty Hammerklavier sonata, we find him not only making sketches for the Ninth Symphony but laying out the ground plan for a tenth, the principle of which was to be the contrast of 'a Bacchus festival (allegro) 'and 'a devout canticle (adagio) . . . the text to be a Greek mythos'. The specifically dionysiac mood had found its most exuberant expression for the time being in the wild finale of the Seventh Symphony (1812), and was to work itself out later in the Hammerklavier sonata and the second and final movements of the Ninth Symphony. With the completion of this and of the Missa Solemnis, in 1823, Beethoven rang the curtain down on a struggle (between the two cardinal principles of his artistic being) to which there is no parallel in the life of any other composer: we have evidence in plenty of the titanic strain under which not only his imagination but his physical powers laboured in the effort to say all that was within him.

But the Greeks knew not only the dionysiac frenzy but the no less valued aftermath of this – what they called the dionysiac silence, when the spirit of the worshipper, at once exhausted, purged, and refreshed, luxuriated in a new illumination, that of ecstatic quietude. It is in this inner field of the dionysiac silence that the works of Beethoven's latest phase live and move and have their being. The old polarity of 'two principles' still survives in them as the basic pattern of his thinking.

How deeply rooted that pattern was in his artistic nature can be seen by a comparison of the Piano Sonata quasi una fantasia in E flat major, Op. 27, No. 1, which dates from 1801, and the Sonata in A major, Op. 101, which belongs to 1816. Paul Bekker has pointed out that the principle of construction is the same in both works – because the imaginative principle underlying them is the same. As Bekker remarks, if Beethoven does not expressly characterize the later sonata, as he has done the earlier one, as 'quasi una fantasia', that is only because for him this was too self-evident to call for mention. In their mood-sequences, their mood-antitheses, the polarity of the 'two principles' that are played off against each other, the two sonatas are the same. The vital difference between them is in the greater depth, the greater inwardness of the feeling in the later work, which comes from a period in which Beethoven was well on his way towards the dionysiac silence that possessed him in his final phase.

The crisis was a purely internal one, arising from an organic change in the nature of the artist, not from anything in the outer life of the man; and, like all great changes, it proceeded slowly. It was a psychical metamorphosis in him which may be compared to a geological 'shift', a slow subsidence which, while leaving the basic rock structure as it was, brings with it a new surface conformation, a new climate, a new flora and fauna. The climate of Beethoven's mind decidedly changed. The old extremes of temperature no longer exist – there is no such difference of that kind between the fast and the slow movements of the final quartets as there is between those of the great works of his middle period. The polarity is still operative, but the poles are not so far apart now as of old: the antitheses are now less violent, less obvious, rather in the nature of nuances of one pervading emotion. The interaction of the contending forces no longer takes place on the external but on an internal plane. He does not need now, for his pattern of opposition and reconciliation, of tension and release, the boldly defined, brightly lit, starkly opposed 'subjects' of the older kind, still less the concretization of the spiritual struggle in human characters such as Egmont, Coriolanus, Leonora-Pizarro. The drama is now played out entirely in the composer's own rapt, self-absorbed soul.

The old academic attempts to 'analyse' the final works in terms of 'expanded' or 'modified' 'sonata form', 'variation form,' and all the other quaint old formulae of nineteenth-century pedagogy will some day have to be abandoned. Beethoven no longer thinks in terms of these forms, superficially as his procedures may resemble them here and there. He now spins outward in all directions from the centre of the insulating web he has woven round his spirit; it is this procedure, infinite in its possibilities, that accounts for the great lengths to which some of his latest movements run. Wagner, in a conversation with his intimates at Wahnfried, drew attention to the capacity for endless proliferation from the nuclear cell of a movement. 'You see,' he said, 'Beethoven, if he had liked, could have stopped here, or here, or here.' That is true; but Wagner might have gone further and pointed out that the composer could in many cases equally well have *begun* here, or here, or here. The 'subjects' of the opening allegro movements of the E flat and A minor quartets, for instance, are not 'subjects' in the old technical sense of that term, begetters of the form and texture that follow; rather do they strike us, from their very beginning, as moments in a train of thought that had already been going on for some time in the subconscious of the composer before he decided to take up pen and paper: what is on the page may begin at this point, but what was in the mind of Beethoven had begun long before then; the 'theme', at its first statement, is only a milestone on a road that stretches as far back as it does forward.

The incomparable slow movements, again, are not 'variations on a theme' but long-drawn-out variations on a mood; Beethoven's texture and procedure are quite different here from what they are when he is writing variations for variation's sake. And by means of stylometric analysis we can trace the underlying currents of his thought throughout a whole work, and show the predominance now of this, now of that aspect of joy – the quiet joy that almost immobilizes motion, innocent joy that finds expression in one dance form or another, artless spontaneous joy that springs into physical being out of its own innermost nature, a profounder joy that needs for the uncoiling of its deep-lying spring a previous coiling of forces rooted in the profoundest tenebrae of the soul, and so on. And always there is the polarity that was the very basis of Beethoven's thinking, because it was the basis of his nature. He saw the world, without and within him, as a series of antinomies that had somehow to be resolved; but the great distinction between the earlier works and the latest resides in the fact that in the latter the contending forces now operate entirely in the innermost being of the man, requiring no reference to externalities.

Of all the mystics of art, the Beethoven of the last few years is the greatest: one has to go back to the thirteenth century Persian poet Rumi to find his parallel, and we can only be grateful for the tremendous inner change, whatever its hidden origins may have been, that took place in him in his final years. But he was hardly more than fifty-six when he died; and inevitably we ask ourselves what his next phase might have been. Is a 'next phase' conceivable? He could hardly have travelled further along the mystical road than he had done already; and we may ask ourselves whether, on the other hand, it was within the bounds of human possibility for him to have gone back once more to the outer world. Has any born mystic ever made that backward journey after

     . . . he on honey-dew hath fed

And drunk the milk of Paradise?

Must we not be driven, after the contemplation of these most
marvellous of musical works, to agree with Hugo Wolf's dark
oracular saying that no man is taken away until he has done his
work?

X

EXCERPTS

From the *National Reformer*, 1892

FROM *THE MEANING OF SCIENCE*

What is science? We are familiar with the definition of it as 'organized knowledge' – knowledge of a high degree of generalization. This being so, it is the extremity of ignorance to assert that science is only concerned with objective description of things, or – a still greater folly – that its province lies only in the material amelioration of mankind. The very essence of science is that it is *not* concerned with facts in themselves, but with facts in their implications with other facts. It ever presses on from the particular to the general, from the many to the one – that is, the goal to which it constantly tends is that of the unification of knowledge. All science is only of value so far as it contributes in working towards this end, and the pursuit of it is due to the impulsion of forces not in the least material, but wholly spiritual. It is not the achievement of some immediate, palpable result that impels the scientist to his work; it is the mysterious prompting within him towards philosophy, towards a deeper and more *imaginative* comprehension of the universe.

THE COMING MENACE

It is a frequent source of consolation to many good Christians to give utterance to their cherished belief that Free-thought sustains a severe blow by the death of this or that prominent Freethinker.

There is a deep-seated idea in the heads of these worthy people that, somehow or other, the mass of Freethinkers are very immoral, deluded, unthinking people, only held together by a common blind admiration for some admittedly great man; and that when he is removed from their midst, the bond of unity between them must be shaken, if not actually broken. Thus after Mr. Bradlaugh's death there was a jubilant crowing from every religious journal, and an equally jubilant braying from every pulpit, that 'Freethought had received its death-blow in England', and that soon the sword of the Lord and of Gideon would everywhere prevail. But crowing and braying, rationally considered, are merely the effect of muscular contractions in the vocal systems of animals not usually thought the epitomes of wisdom, and, indeed, are not casually connected with any intellectual stimulus whatever. One hardly looks to these organisms for wisdom, anymore than one looks to a Christian journalist or a Christian preacher for an accurate weighing of social or moral forces. Freethinkers are not likely to be alarmed by the crowing and braying on this point. They know that great as is the loss of any foremost man, it is not irreparable. Freethought still lives, and would continue to live and thrive, even though every Freethinker in the world were to die tomorrow. For Freethought is not a creed but an attitude – an advanced intellectual attitude towards the current conceptions of society. As such, it must and will exist all at times and in all places; in the most elementary society there are Freethinkers, men who are a step in advance of the ideas of those around them. So long as men are born into the world with minds of different calibre, so long will there be Freethinkers, whatever name they may choose to call themselves by.

The real danger to Freethought lies elsewhere, and is a danger that will only make itself apparent as the movement advances. Old as Freethought is in England, measured by the number of years it has existed, it is only young as measured by its strength and stature relative to the remainder of society. It only needs a backward glance at the history of similar movements to see how much of an advantage is enclosed within this seeming disadvantage. During the period in which a new movement is, numerically speaking, in a minority, there is a bond of union between the members that can rarely be maintained after they have become a majority. There is always more activity, more moving force, in the party of opposition that is endeavouring to wrest a place of vantage from the holders, than there is in the holders themselves. Persecution is the most powerful of all factors in binding men together. To have suffered together, to be willing to die together for the common cause, is to animate men for the time being into an impregnable brotherhood. Individual differences are lost sight of; unconsciously men obey the physiological law that a complex life can only be maintained by all the parts working harmoniously to one end. Men are tried by fire, and all the baser metal is burned out of them; the nobler metal is melted into one conquering golden stream. The history of all great moral or social movements teaches us how, in such a time as this, men are fused into one, to the effacement of all individual differences, and the achievement of their end is due to this very self-abnegation; and it teaches the further fact that when the minority become a majority, along with the disappearance of the need for self-restraint there goes a disappearance of that submergence of self which was the most potent factor of success.

A NOTE ON DEATH

To a man who cares more for truth, whatever may be its emotional issues, than for a falsehood that brings along with it shapes of hollow and deceptive beauty, there is nothing in the inexorableness of science that can sadden or embitter him. And the more he adopts that stern heroic way of looking upon the immense and all living things that has foolishly been called materialism the more his spirit is chastened and his heart strengthened; he looks through everything – through matter and mind, through the organic and the inorganic – to the marvellous moving forces of the universe, and becomes a grander being, in proportion as he abandons his own petty claims to the lordship of creation, and he sees himself to be what he really is, and nothing more – a mere part of the whole great scheme of things. Mr. Ruskin has snarled and screamed at what, with the customary presumption of the religious man, he is pleased to call 'the pride of Science'*; and the devotees of Christ strive, or strive to strive, not always with any measure of success, after 'humility of spirit', saying with Tennyson that this whole weak race of venomous works is not worthy to live. Yet to a quiet observer it would rather appear that these humble Christians, with their exaltation of man above all other living things – him for whom the sun was made to give a light by day and the moon by night – and then contemptuous closing of the eyes to what they call 'dead matter', are much prouder and more presumptuous beings than the scientist who sees in man only one link in the whole great chain of creation, and who is content to humbly take his place among other existences, knowing that he is allied with them and born of them.

From the Free Review, 1893–1895

IBSEN

Realist as he is, according to his conventional classification, in his later choice of subjects, he is at heart an idealist of the most pronounced kind. He began as an idealist of the most pronounced kind. He began as an Idealist, writing works such as the early poems, *The Comedy of Love*, *Brand*, and *Peer Gynt*, in which the idealism is unmistakable; and through even the Social Dramas, with their apparent realism, this ideal element still persists; while in the *Master Builder*, if the allegorical reading of that play be correct, Ibsen himself indicated his irradicable idealism.

The Stones of Venice.

'He is everywhere alone, even among other men. He is always
the introspective thinker, to whom the thought is of more value
than the reality which has given it birth. He seeks reality merely to
fertilize his own inner life of feeling and intellect; as soon as this
end is accomplished, reality has lost its importance in his eyes'
(said Jaeger). And he consoles himself for the changing phantas-
magoria of all external things with the reflection that thought is
at least eternal; Spring and summer and autumn may die, but the
memory of them endures.

Even in *Cateline* – his earliest play, written when he was about
twenty-one – the notion of Will plays a leading part in the
evolution of drama; the reason of 'Cateline's' failure was that his
own strength of will was not assisted by the weaker men around
him; individually he could have achieved something by the very
fact of his *willing* to achieve it, but he was held in check by
the inertia of his surroundings.

Brand is simply the outcome of the innate and inflexible
Puritanism of his nature. 'Will' is preached to the fullest; and
Ibsen has every opportunity of stating the case for individualism,
with all the added persuasiveness of a moving poetical presentation. And yet Ibsen fails his own crest, to so speak, by making
Brand fail in his work, and die without having achieved anything.

The misfortune, indeed, of a poet attempting any social
evangel by means of confining with mere words, is that he himself is almost certain to complicate the issues so greatly as to
diminish the force of his own preaching. Dramatic necessities are
inexorable, and will not be bandied about at the will of social
theory; and it was only to be expected that when Ibsen came to
incarnate his individualism in imaginative literature he should
become at times contradictory, at times inconclusive, and at
times absolutely self-damaging. But monadeist as Ibsen is, and
whatever may be his shortcomings in moral philosophy, he is
certainly not the immoral satyr he is popularly supposed to be.
The judicial critic, indeed, is compelled to sum up that Ibsen's
moral doctrine errs less on the side of indulgence than on the side
of repression.

Hedda Gabler, which is such a thorn in the side of the sentimental or didactic critic, is of intense interest to the student of
psychical morbidity.

KIPLING

He works in flashes, making up a concentrated brilliancy for
what he appears to lack in the sustention of energy. And as the
flashes are short in duration, they are correspondingly intense.
His best work, indeed, has always been the description of abnormal states of mind, plainly done under the momentary stimulus
of abnormal cerebral disturbance. We need not go into the question of how far all genius is allied to madness, but we can safely
assert that the exceptional brilliancy of insight into certain
psychical states that Mr. Kipling displays at times, can only be
made possible by a correspondent weakening of mental power in
other directions. His very excellences inevitably bear with them
their correlative defects. To work at so high a rate of cerebration
simply means, in most men, a concentration of energy in one
field and a withdrawal of it from another. Almost alone among
modern artists stood Wagner in his power of lengthy sustention
of abnormal cerebration. Mr. Kipling would be almost more
than human if he had had at once this brilliancy of insight into the
abnormal and the faculty of wise, dispassionate observation of life.

RICHARD LE GALLIENNE'S *RELIGION OF A LITERARY MAN*

Economy is all very well up to a certain point, but the devil
cannot possibly be dispensed with. The old theologians hung all
the evil of the world upon his shoulders, which was convenient
and simple, and then dodged the inevitable question, 'But who
made the devil?' by telling you that you must have faith, and
that these things are a mystery. Mr. Le Gallienne, leaving the devil
out of the universe, is hard put to it to solve the old problem of
how evil comes into the universe at all. This, of course, has
always been the crux of Theism; and after eighteen centuries of

Christian ethic, the Theist of today cannot answer the question otherwise than it was answered by Cicero, by Maximus of Tyre, by the Stoics generally. The argument was that as God was good, evil was only apparently evil, and subserved some good purpose, could we but know it – which was not explaining the existence of evil, but denying its existence.

MASCAGNI AND THE OPERA

Ever since men began to theorize upon the musical drama, their favourite problem has been that of the relation between poetry and music, their respective spheres, and the manner in which they can be most efficiently blended.

★   ★   ★

It would be hard to find a parallel to the extraordinary popularity which *Cavalleria Rusticana* has enjoyed from the first.

★   ★   ★

Mascagni's popularity among the people seems to be due to precisely those qualities in his music that repel the connoisseur. The Siciliana in the overture is a meeting-place for both orders of mind; but after that the critical and uncritical part company.

★   ★   ★

Who that has spent time on the Old Italian Opera does not preserve a lively recollection of these choruses, with their commonplace melody, their good, thumping rhythm, their liberal supply of the obvious, which, according to Mr. Oscar Wilde, has been exhausted by Providence and Walter Besant.

★   ★   ★

Everywhere it was recognized that Mascagni was not merely a musician, like Gounod, but a musician born for the stage, as Gounod was not.

★   ★   ★

Looking back at *Cavalleria Rusticana* from the point of view of the new experience given us of Mascagni by *L'Amico Fritz* and *I Rantzau*, we have all the more warrant for saying that a great part of the success of his first work was due to the harmonizing of Signor Verga's sombre art with Mascagni's own dramatic feeling, and the skilful way in which the librettists had turned the prose story into an opera-text.

The irrelation and loose articulation of *I Rantzau* is incredible to anyone who has not taken the trouble to study the score carefully. One of the most important *motives* in the whole opera does not appear in the overture at all, though the overture is nothing more than a *potpourri* of the themes of the opera, in the style of *Oberon* and Wagner's earliest works.   (1894)

AMIEL

It is the voice of Geneva speaking; and the strange thing is that it should come from the mouth of a man who is at other times partly Schopenhauer, Hegel, Stoic, Epicurean and Oriental quietist. The dualism of Amiel's nature was his destruction; he cannot harmonize everything within him, and yet tortures himself because of his failure, ultimately seeking a fictitious harmonization by strangling philosophy in the arms of religion. Geneva is at the bottom of him, suggesting dark problems of sin, and evil, and death, and salvation. And since he cannot attain the inward peace he strives for, and since he cannot flout God in the face, and show him the cardinal blunder he has made in the clumsy creation of mankind, he takes a thin ascetic comfort in the Christian theory of the innate perversity of man, *ad radicale Böse* of Kant. This in turn troubles him, for how is it to be harmonized with the general beneficence of the scheme of things? Finally he takes refuge from the questioning spectres that haunt him, in the Christian doctrine of the forgiveness of sins. This is indeed the pressing problem to Amiel. 'The best measure of the profundity of any religious doctrine', he says, 'is given by its conception of sin, and the cure of sin.' Is then the Christian doctrine so perfect a thing in this respect? Was there ever a more grossly immoral doctrine than this of the forgiveness of sins, a doctrine more based on selfishness, on cowardice, disregard for others, callousness at the evil inflicted so that the individual soul but makes its peace with God? It is the most striking proof of the innate incapacity of the religious mind to think honestly upon moral questions, that such a doctrine as this should ever be regarded as the be-all and the end-all of moral obligation. Of all the specious lies that have ever blinded humanity to the real issues of ethics, this is surely the worst. It is an immoral doctrine because it avoids the real question of obligation; it shifts the moral centre of gravity from man to the skies; and such a displacement as this is regarded, even by thinking men, as compatible with notions of justice not merely human but divine.

Thus Amiel hovers between Buddhism and Christianity, between absorption and duty, and between hope and fear. He hugs his cross to his breast in obedience to the will of God, and he never perceives that such a doctrine as this bears only on death, not on life. Practically, it is identical with the fundamental axiom of Schopenhauer, that the supreme happiness is in the negation of the will to live. After long attempts to reconcile his philosophy and his religion, Amiel finally lets them drift apart, taking up definitely with religion. Towards the end, when his disease is hurrying him on to a death of pathetic suffering, he hovers between obedience and revolt for a moment, even breaks out into Stoicism, and then brings this round in a curve to resignation to the supposed beneficent ordering of things.

*　*　*

Such was the complex and contradictory being called Amiel, whose epitaph might be 'He died through a confusion of ideals'. With him synthesis became a vice and psychology a snare, for through a wrong application of them he lost his hold on the reality of things. He himself looked back with regret upon his wasted life, and thought sadly of the tragic withering of the promise he had shown in youth.   (1895)

From the *Speaker*, 1901–1904

THE NEED FOR BANKING REFORM

(9th February, 1901)

Without committing oneself to any disputable theory of economics, it is easy to see that, as at present constituted and worked, our banks do not do half as much as they might for the general good of the country. On the one hand, we oscillate between over-trading and depression, between undue expansion of credit and undue restriction of it; on the other hand, our normal practice is to place credit at the disposal of those who make absolutely no good social use of it – who use it simply for Stock Exchange and other gambling – while we deny it to the honest worker if he happens to be poor as well.

Banks, of course, would sooner lend £10,000 to a mere Stock Exchange speculator on marketable stock, with a good margin, than lend £100 to a small trader on the contents of his shop, because the security is easily realizable – "liquid" is the banking term – in the one case and not in the other. And, so long as banks are run simply for the benefit of the shareholders, this kind of thing cannot be altered. But is it good for the community that its funds or its credit should be put to such purposes as this?

THE NEW SCHOOL OF BRITISH MUSIC

Frederick C. Nicholls

(18th January, 1902)

The tendency of the modern young men, almost without exception, is towards the orchestra and the larger forms of music. For the piano a great many of them have an unmitigated contempt. Modern music is, of course, developing in every direction; but the greatest progress has been made in our sense of musical colour, owing to our having, in the present-day orchestra a huge paint-box with which we can be incessantly experimenting. Hence the young composer, when he sits down to write music of his own, has his brain throbbing with the gorgeous tints of Wagner, Tchaikovsky, and Richard Strauss. The piano, or the single voice with piano accompaniment, is a medium too pale, too cold, too virginal for his incandescent thoughts. He feels, when restricted to these, much as a scene-painter would feel if he were asked to do his work with a child's paint-box and a tiny camel's-hair brush. It is a rare thing to find an Englishman writing well for the piano now. Mr. Elgar and Mr. Wallace fight shy of it; Mr. Bantock and Mr. Coleridge Taylor essay it with only partial success; Mr. Percy Pitt writes for it as if it were an orchestra; Mr. Holbrooke knew how to write for it delightfully at one time, but is fast forgetting the art, seduced by the more glowing colour of the orchestra. Erskine Allon knew the piano and wrote well for it, but he is dead; and I can think of no present Englishman, with the sole exception of Mr. Nicholls, whose piano writing really conveys the soul and the idiom of the instrument.

I have two sonatas, a quintet, a big symphonic poem for the piano, and, in addition to some odd sheaves of pieces, a little volume of thirteen waltzes, and another containing a series of tone-pictures based on Heine's *Florentine Nights*. It is of the two last-named collections that I more particularly wish to speak. I am convinced that any intelligent musician into whose hands these tiny volumes came would at once recognize in them the work of an artist of rare distinction and originality.

HOLBROOKE

(15th February, 1902)

I may be wrong, but I myself feel that Mr. Holbrooke's four symphonic poems will one day be recognized as something absolutely new in English or in any other music. They have an atmosphere, a psychology, that are his and his alone. They are not imitated; this atmosphere and this psychology are not in Wagner, or Tchaikovsky, or Richard Strauss. Morbidity – to employ a much-abused word – has never been made so truly beautiful as here. The boy who could write that exquisite ending to *The Raven*, with its supreme nobility of conception, its rare pathos of speech; who could bring the very heart into one's throat at passage after passage of *The Skeleton in Armour*; who could give an even more intense life to the mournful beauty of *Ulalume*, has surely added something to the world's store of great and lovely things.

RICHARD STRAUSS

(11th April, 1903)

Programme music is simply music written under a more definite stimulus than abstract music; and every song, every opera, every oratorio that has been penned comes from the same psychological fountain-head as the symphonic poem. On the one side stand such abstract tonal expressions as the sonata and the fugue; on the other side are all the musical utterances into which a more definite idea of some kind or other enters, and of which programme music is only the most fully developed instrumental form. To condemn programme music in the mass as a sin against the aesthetics of music is to analyse the art only superficially. What we can justly condemn is the vain attempt to represent in music what is really unrepresentable in sound; as soon as programme music goes to this extreme it becomes absurd. But we are finding out every day how many fresh things can be said in music, how greatly the representative, as distinguished from the merely expressive, side of the art is developing; and this evolution is really not to be cut short by the haphazard use of an epithet that has come to be looked upon as opprobrious. You cannot put the clock back simply by reasoning wrongly about the forces that move the pendulum. . . .

★   ★   ★

Don Quixote, one of the most human and at the same time most musical works in existence. . . .

★   ★   ★

No setting of a poem or of a libretto is a success that does not take up the subject and transform it by re-thinking it in terms of music. Judge *Also sprach Zarathustra* by this standard and it comes out, I think, triumphantly. . . .

WOLF

(19th November, 1904)

The set, regular, square-cut phrases and rhythms of *Penthesilea* seem hardly to have come from the same hand that later on achieved such marvellous flexibility and variety of musical speech. The explanation, I suppose, is that Wolf was never at his best except when he had a poem to work over line by line. Look at the song "Die Spinnerin," composed in 1878, when he was eighteen, and you will see that it is years more mature in feeling and technique than the *Penthesilea* of 1883. Apart from some spasmodic efforts, it was really the Mörike poems, in the early part of 1888, that set free all the flood of music that was in him, just as a spark liberates the dormant energies of gunpowder. *Then* the real Wolf began to live. He was a vocal writer, pure and simple, with every gift the genuine vocal writer ought to have; and there was no poem, of whatever form or whatever content, that could keep its secret from him. But the poem itself – lyric or elegy or drama – was a prime necessity if his imagination was to be stirred to its depths. Opera gave him the same opportunities as the song, and *Der Corregidor* is a continuous feast of delight; but it is probable he would never have done anything remarkable in the purely instrumental forms.

From the *Weekly Critical Review*, 1903

MUSIC AND MORALS

Whence comes this proneness of some people to take art as seriously as they do life, to be annoyed at a paradoxical play of Oscar Wilde, to be rendered unhappy by the Pathetic Symphony, to be paralysed in action by Turgeniev or James Thompson? Is it not just a sign that they have failed to take the thing in *as art*, that they have half dragged it out of its own sphere and half thrust it into a sphere whose standards of value, or right or wrong, by no means concern it? Let us note in the first place that people of this kind are sometimes inconsistent even in their failings. I myself know a man who can drench himself without a moment's pang of discomfort in the pessimism of music, but is seriously disturbed at the touch of pessimism in poetry and fiction. He can listen to the Pathetic Symphony or to other music of that kind with unmitigated artistic enjoyment; but it is almost impossible for him to read Turgeniev or Dostoievsky or Leopardi, and he seeks intellectual nutriment in the facile optimism of Dickens. There must be hundreds like him, all, in their one-sidedness and inconsistency, proving that this tendency to look upon art as reality is due to a confusion, temporary or permanent, between the organs of practical and those of aesthetic life – for if it is possible for them to be morally and philosophically detached with regard to fiction or poetry. . . .

* * *

La Rochefoucauld was cynically right when he spoke of the secret joy we feel at the thought that misfortune has overtaken other people – taking the statement, of course, with the liberal reservations which we all know have to be made. Civilized man, however, differs from the savage in that he reserves the delight of malignity for his aesthetic moments, instead of seeking them in actual life at the expense of actual people. It is of the essence of tragic satisfaction that it shall never be allowed to step beyond its own sterile circle and give our real life a bias in this or that direction. . . .

THE CRITIC'S FRAILTY

The fact is that the critic is even more painfully the product of his epoch than the composer. He is blinded by the dust of the fights that are raging round him, he cannot see problems and principles, but only individuals and antagonists. . . .

* * *

Think of all the criticism that has been written upon music, from that of Bach to that of Wagner, and try to discover how much of it would stand a chance of being read if it were brought out again now! It is solacing to remember that they do not reprint everything a critic has written, as they do with composers – that there are no Breitkopf and Hartels to being out *gesammelte* editions of the celebrated critics X & Y & Z, including the work that anyone would be proud of and the work that anyone would be ashamed to own – which is the inconsiderate way they have with Bach and Mozart and Mendelssohn and Beethoven. Indeed, when I reflect upon some of the more than usually foolish things I have done in the way of criticism, my only consolation is that few as are the people who read me now, there will be fewer still to do so a hundred years hence.

SHAW AND SUPER-SHAW

The trouble with *Man and Superman* is that Mr. Shaw is
here serious to a degree that is really rare with him. He will not
let us take his amusing comedy as it stands, but he must needs try
to drag us into agreement with a preface of doubtful and an
epilogue (the "Revolutionist's Handbook") of still more doubtful
argumentation. Frankly, Shaw the humorist is more impressive
than super-Shaw the philosopher; and in saying this I have no
desire to do injustice to his obvious seriousness of purpose.
Undoubtedly he is in deadly earnest; undoubtedly he feels most
bitterly the pain and misery and bestial stupidity of mankind.

From the *Nation*, 1908–1912

OPERA IN ENGLAND

English singers, given the proper environment, have a capacity
for opera at least equal to that of any other race; and the question
was always presenting itself whether better use could not be made
of the talent the country undoubtedly possesses, and whether
something could not be done to bring more of it into the light of
day.   (1908)

ELGAR

Each section of the *Enigma* variations is a gem, but the work
remains a collection of unrelated pictures, not an organic whole.

*   *   *

The symphony is [the first], indeed, remarkable for the unity of
impression it gives, in spite of the wide emotional field it covers.

Besides this use of a central theme throughout the work, subsidiary themes from one movement recur in others, and the melody of the adagio is a note-for-note reproduction – of course, in different phrasing – of that of the scherzo. Here, perhaps, the intention is better than the achievement. I take it that it is really the scherzo that has been evolved from the adagio, not vice versa. It is more likely that Elgar should have written the noble and beautiful slow movement, and then whipped the theme up into that of a scherzo, than that he should have written the theme in its rather inexpressive quick form, and then discovered that in a slower form it would make highly expressive music. Here, perhaps, the unity of the tissue does not quite compensate us for getting a scherzo theme inferior to what Elgar could no doubt have written under other circumstances. The gradual metamorphosis of the scherzo into the adagio is, however, admirable in every way, emotionally and technically. The thematic material of the symphony is refined and expressive almost throughout, perhaps the solitary exception being a theme in C sharp minor in the scherzo. What may be called the central theme of the work, the melody that begins and ends it, is one of those rare things that seem to have more and more meaning in them each time we sing them to ourselves. (1908)

OPERA AND THE ENGLISH

We English are probably the most extraordinary people under the sun; instead of listening to music for ourselves and enjoying it, we prefer to read what someone else has to say about it. How otherwise can we explain the fact that so many books are published – apparently with enough success to induce publishers and authors to continue in the business – upon all kinds of composers of whom the average Englishman knows nothing, and can never know anything so long as the present conditions continue?

(1908)

FEUERSNOT

The opera shows to perfection Strauss's power of adapting his musical idiom to the subject in hand – a faculty for transformation of style that he shares only with Wagner and Hugo Wolf. It contains some of the loveliest music he has written, music, such as that of the children, with a sweetness and a tenderness in it that only peep out here and there, in the remainder of his work, in one or two of the songs. One wishes, indeed, that he would let us see more of this side of him – stop his contortions and jugglery and grimacing, and talk to us in plain language about something that really matters. 'Music must progress,' he said in conversation the other day, 'until it can depict even a teaspoon.' It is pretty safe to predict the ending of a composer, however gifted he may be, who sees 'progress' mainly along the line of the perfected orchestral suggestion of materialities.

Greater complexity of tissue does not necessarily mean greater depth of meaning, as anyone can see by comparing the *Symphonia Domestica* with *Tod und Verklarung*, or some of the wilder parts of *Elektra* with *Feuersnot*. The latter work, in fact, occupies somewhat the same place in Strauss's operatic development as *Don Quixote* does among the orchestral works. In both genres he has since done amazing things, but he has been less and less able to keep the cruder elements of his nature in check. In *Feuersnot* we have all that is best in Strauss – his fertility of ideas, his power of characterization, his magnificent architecture with the minimum of extravagance and ugliness.

(1910)

NIETZSCHE'S CRITICISM OF WAGNER

What, indeed, does the whole of Nietzsche's polemic come to but this – that Wagner's music gave him disagreeable sensations, for which he tried to account in terms of a world philosophy? With characteristic complacency he calls his own cravings 'the plentitude of life', and Wagner's 'the denial, the loathing of life'. The bystander smiles. He confesses that he needed music as a medicine against his melancholy; it was for this he turned, with a sigh of relief, to the nimble, sunny, clean-built art of the South. We would not deprive him, or any other sick man, of his medicine; but is his dyspepsia a reason why we, with sounder stomachs and cleaner nerves, should not eat the food that agrees with us? Here and there Nietzsche scores a good point. He is refreshingly breezy on some of Wagner's obvious weaknesses, his theories of redemption and of woman the redeemer; and his hyper-sensitive invalid's nose is keen for a whiff of the under-ripe or the over-ripe in Wagner's art, such as the 'brutality' of the *Tannhauser* overture. Some of his criticisms upon the texture of the music anticipate Debussy's well-known gibes. But he makes some amateurish blunders. He blindly insists that Wagner is only a miniaturist multiplied; he has no eye for the grand architecture and the far-flung strands of thought in the operas. He rails like a Conservatoire academic against Wagner's supposed asymmetry of rhythm and his 'endless melody', unable to see that these do not represent formlessness, but merely a more subtilized manipulation of form, just as in a modern painting balance and unity of design are secured without the Primitives' resort to mathematical squareness, or as Swinburne's metres imply a finer sense of rhythm than those of Pope. There is a good deal in the pamphlets of what looks like hard hitting, but the blows fall, not on Wagner, but on a stuffed scarecrow of Nietzsche's own that he mistakes for Wagner. It is always interesting reading, though; for Nietzsche's active imagination keeps springing a new image in almost every line, and his quick, nervous style gives one a new opinion of the German language. There is something vital in a man we can disagree with and yet enjoy so hugely. (1910)

BEETHOVEN

To the psychologist Beethoven's is one of the most interesting lives, in spite of – or perhaps because of – the fact that it is almost devoid of outer incident. It does not stand in the limelight

like Wagner's, does not come down to the footlights and bawl its
story at us till the least concerned of us cannot help but hear; it
has not even the romantic garnishings of the lives of men like
Chopin and Liszt. Beethoven, for the greater part of his career,
rarely moved out of Vienna; and for a composer – and such a
composer in such a time – he was fairly well treated by the Fates,
his work being appreciated to an extent that is really surprising,
and his material lot being felicity itself in comparison with that of
Mozart or that of Schubert. Yet his life was on the whole the
most tragic in the history of music, even when one remembers
the poverty and misery and the too-early deaths of the composers
just named, and the pitiful endings of Schumann and Hugo Wolf.
No other musician has had to face so awful a trial as deafness
during practically two-thirds of his working life. What that
meant for him we can, with all our sympathy, only dimly guess.
It must have been heart-rending for his friends to see such a sight as
Beethoven playing the piano and frequently drawing no sound
at all from the keys, so lightly did he touch them in the more
expressive passages, while he himself was unconscious of the
silence, the rapture written on his face showing that his spiritual,
if not his physical ear, was listening to the divinest strains; but
Beethoven himself, except in moments of forgetfulness like these,
the anguish of that perpetually lamed sense must have been something beyond our power of imagination. The wonder is not that
he should have thought of suicide so early as 1802, but that he
failed to carry the idea unto execution.   (1912)

GRANVILLE BANTOCK

It argues no small imaginative and technical power for a
composer to able be to keep us deeply interested in a piece of
unaccompanied choral music for something like forty minutes.

★   ★   ★

There is no more expressive choral writing in Europe today,
indeed, than Mr. Bantock's.

★   ★   ★

I can think of none, since Bach, whose choral music talks so gravely and wisely of the profounder issues of life and death. Mr. Bantock's *Omar Khayyam* is particularly rich in music of this type; .... (1912)

From the *New Witness*, 1916–1918

ON THE CRITIC AND MUSICAL CRITICISM

Had Samuel Butler been alive in the great days of the Greek drama, had he been critic, say of the *Athens Daily Mail*, and had he said there, as he does in one of his books, that Aeschylus was an old humbug whom the world rates far above his merits, that he probably bribed the dramatic critics of his time to say the best they could for him, and that we can account for his getting his plays produced only on the supposition that he married the daughter of a theatrical manager – had Butler said these things then and there, Aeschylus would have spluttered with rage at the insolence of the critic, and would have had something very nasty to say about the uselessness of criticism, except when practised by 'creative artists'.

Time blunts the edge of many an effect in music that seemed to its own generation the last word in poignancy: if the celebrated monologue in Gluck's *Iphigenia in Tauris* seems to us a little blood-less after Wagner and Strauss, how can we be expected to thrill to it now at secondhand, through the recorded thrill of some journalist of Gluck's time? But the journalist of that time did good service in pointing out the feature in the aria that might have escaped the casual listener; and if musical criticism is good enough to be of some slight use in its own day it has perhaps fulfilled its function. It is a common grievance of the musical critic that he generally has to do his work with one eye on the clock. Perhaps that is just as well, after all; it may keep him from the too fond vanity of fixing both eyes on eternity.

*   *   *

K

. . . Pater's famous rhapsody upon the Mona Lisa has the very slightest connection with the picture; to many artists it means nothing at all – it would probably have meant nothing at all to Leonardo: one does not need to have seen the picture to enjoy Pater's words about it, and when, after having read those words a hundred times, we stand once more before the picture, the words never recur to us, or do so only in proportion as we lack the painter's eye for the painting. Pater might conceivably have been wrought to the same ecstasy by a poor picture, in which case his dithyramb upon it would have been no less fine as mere literature, just as a love lyric loses nothing in beauty for the world at large from the fact that the maiden who inspired it was more fair in the poet's imagination than in reality. Pater's passage is hardly at all a transposition of the picture itself into another medium: it is simply the literary expression of a mood in himself that this particular picture had the good fortune to evoke: the picture merely made visible something that was already written in him in invisible ink. Had it been a shade less well done, the rhapsody would have been as insufferable as the conventional rhapsody of the feminine scribe upon music.

★   ★   ★

. . . it always makes us doubt another man's sanity to find that he has read into a given page of music a series of images quite different from our own. . . .

★   ★   ★

The first precept for the critic surely is that he shall paint with his eye in the object, and the portrait shall be unmistakably that of the sitter.

★   ★   ★

Really musical people, for instance, can never see anything erotic in the music of *Tristan* as half-musical people generally do; while these latter people can never see what it is in the music of *Tristan* that makes it, to the musician, so glorious an experience to live through.   (1917)

PUTTING THE CLASSICS IN THEIR PLACE

We have never had a real iconoclast in music. We have, it is true, in abundance, young musicians who dislike Bach or Beethoven or Mozart or Wagner; but their repugnance is so obviously a purely temperamental matter that we take no notice of it. It would really do us good for a genuine iconoclast to arise among us – one who would break graven images impartially and rationally, because he thought graven images bad for our souls, and who would have some sort of workable criterion for knowing a veritable graven image when he saw it, and not confusing it with a piece of individual sculpture. We critics are always complaining of the lack of real originality among composers; but how many critics are really original? The great test of the critic is supposed to be his scent for the right or the wrong thing in new music. I should say that a greater test is his scent for the real or the sham thing in the old music. It is really less difficult to see a modern composer as he really is than to see a classic as he really is; the classic comes to us in such a cloud of transmitted adoration that none of us, do what we will, can turn the same critical searchlight upon him that we do upon Strauss or Debussy. Let us take a couple of specific instances. A few years ago Strauss produced a short orchestral work – a 'Festal Prelude' for the opening of a new concert room in Vienna or somewhere. Virtually the whole of the British press 'turned it down', as the vernacular has it: I myself not merely turned it down but stamped on it, for it was a truly wretched piece of hack-work. But there is an early Beethoven *Rondino* for wind that Sir Henry Wood is very fond of giving, no doubt for the chances it affords to good wind players to show what is in them. 'Autolycus' candidly calls the *Rondino* a dull work. So it is. If one of our young British composers were to produce such a work at Queen's Hall, the critics would with one accord say things about him that would make his ears tingle for a month after. Yet very few of us say, the morning after a concert, that we think the *Rondino* dull; and if we do drop a hint to that effect, it is in a half-apologetic way, as

if we knew we were doing the wrong thing in supposing that so
great a man as Beethoven could ever be third-rate.

★   ★   ★

The young composer of today is not even given the dog's
privilege of a first mistake: the classic can get the majority of us
to accept almost every one of his mistakes as a Delphian oracle.
Gott in Himmel, how dull Bach sometimes is! Yet let anyone show
me, if he can, the book in which Bach's occasional faults of dull-
ness and over-statement are frankly laid bare.

★   ★   ★

Is there one orchestral work by a relatively unknown British
composer, given during the last ten years, that is of so fine a
quality that were the public to hear it twenty times, instead of
once, they could clamour to hear it a hundred times?

★   ★   ★

Music in the newspapers should be the affair of experts who
will treat it not as a matter of mere performance but as a matter of
culture, who will interest the public in new good music as the
literary expert interests it in new good books. Where would our
young poets be if it were not for the publicity given to their work
in the best critical reviews? *Per contra,* what would become of a
volume of songs by an English Wolf or of piano works by another
Albeniz or Granados if it were issued in this country? There are
not five newspapers in Britain in which it would be reviewed at
the length and with the care and authority that a volume of poems
by a new poet of genius would. How can it be expected, with the
musical portion of the Press mishandled as it is at present, that the
majority of music-lovers should know what is going on in
music, that they should be interested in new ideas, and that they
should be stimulated by criticism to buy new music and test it for
themselves? English music suffers not from a variety of diseases
but from one central disease only – the lack of a cultured public;
and the biggest force in supplying the culture in a free and independent and progressive form must be, as it is in literature and the
other arts, a truly critical Press.

Beethoven meeting Paër after a performance of the latter's opera *Eleanora*, said to him, 'I like your opera: I think I will set it to music'. That was perhaps not very nice, at the moment, for Paër; but as the result was *Fidelio* and in the sequel, the *Leonora No. 3 Overture*, the world has given Beethoven a full indemnity.

*   *   *

Many of Chopin's melodies are obviously so much more violinistic than pianistic that one wonders why Chopin himself did not perceive that fact.

*   *   *

Paganini would probably not have understood a page of the variations that Brahms has written upon a well-known theme of his, and would have protested against what would no doubt have seemed to him an impertinent desecration. But Brahms was right. He shows us nothing in the theme that was not latent in it all the time, though Paganini had not the wit to see it.

(1918)

DEBUSSY

Debussy has always struck me as containing something pathetically childlike, not to say childish, in his make-up. The prose is often that of a smart schoolboy! I think I have said once before, somewhere or other, that his gibes at Wagner remind me of an urchin who scribbles an obscenity on a public monument and then walks away whistling for pure pride and joy in his own smartness. (1916)

The first paradox of Debussy is that his very originality prevented him from being as great as perhaps he might have been had he been slightly less original; and the second paradox is that for so thoroughly independent a thinker he was strangely dependent upon the thought of others – more dependent upon others than other geniuses have been who were, on the surface, rather less 'original' than he. (1918)

THE MUSICIAN AND HIS ENVIRONMENT

If I were to attempt to trace my own development, I should find that the thinking and feeling part of me was made up, before I was twenty-five, of not only the usual English influences but of very powerful influences from Greek sculpture, from English and French and German philosophy, strong tinctures of Renaissance art and of French literature, particularly of the eighteenth century and of the Romantic period, and of course the music of all nations and all periods. The mind cannot be parcelled off into watertight compartments. . . .

I think I can trace what I take to be one of my dominant traits in musical feeling – my passion for what I call, for want of a better term, musical logic, for closeness and coherence and the inevitable continuity of musical thought – to two great culture influences in my early life that have seemingly nothing to do with music – an early acquired habit of reading hard in philosophy, and the most intense love for sculpture, the art in which form speaks most lucidly and most concisely.   (1917)

A SCHOOL FOR CRITICS

The fact that there are hardly five decent musical critics in Europe, while there are at least five thousand decent fiddlers, would seem to show that the good critic is a type a thousand times as rare as the good fiddler.

The trouble with a critic is that he has to be his own pupil and his own master, and that by the time he has learned enough of the business to be able to teach himself he is either ripe for the grave or unresponsive to music from too much hearing of it.

The peculiarity of music is that its very language alters from generation to generation; and much of the misunderstanding that falls to the lot of men like Wagner is due to their speaking in polysyllables, as it were, to a certain number of good people who can think only in words of one syllable, or to people who might be able to follow Mrs. Hemans but would be confused by Shelley.

Wagner not only founded the modern music drama and the modern symphonic poem; he also founded, unknown to himself and his contemporaries, modern musical criticism. That so little has as yet been built on his foundation is our fault not his.

(1916)

BEETHOVEN

Fate seems to have shaped him with the conscious and deliberate hand of an artist bending a mass of inchoate material to the realization of a vision of his own. It pruned him as a horticulturist prunes a tree, destroying a dozen shoots that one may bear the richer fruit. We can only dimly speculate on what would have become of him had disease not laid her ugly and terrible hand on him at the beginning.

Music shows us the soul of things at first hand.

The *Eroica* or the C-minor Symphony is as truly a reading of earth as anything that Shakespeare or Wordsworth could give us.

Wagner was right: there is no music that suggests the clair-voyant like Beethoven's.

I fancy we have, by a sort of paradox, another evidence of the clairvoyant nature of Beethoven's genius – a genius that was simply the medium through which a power beyond himself delivered its oracles – in the very slowness of some of his conceptions. His sketch-books show us that his themes were, as a rule, arrived at by a series of experiments: as first set down they are often incredibly commonplace; then they are altered by a touch here and a touch there, until, after a score of hackings and hewings, they take the shape in which we now know them.

(1917)

BIZET

Carmen had to be written; no one else could have done it, and the world would obviously have been incomplete without it: yet Bizet would probably never have repeated that success, and there is a species of philosophic beauty in his death within a few months of it.

*   *   *

It (*The Fair Maid of Perth*) manages to hold the sympathetic attention of the musician almost as much in the theatre as it does in the study. The explanation lies, no doubt, in the pure if slenderly-built genius that undoubtedly infuses a good deal of it.

(1917)

THE RUSSIAN SONG

... the wonderful 'Savielina' of Moussorgsky – one of the most extraordinary songs ever written. The words are the composer's own. He was looking out of the window in a house in the country one day when he saw the village idiot – poor, ugly, ragged, God's fool but an offence in the eyes of men – begging a disdainful village beauty for a moment of love. A wave of Dostoevskian pity – that marvellous Russian pity – surged through Moussorgsky and this song welled up in him. It is in five-four time, with five crochets – never more and never less – in each bar. In the whole of two hundred and twenty-five crochets there is not a breathing space marked for the singer. He has to snatch a little breath when he can: the song is thus exceedingly difficult to sing, which is no doubt one of the reasons why we never hear it. If we can forget

the poor singer, we can only admire the intentions that lie at the
root of the song and the persistence with which Moussorgsky
holds to them. The unchanging rhythm and the absence of any
pause in the vocal melody suggest, as no other devices could do,
the breathless eagerness of the poor idiot: he begins with a
stammered phrase, is obsessed by it, has not the art to vary it,
pours out his incoherent soul in it, and at the finish stops as incon-
sequently as he had begun; the breath and nerve drawn out of
him. That is all, and he is physically done – a candle that has
spluttered out in the socket. The whole thing is something unique
in the literature of the song. (1917)

MOUSSORGSKY

Moussorgsky was the great folk-composer of Russia; he saw, as
no composer has done before or since, into the very hearts of his
simple countrymen, and out of the songs and dances of these
unsophisticated beings he made a musical language that is at once
theirs and his – theirs raised to the *Nth* by sympathetic genius.

*　　*　　*

The supreme instance in modern music of this ability to make
one's own technique – a technique never dreamed of by any
practician, and still less by any theoretician, before their time – are
Wagner and Wolf. Debussy and Stravinsky have done the same
thing but on a smaller scale. One of the Russians of the mid-
nineteenth century had the capacity for it all-round, though
Moussorgsky struck out a melodic and harmonic idiom of his
own, and Rimsky-Korsakov an orchestral idiom of his own.

*　　*　　*

The Dargomijsky ideal of opera as a reproduction in music of
the accents and inflections of the speaking voice is nothing but the
amateurism of a man who is only half a musician.

*　　*　　*

His (Moussorgsky's) own field in music was a very narrow one.
He cultivated it to perhaps the utmost perfection to which it

L

would be possible to bring it; but he no doubt felt himself the narrowness of it, and was always being tempted to leap the fences. His nature was at bottom extraordinarily original. Where his imagination and his technique enabled him to realize that original-ity to the full, the results are wonderful. But he had many impulses to originality that never succeeded in getting past the purely ratiocinative side of him, never became an unconscious part of the blood and bone of his thinking. Some of his work stands midway between these two extremes of inspired unconsciousness and uninspired deliberation.

*   *   *

We may almost say that Moussorgsky was a Russian Synge. He studied the simple Russian peasant as Synge studied the peasant of the West of Ireland, assimilated the peasants' language till it became the very blood and bone of his own thinking, and he drew the peasant from life and to life in a language applicable to him and no one else. He had Synge's contempt for all that is ready-made in art, for the facile effects of the standardized emotions and the transmitted speech. He would have called this, like Synge, 'town writing'. He would have said with Synge, that 'before verse can be human again it must learn to be brutal'. He might not have agreed that 'when men lose their poetic feeling for ordinary life, and cannot write poetry of ordinary things, then exalted poetry is likely to lose its strength of exaltation, in the way men cease to build beautiful churches when they have lost happiness in building shops'.

*   *   *

Khovantchina, in spite of many pages that we can never forget, strikes us, on the whole, as little more than a watering-down of *Boris*.

*   *   *

Moussorgsky is the only case known in musical history of a composer with a clear enough consciousness of himself to know how far genius can be trusted unassisted.

RIMSKY-KORSAKOV

Rimsky-Korsakov is one of the most baffling problems in musical history. One rarely comes across anything in his work that suggests genius – except, of course, in his orchestration – and yet one is always attracted to him and interested in him. If he is not a genius, he is at any rate a talent of the first order.

*　　*　　*

I make bold to say that it was precisely because Rimsky-Korsakov tried to think too hard like Moussorgsky and the other nationalists of his day that he found such difficulty in discovering his real self – that had he been born in an epoch that was less the slave of a fixed idea he would have been a greater composer.

*　　*　　*

Rimsky-Korsakov's nature was a subtler and far more adventurous one than Moussorgsky's, but he was without Moussorgsky's gift – the gift of genius – for finding at once his right orientation.

*　　*　　*

Rimsky-Korsakov does wonders with the folk-song in *Le Nuit de Mai*; here is a purely Russian popular subject, and the virtuoso in him made it possible for him to limn every one of his characters in the traditional popular idiom.

*　　*　　*

Rimsky-Korsakov had dreams of a musical logic that should flow through and unite organically all the parts of an opera. In *Le Coq d'Or* these dreams were largely realized; in *Ivan the Terrible* he is for ever pursuing them and for ever losing them.

SCRIABINE

Scriabine is always naïf enough to let us see, by the indications in his score, what it was in his mind to say; and it is not our fault if, comparing the indications with the music, we are occasionally

more disappointed with the latter than we should have been had
the composer been content to leave it to speak for itself. When he
writes, for example, '*Monstrueux et Terrifiant*' over a clear little
theme that is no more monstrous and no more terrifying than a
white mouse, we cannot help being a little more severe on the
theme than we otherwise would be. The score of this third symphony of his is besprinkled with markings that over-describe the
music just as grossly: Scriabine may have felt in these themes all the
horror, the despair or the sublimity with which he labels them;
but for the unprepossessed listener there is hardly one of them
that, judging it by specimens of the horrible, the despairing or the
sublime in other men's music, can be said to answer to its label.

(1918)

GLINKA

Glinka has become largely a myth. He was never a really great
composer, and he is of scarcely any significance in the history of
any music but Russian music. He is not big enough in any way to
be a world figure; and the greater music of Western Europe in the
last eighty years would have been precisely what it is now had he
never lived; but a lucky coincidence of certain qualities in himself
and of certain needs in the Russian musical life of his day enabled
him to set a movement going that would have been impossible to
a composer ten times as big as he in a country with a more
developed music.

A sensible nation, like a sensible man, talks as little as possible
about its past. . . . .

A Life for the Tsar is merely fluent commonplace, that will never
stand the ghost of a chance, let the propagandists of all things
Russians work their fountain pens to the hardest, of imposing
itself upon the experienced operatic public of our own epoch. I do
not know what a great interpreter like Chaliapin could make of

the character of Soussanine, but as Soussanine appears in Glinka's score I can see nothing very striking about him.

* * *

Glinka never evolved a purely Russian style Russian folk-song, for the simple reason that he never succeeded in evolving any style whatever of his own. His operas are a mixture of half-a-dozen styles – fragments of genuine folk-song, essays of his own in the folk style, the commonest tags of the Franco-Italian opera, whiffs of German Romanticism, coquettings with Orientalisms, and – but only occasionally – strokes of real and striking individuality.

* * *

I can nowhere see genius in Glinka.

* * *

Russlan and Ludmilla, like *A Life for the Tsar*, is a medley of incongruities. (1917)

MANFRED (SCHUMANN)

Musicians will always be eager to hear the *Manfred* music, for it is among the very best that Schumann wrote. This phase of him is hardly known at all in England, where the only Schumann the amateur knows is the Schumann of the early song and piano pieces. The greater Schumann is to be found in some of the works of his last fruitful period, before his mental trouble had seriously affected him.

* * *

Schumann had little dramatic sense; but he had lyricism and he had philosophy, and wherever, in his later larger works, he gets an opportunity for one of these he is astoundingly modern.

In *Manfred* he (Schumann) is much more of our own day than Byron is. And he is helped by the haphazard nature of his cooperation with the poet. In *Faust* and *Genoveva* his liability to cover the whole range of dramatic expression keeps him some-times plodding on page after page, with the emptiest of platitudes. In *Manfred* he could select; and he has chosen virtually nothing from the drama that could not call out the whole face of his genius.   (1918)

THE VALKYRIE

What struck me in *The Valkyrie*, after not having heard the opera or looked at the score of it for four or five years, was the superb ease and confidence of its style. The Wagnerian manner-isms, the Wagnerian *longueurs*, were unmistakably there; but they seemed very trifling things. The dominant impression was of a medium of musical speech that was equal to any demand that might be made upon it, a style that, as it were, is ready to go any-where and do anything, to be realistically descriptive, atmospheri-cally suggestive, philosophical, or purely emotional, and to keep all four orders of expression in constant interflow. There is no music of the present day that has anything like this universality of scope; for the satisfaction of the various sides of our imagination we have to go to various composers. When the man comes who can sum up all the musical thinking as Wagner summed up that of his own day, the man who shall be master of the whole field of modern feeling and modern style, we shall have then, but not till then, something as wonderful in its own genre as *Tristan* and *The Mastersingers* and *The Ring* are in theirs.   (1918)

PUCCINI

No artist, of course, ever achieves such popularity, and such enduring popularity, among art lovers of all kinds without there being excellent reasons for it. Puccini's genius is a very limited one, but he has always made the very most of it. His operas are to some extent a mere bundle of tricks: but no one else has ever performed the same tricks nearly so well.

The failure of *The Girl of the Golden West* is largely due to the fact that there he aimed at making the general tissue of the music more organic throughout, instead of relying upon his power to bluff us through the less vital portions of the work by means of those delightful irrelevant little orchestral garrulities that in *Manon* and *La Bohème* keep us too constantly and too agreeably interested for us to have either the time or the inclination to be critical. Puccini's music has none of the philosophical pity of *Parsifal* nor of the wistful pity of *Pelleas and Melisande*, but for blubbering, whimpering pity there is no music to compare with it. We weep with his little people because there is nothing so infectious as tears – even the tears of weak self-pity.

Both *La Bohème* and *Madam Butterfly* are masterpieces in the miniature style.   (1918)

SALOME

Had Wilde not been convicted and sent to gaol for practising a nasty vice, it is pretty safe to say that no one would ever have thought of reading nastiness into *Salome*, just as no one would have thought of reading nastiness into *Parsifal* but for the fact that the friendship of Wagner and King Ludvig was the friendship of two men. . . .

Artists should ask themselves betimes whether the heresy hunt having died out in religion, it should be allowed to be revived in art – whether they will tolerate their art being pronounced malodorous simply because it smells evil to some poor fool with a polypus in his nose.   (1918)

THE PERFECT ACCOMPANIST

The perfect accompanist, could we evolve him, would be very much our ideal musician. The wider any musician's knowledge is, the better; but roughly speaking we cannot expect any more of the singer or the pianist or the violinist than that he should be thoroughly conversant with his own branch of art and the music that has been written for it.

In Ippolitov-Ivanov's song, 'Far on the road we two journeyed together', the 'scoring' – for so we may truly call it, although the accompaniment is purely for the pianoforte – is obviously for the woodwind in octaves (with that strange mixture of fullness and hollowness that we sometimes get when clarinet, say, and bassoon are doubled at the octave) with horn chords in between. The intelligent accompanist will not need to have all this set down for him on his copy. He will enter imaginatively into the mind of the composer, who, though he himself may not have been conscious of it, must have been possessed by the memory of some such combination of timbres in the orchestra.   (1918)

BANDBOX OPERA

I have long dreamed of the possibility, or at least the desirability of the country being studded with bandbox opera houses.

Not in the life-time of any of us now living, I am afraid, shall we see full-sized opera houses in even half-a-dozen of the larger towns.

. . . the average English music lover knows next to nothing of that most delightful guise, the *Opéra Comique*.   (1918)

NONSENSE MUSIC

Music has talked such admirable sense for so long that I wish a composer or two of genius would arise who would make it talk equally admirable nonsense. For really, for so human an art, music has been preternaturally serious: whereas our shelves are covered with masterpieces in the serious genre, the works of genuine and enduring musical humour could probably be counted on the fingers of both hands. There has been plenty of music written to humorous subjects, but it has mostly not been humorous music – not music, that is to say, that we could recognize as humorous apart from its subject. And so far there has been practically no nonsense music, by which I do not mean the mere piling up of absurdity, but that blend of sense and absurdity that we get in Carroll, in Lear, and in Gilbert at his best – the world obviously seen upside down, but still recognizable as the world, and almost as rational seen standing on its head as standing on its feet.

Satie has, I should say, a good deal of the right sort of topsy-turvy imagination for the nonsense worker, without the musical ability to realize it.

When, in the *Holothurie* of the *Embryons Desséchés*, Satie marks a passage '*Comme un rossignol qui aurait mal aux dents*' the joke remains a merely verbal one. These *Embryons Desséchés* however, contain some of his best fooling. They may be described as days in the life of certain inhabitants of the deep. We really seem to get to know the *Holothuria* ('whom the ignorant call the sea-cucumber'), the *Edriophthalma* ('Crustaceans with sessile eyes, that is to say without stalks and immovable; naturally very sad, these crustaceans live in retirement from the world, in holes dug in the cliffs'), and the *Podophthalma* ('Crustaceans whose eyes are on movable stalks; they are adroit and indefatigable hunters, etc.'). We see the *Holothuria* taking his promenade in the rain, and gluing himself with a sigh of satisfaction to a rock; and we quiver with him when the bit of moss tickles him ('*ne me faites pas rire bien de mousse: vous me chatouillez*'). Best of all is the musical description of the sombre meeting of the *Edriophthalma* tribe, where a *père de famille* addresses them in mournful tones; and they all weep to the strains of what Satie describes as '*citation de la célèbre mazurka de Schubert*' but that is, of course, a delightful burlesque of the slow section of Chopin's Funeral March. Here there is something for us to go upon. The nonsense has the basis of sense that all good nonsense must have. The trouble with Satie is that as a rule he is not musician enough to stand musical sense on its head, in the Carroll or Lear style, and keep it still recognizable. What he too often gives us is not pure nonsense, but merely damned nonsense.

(1918)

TEMPO

Wagner's marking for Elizabeth's Prayer is crotchet = 60, quickening to 66 and then to 72, with a final return to 60. I think it will be found in practice, that comparatively few Elizabeths keep within these figures.   (1918)

THE UNFINISHED IN MUSIC

We have, in Hugo Wolf's last opera *Manuel Venegas*, the case of a dead composer's incomplete manuscript being published as he left it; and I know nothing more pathetic than this fragment. It ends abruptly in a casual bar with an unresolved discord; and so helpless are we in the face of the unfinished music that, so far from our imagination being able to surmise the remainder of the scene, it is incompetent to give, for the mere resolution of the discord, a suggestion so plausible that any musician would accept it as being the probable truth.   (1918)

THE SMALL POEM IN MUSIC

What is the shortest complete musical work that has ever been written? So far as I know, it is one of Theodore Streicher's four settings of the *Sprüche und Gedichte*, of Richard Dehmel. As so often happens, the very new thing has been done for the first time by a composer not of the first class. This little opus of Streicher's consists of four songs – if we can call them songs: perhaps aphorisms in music would be a better title for them. The fourth is of average length; but the first runs only to eight bars,

the third to nine bars and the second to no more than four bars –
which last I take to be the record in musical brevity. One or two of
the little pieces are not wholly unsuccessful, though we always
have the feeling that it was hardly worth while setting so much
apparatus to work to say so little; it suggests a man taking half-an-
hour to get a string of his violin in tune and then publicly playing
a semiquaver on it; for few as the notes are in the smallest of these
works, the *Leitspruch*, they seem rather many for the impression
that is finally left on us. The collection as a whole does not
destroy our belief in the possibility of musical song reduced to the
nutshell; it only makes us wish that some man of genius would
try his hand at the genre.   (1918)

From the *Musical Courier*, 1919

SIR HUBERT PARRY

When a composer dies it is customary for concert societies to
devote a whole memorial concert to his works. Within the last
few years there have died Scriabine, Reger, Debussy, and
Granados. From the works of any of these men an interesting
orchestral or choral evening could be made up. Even Saint-Saëns
could fill out an evening. But what survives on the world-stage
of Parry's music? The *Blest Pair of Sirens* alone. All the orchestral works, all the other choral works have vanished, except from
the smaller provincial concert-rooms. Of his many songs, not one
has taken any real hold upon either singers or public. As a composer he has already ceased to be for the simple reason that as a
composer he never was.

Parry's music is not an artist's picture of the emotions with
which it deals; it is only a guide book to the emotions, a conscientiously constructed chart to them, done by a plodding
cartographer without the visionary inner eye.   (1919)

From the *Sunday Chronicle*, 1923

ON FLOGGING

If flogging really does act as a deterrent, I see no good sentimental reason why it should not be administered. Are not the
people who object to it a little inconsistent? Do they not show a
certain lack of imagination? They can enter shudderingly into
the feelings of a man who is getting the lash. But surely, to anyone
with a lively imagination, the thought of what some criminals
must suffer during a long imprisonment is just as dreadful?
Stinie Morrison, it is evident, suffered intensely – as a caged beast
would, no doubt, but all the same in a way that moves us to
pity. If, in the social interest, we are to stifle our pity in the one
case, why should we not do so in the other?

Indeed, if flogging is a deterrent (remember, I am not saying
whether it is or is not), there are many criminals who perhaps
better deserve a flogging than some of those who get it. Why flog
some poor wretch who, perhaps in desperation, inflicts a bodily
wound on the man he is robbing of a few pounds – a wound
from which the man soon recovers – and not flog a Bottomley or
a Jabez Balfour, whose cold-blooded depredations may possibly
condemn thousands to years of misery, or drive some to suicide?

But the real argument of the advocates of flogging is that it
deters certain criminals from committing certain crimes. I really
cannot see, on these lines, why it should not be equally efficacious
with other criminals and other crimes. If flogging were made the
penalty for other crimes, would not an eminent financier think
twice before he falsified a balance-sheet if there were a chance of
his getting flogged when he was found out?

The criminal who uses violence is often a blunted being, with
a physical organization as insensitive as his mental or moral
organization, with a hide so tough that an ordinary hiding is
wasted on him; whereas the eminent financier is probably a man
of refinement and culture, soft tissued as the result of soft living,
a man whom the very thought of a flogging would probably
keep honest in the moment of greatest temptation.

XI

FROM *A MUSICAL CRITIC'S HOLIDAY*
1925

A MAN OF Chaucer's day – we might even say a man of Aeschylus's day, had Europe known but one language for the last three thousand years – would find little difficulty in deciding whether *Hamlet* was a great work or not. The man of Herrick's time would find no difficulty in taking his bearings in the lyrical poetry of today. But what would a man of the twelfth century who knew (apart from folk-songs and dances) no music but plainsong and the first experiments in organum have been able to make of a mass by Palestrina or a madrigal by Gesualdo? What would Peri or Caccini, or any other of the Florentine reformers, or even Monteverdi himself, have been able to make of *Tristan* had he been brought to life about 1870 and suddenly set down in a German opera house? Would the composer of *Sumer is icumen in*, had he been reanimated in Leipzig in the early eighteenth century, have been able to follow the complex figuration of a Bach chorale prelude? What would John Bull have been able to make of one of the late Beethoven quartets, or even of the *Eroica*? Would Corelli have been able to make head or tail of Bela Bartok's second violin sonata? Would the composer of any of the old German chorales be able to find his way about in a song like Hugo Wolf's *Auf dem grünen Balkon*? What would a great sixteenth-century contrapuntist like Byrd make of Schönberg's *Pierrot Lunaire*?

★　★　★

We know that almost every harmonic innovation has puzzled, and perhaps shocked, some contemporary listener or other. But the shocked ones have mostly been pedagogues and theorists, whose freedom of assimilation was hampered by their belief that the 'laws' of their schools and their text-books were rooted in Nature itself. But whatever a few people of this kind may have said about the harmonic innovations, these presented no difficulty to the average man who, having escaped the petrifying intellectual influences of an academic musical education, listened with his ears and his imagination alone. Unfortunately the musical histories tell us nothing about these people – what, indeed, is there to tell about them? – while the historians go on making an absurd fuss over some pedant or some ignoramus whose inanities happen to have been recorded in print.

★   ★   ★

The plain man, knowing nothing of harmonic analysis or the 'laws' of harmonic combination and progression, is as a rule happily ignorant whether a new texture is new or not, or in what respects it is new; all he knows is whether it pleases him or not, whether it does or does not carry on the composer's thought logically. There are tens of thousands of unschooled hearers, for instance, who have no notion that the harmony of Scriabine's *Prometheus* and of other late works of his is largely based on a chord-system of superimposed fourths. But it is not necessary for them to know this, any more than it is necessary for the lover of a simple song to know that some of its harmonies are tonic, some dominant, some sub-dominant, and all the rest of it. All that is required is that he shall be able to follow the composer's thoughts as expressed in the harmonies.

★   ★   ★

Vocal music has gone stepwise from the simplest folksong to the subtly wrought songs of Hugo Wolf, and from the most primitive piece of 'imitation' to the intricate voice-weaving of the madrigal. Instrumental music has gone stepwise from the primitive dance tune, with its simple balance of parts, to the fugue of Bach and the symphony of Beethoven, Brahms, Franck and Elgar. Opera has progressed stepwise from the *Euridice* of Peri, or those still earlier quasi-dramatic tentatives of the sixteenth century with which modern research has made us acquainted, to the opera of Verdi, of Wagner, of Strauss, of Moussorgsky, of Debussy. In none of these instances has progress consisted of anything but putting old material to new uses, expanding it and adapting it as was necessary.

*   *   *

No critic who thinks at all about his work can feel anything but depression after twenty years or so at it.

*   *   *

There has never yet been a composer so greatly in advance of his time that only an initiate here and there – one or two out of a vast population of cultivated musicians and music lovers – could understand him.

*   *   *

Is it not part of the business of the critic to distinguish between the works that are masterpieces and those that are not, and to make it clear that a given work is to be put in the one or the other class?

*   *   *

The chief object of the critic is surely to get other people to see the thing as he sees it; in other words, to get us to believe that he is right in calling this work good and the other bad. And how is this appeal of his judgment to ours to succeed unless he and we agree on certain standards of goodness, or rightness, that are independent of our own little subjectivities?

*   *   *

The artist can be, to a large extent, a law unto himself. The critic cannot. . . .

          ★   ★   ★

The truth is that the modern composers are mostly 'too complicated', resorting to ingenuities and piquancies and audacities because they know that if they were to talk simply about simple things their poverty of idea would be found out. Still, there are works that are recognized as excellent, even at a first hearing, by both critics and public: for example, Gade's first symphony, 'which pleased at its first performance in Leipzig, and goes on pleasing everywhere'.

I am pulled up with a jerk; my blood runs cold.

Gade's first symphony! Where is that symphony now? as Hans Breitmann might ask. I begin to ask myself whether our good Lobe's judgment is quite so infallible as he thought, especially when I find him, in this same chapter, hinting that the bigger works of Schumann were among those that indiscreet admirers regarded as too 'deep' to be understood all at once. Well, Schumann's symphonies may not be in the very front rank of their genre, but at any rate they are still alive, which is more than can be said, I am afraid, for the Number One of the estimable Gade.

          ★   ★   ★

It is all very well to say that the difference between good music and bad music is that the former is sincerely felt and the latter is not; but what is 'sincere' in this connection? Is it not probable that Ethelbert Nevin was as sincerely moved when he wrote *The Rosary* as Wagner was when he wrote *Tristan*?

          ★   ★   ★

The test to which we put a critic of the past is this – did he see his own age *sub specie aeternitatis*? Did he pierce through all the little things of the day that did not matter and get to the heart of the things that really did? This is the test, we may depend upon it, to which each critic of today will be put who may have the curiosity to make research into contemporary critical opinion.

          ★   ★   ★

Every new movement, not only in art but in politics and in social affairs, throws up a large number of not very intelligent people who are infected by the excitement around them and stimulated by it to a self-expression that may be excellent as a safety-valve for themselves, but does not add very much to the world's store of wisdom.

*   *   *

Nowhere does history repeat itself with such monotonous uniformity as in this eternal resurgence of the romantic in art.

*   *   *

Theophile Gautier's *Histoire du Romanticisme* has this value among others, that it shows us how a movement of revolt appeared in later years to one who had taken a prominent part in it. Gautier himself has to admit that in the trail of the half-dozen artists of the time who really mattered came an army of little people of whom their contemporaries and they themselves took much too flattering a view. Even Petrus Borel – a fourth-rate mind if ever there was one – inspired the young Gautier with 'exceeding awe'; he treated Borel, he says, 'with an amount of respect quite unusual between young fellows of nearly an age ... I thought him remarkably clever, and had concluded that he would be the particular great man of our company. He was slowly elaborating the Rhapsodies in mysterious secrecy, intending that they should suddenly blaze forth like lightning, or at least dazzle the outstanding bourgeoisie', the Borels we have always with us; who does not recognize a hundred specimens of the type in the music of today? They are always about to blaze; always, like Mr. Snodgrass, taking off their coats and announcing that they are going to begin. And an admiring world waits expectantly; but the coat never gets any lower than the shoulders, the blaze never becomes more than the spluttering of a squib.

*   *   *

Is any age capable of distinguishing between its own first-rate composers and its second- and third-rate? Have not past generations blundered badly in this respect? And is our own luck likely to be any better in the eyes of our successors?

*   *   *

What are we to make, for instance, of the case of Telemann, that has been set forth so fully for us in M. Romain Rolland's essay on 'A Forgotten Master', in his book, *Voyage Musical au Pays du Passé*? Telemann's vogue was infinitely greater than that of his contemporary Bach. Yet Bach today is – Bach; and Telemann is forgotten except by an historian here and there. Has it been thus in every age, the glib talent being acclaimed and the seminal genius being ignored or opposed?

*   *   *

Mr. Bernard Shaw has had some devastating things said about him in his time. Suppose some historian, fifty or a hundred years hence, were to dig out a few of these and attempt to prove from them that Mr. Shaw met with nothing but misunderstanding and vilification during his lifetime; would not that be a sad perversion of the real fact, which is that Mr. Shaw is recognized all the world over as one of the half-dozen most vital minds of our time?

*   *   *

It is high time someone undertook a genuine history of musical opinion. What has hitherto passed for this seems mostly to have been written by children for children.

*   *   *

In recent years the great object of sympathy, among recently dead composers, has been Hugo Wolf. The legend is already well established that it was left to the decade that followed his premature death to atone for the scandalous neglect of his contemporaries. Only the other day a newspaper correspondent, combating my views that history records no case of a great musical genius being so far ahead of his time that his contemporaries could not do him justice, confronted me with Hugo Wolf. 'One can confidently assert', he said, 'that practically nothing but

nonsense was written about him in his own day.' History, however, does not support this confident assertion. Excellent and
appreciative articles on Wolf's music were written during his
lifetime by several people, including Emil Kauffman, Josef
Schalk, Michael Haberlandt, Edmund Hellmer, Karl Hallwachs,
Paul Muller, Karl Crunsky, and O. E. Nodnagel. It may be said
that these were mostly members of the Wolf circle. Precisely; but
they had become members of the Wolf circle through their
enthusiasm for his music. And if it be asked why Wolf's music
made so little general headway during his lifetime, the answer is
that comparatively few people could, in the circumstances of the
case, have any acquaintance with it. Few of the German singers
who knew anything about the songs cared to sing them; we all
know what singers are. The songs were difficult, and the average
singer, not seeing sufficient opportunities for applause in them,
could hardly be induced even to study them. The accompaniments
are often so difficult that even today the ordinary amateur can
make little of them.

*   *   *

Criticism has practically nothing to reproach itself for with
regard to Gesualdo. He has always been seen by those who have
studied him (except Burney) steadily and whole. His case certainly
will not support the theory that there are geniuses so far ahead
of their own or the next century that many generations have to
go by before they can be rightly judged.

*   *   *

How, indeed, could or can the few 'make' a composer? Music,
let me repeat, is an art that people enjoy in masses. They pay their
money to be interested and pleased, and if they are not interested
and pleased, nothing will make them go through the same
experience again. Professional criticism is powerless either to
make or mar a reputation; if people like a man's music, not all
the unfavourable criticism in the world will keep them away
from it; if they do not like it, not all the favourable criticism in the

world will send them to it after one or two unrefreshing experiences of it. Indeed, the plain man reads very little musical criticism; and as the critics invariably disagree with each other, 'criticism' cannot claim either the credit of making an audience for a new composer or the discredit of keeping audiences away from him.

*   *   *

Genius of a kind, or at any rate a decided talent, cannot be denied to Gesualdo; but it is impossible to see more than average talent in the work of most of the monodists of the first generation after 1600. When the men of greater talent got to work, they simplified the texture of their music; a Carissimi could not or would not work in the experimental harmonic idiom of a Saraceni. May we not be sure that something of the kind will happen again? The minor men of today are experimenting with all the ardour of their predecessors of the sixteenth and seventeenth centuries. They are producing, like these, more harmonies than they quite know what to do with.

*   *   *

By slight effort of the historical imagination we can place ourselves at the point of view of the sixteenth-century musician, and realize that the prospects of atonality or quarter-tones cannot be more exciting to us than the prospects of chromaticism were to them. Yet the great masters did ninety-nine hundredths of their work in sublime disregard of what was felt at the time to be the new spirit. And it is easy to see why this was so. We can imagine a Palestrina saying to himself: 'Yes, this is extremely interesting, and some day something may come of it. But at present it is not for me. If my musical faculty is to function freely, I must be content with the normal language of music; I must not try to build with materials of which I do not fully understand the use, and which, indeed, I shall have, in part, to make as I go along.' And we may be pretty certain what would have happened had there been musical journalism in those days. Palestrina would have been derided as a conservative, a reactionary. Extravagant praise would have been poured out on the experimenters in chromaticism, and, feeling it to be 'in the air', and fearing to be stigmatized as old-fashioned, the feebler heads among the younger men would have launched out into extravagances of which they themselves could see neither the first reason not the ultimate end, but that would at least have earned for them the praise of being thoroughly 'progressive'. Progress there certainly would come in time from these experiments, in the sense that a new language would be made for music. But little great music – music, that is to say, recognized as great by posterity – could have come out of it at the time. The theoretical future might be with the experimenters; the practical future was with the immovable 'conservatives', who, masters of a material and a technique that they thoroughly understood, built fabrics that all the revolutions of time cannot shake from their foundations. The phenomenon is not a chance one. It obeys a law; and we may be sure that the law is operative today. Criticism need have no fear of stultifying itself in the eyes of future generations if it tests contemporary musical activity in the light of this law.

★   ★   ★

If the age makes a mistake at all, it is in the direction not of failure to recognize the truly vital minds but to over-estimate the minds of only partial vitality, such as a Telemann or a Spohr. Of a thousand men who are writing music in any country in any given decade, not more than half-a-dozen are likely to receive much attention from posterity; and the critic who says that the vast majority of the new and original works of today will be forgotten in a few years need not fear being proved to be wrong a century or so hence.

★   ★   ★

The people who disliked Wagner in 1870 or 1880 mostly did so not because his music was intellectually beyond them, but because, having got into them, it set up unpleasant emotional or moral reactions. It was not a matter of the novelty of the sensation but of the disagreeableness of it; there are anti-Wagnerians in plenty today, musicians to whom *Tristan* is musically no more complex, no more difficult, than *Don Giovanni* is, but who see nothing in it but a long erotic convulsion, and who turn away from it for their soul's health. 'The whole man thinks' is as true in music as in ordinary psychology; music sets up different reactions in each of us according to our physical and mental and moral chemistry. But the extremes of musical temperament in a population cancel each other out, and we are left, as I have argued already, with a body of plain, sensible, instructed music-lovers whose taste is fairly catholic. Mr. Arnold Bennett would no doubt call these people the passionate few. I should prefer to call them the intelligent average.

★ ★ ★

We can see that Stravinsky stands head and shoulders above all his imitators and hangers-on; and we can hazard our soul's salvation on the wager that, even though a good deal of his work should become for future ages only what much of Monteverdi's is for ours – evidences of an interesting stage in musical development rather than creations eternally valuable as art – posterity will confirm our judgment that *Le Sacre du Printemps* or *L'Histoire du Soldat* is to similar efforts of the day in the same genre as Monteverdi's *Orfeo* was to the average dilettante essay of the time in the new Florentine 'drama with music'.

INDEX

WORKS BY ERNEST NEWMAN

ORIGINAL WORKS

1895 'Gluck and the Opera.' A study in Musical History.

1899 'A Study of Wagner.'

1904 'Wagner.'

1904 'Richard Strauss.' With a Personal Note by A. Kalisch.

1905 'Musical Studies.'

1906 'Elgar.'

1907 'Hugo Wolf.'

1908 'Richard Strauss.'

1914 'Wagner as Man and Artist' (revised 1924).

1919 'A Musical Motley.'

1920 'The Piano-Player and Its Music.'

1923 'Solo Singing.'

1925 'A Musical Critic's Holiday.'

1927 'The Unconscious Beethoven.'

1928 'What to Read on the Evolution of Music.'

1931 'Fact and Fiction about Wagner.' A Criticism of 'The Truth about Wagner' by P. D. Hurne and W. L. Root.

1934 'The Man Liszt.' A study of the tragi-comedy of a soul divided against itself.

1933-47 'Life of Richard Wagner.' 4 vols.

1940 'Wagner' (Novello's Biographies of Great Musicians).

1943 'Opera Nights.'

1949 'Wagner Nights.'

1954 'More Opera Nights.'

1956-58 'From the World of Music' (3 Vols).

TRANSLATIONS

1906 [N.E. 1925] 'On Conducting' by Felix Weingartner.

1911 'J. S. Bach' by Albert Schweitzer.

1912 ff. Wagner Libretti: 'The Flying Dutchman,' 'Tannhäuser,' 'The Ring,' 'Tristan,' 'The Mastersingers,' 'Parsifal.'

1929 'Beethoven the Creator' by R. Rolland.

311

WORKS EDITED AND WITH INTRODUCTIONS

1909 'Handel,' by R. A. Streatfield.

1911 'Brahms,' by J. A. Fuller Maitland.

1912 'The Life of Mozart,' by Edward Holmes. Intro. E. N. (Everyman's Library.) Edited. The New Library of Music (Methuen).

1926 'Thirty Years Musical Recollections,' by Henry Chorley. Edited by E. N.

1928 'Franz Schubert's Letters,' by F. P. Schubert. Foreword by E. N.

1929 'Evenings in the Orchestra,' by Hector Berlioz. Introduction by E. N.

1930 'Cosima Wagner,' by Du Moulin Eckart, translated by C. Alison Phillips. Introduction by E. N.

1932 Introduction and Analytical Notes to the Musical Works of Sibelius (Sibelius Society).

1932 'Memoirs of Hector Berlioz,' edited, annotated and translation revised by E. N. (New York).

1933 Introduction and Analytical Notes to the Songs of Hugo Wolf (Wolf Society).
     Introduction to Novello's Edition of Brahm's 'German Requiem.'

1946 Introduction to Ethel Smyth's 'Impressions That Remain.' (New York).

1950 Introduction to R. W. S. Mendl's 'The Soul of Music.'